President Eise
Close Encounters

Paul Blake Smith

Foundations Book Publishing
Brandon, MS 39047
www.FoundationsBooks.net

President Eisenhower's Close Encounters
By Paul Blake Smith
ISBN: 978-1-64583-038-2

Cover by Dawné Dominique Copyright © 2020
Edited and formatted by: Steve Soderquist

Published in the United States of America
Worldwide Electronic & Digital Rights
Worldwide English Language Print Rights

Taking seriously the greatest of all UFO stories, that as president Dwight Eisenhower secretly met with alien beings and negotiated with them to stay aloof to avoid social upheaval on earth...

Endorsements

"A persistent historical question is whether President Dwight Eisenhower in the mid 1950's secretly met with representatives of Alien species and even entered into a formal treaty with them. Until now no one has thoroughly researched the question. Paul Blake Smith in President Eisenhower's Close Encounters leaves no stone unturned in his search for the truth. Utilizing a vast number of sources this skilled researcher and writer concludes that there was not just one such meeting but perhaps three that took place over two years. His many revelations are exciting and convincing."

—Douglas Caddy, attorney and author of "Being There: Eyewitness to History," Watergate lawyer

"Paul Blake Smith carefully lays out for us why the Eisenhower-ET stories may hold water, and a timeline of events that takes a very messy puzzle and begins to reveal a clearer picture of intrigue, educated theory, and just plain good storytelling."

—Ryan Sprague, author of "Somewhere in the Skies," podcast host, and co-host of CW Network's "Mysteries Decoded"

"The U.S. government has officially denied for decades that it has any knowledge of an extraterrestrial presence here on Earth. Author Paul Blake Smith demonstrates through painstaking research and explosive new information that the government is lying to us. Be sure to pick up a copy of President Eisenhower's Close Encounters before someone decides to make this book disappear."

—Gabriel Campisi, author and movie producer of "The Horde," "Attack of the Unknown," and "Gaslit."

"Paul has researched an overlooked allegation with a fascinating new book that every UFO buff and hardcore fan needs to get a copy and read today."

—Ryan S. Wood, author of "Majik: Eyes Only," and producer of the SyFy Channel special "The Secret: Evidence We Are Not Alone," and webmaster at www.MajesticDocuments.com.

"Paul Blake Smith dug up enough new evidence in his 2016 book *MO41: The Bombshell Before Roswell* to convince me that the U. S. government's first UFO crash retrieval was in April 1941 — NOT July 1947 Roswell. Now in his new book, *President Eisenhower's Close Encounters,* Paul explores a stack of hard and circumstantial evidence that points to President Dwight Eisenhower meeting a non-human intelligence in February 1954. A secret treaty was negotiated by the Classified Executive Order. This book is a must-read for everyone who wants more truth about UFOs and E.T.s."

—Linda Moulton Howe, Reporter and Editor, Earthfiles.com <http://earthfiles.com/> and Investigative Reporter, *Ancient Aliens *on The History Channel.

Dedicated to those who seek the truth in all matters.

Table of Contents

Foreword

by Ryan Sprague

America changed in 2017. It may not have felt like it to most, but under the surface of overwhelming information bombarding our eyes, ears, and minds at a constant rate, a story broke that would alter the entire perception and conversation on a topic once pushed to the furthest corners of the fringe; UFOs. And here we are today, talking about UFOs across dinner tables, over coffee with co-workers, and even amongst the most skeptical of friends who always had a stock answer for those saucers in our skies. A bombshell article released through the *New York Times* shot across the world with the headline, *"Glowing Auras and 'Black Money': The Pentagon's Mysterious U.F.O. Program."* With astonishing admittance by the Pentagon and even the Secret UFO Program's director, Luis Elizondo, we learned that the United States was studying UFOs in a very serious manner. This isn't earth-shaking at first glance, but it does go to show how unreliable the government can be when it comes to telling the public the truth, the whole truth, and nothing but the truth.

Project Blue Book, the official study of UFOs conducted by the United States Air Force, determined that UFOs posed no threat to national security and that no evidence suggested an extraterrestrial intelligence behind their presence. And this would be the final governmental investigation and final word on the topic. Yet, through the diligence of tenacious journalists, this clearly would not be the case. So we now live in a time where practically everything the government has told us about UFOs is put into question. From the

Roswell UFO incident of 1947 to the Washington D.C. UFO flap of 1952, tracing up to the recent 2004 Navy UFO sighting dubbed the "Tic Tac UFO." And while conspiracy theorists can now tout that they were right about everything, it takes a rare breed of researcher to bring forth information based on dedicated research and not just hearsay. And that's exactly what author, Paul Blake Smith, has done in this carefully compiled compendium of a book.

On February 19, 1954, while on vacation in Palm Springs, President Dwight Eisenhower, the 34th commander-in-chief of the United States, made an abrupt and unplanned trip in the middle of the night. Where he went and who he met with has been a source of contention and speculation for decades now. Many came to the fantastic conclusion that Eisenhower had been rushed to nearby Edwards Air Force Base for an unplanned and clandestine meeting with beings from another planet. To many, this would easily be laughed off as pure fantasy and there had to be a more logical and prosaic explanation for Eisenhower's midnight excursion through California. The official statements proclaimed that Eisenhower was swept off to an emergency dentist to repair a chipped tooth. But that story soon began to unravel, and in its place came a dramatic story of treaties negotiated between the United States and beings from other worlds. Science fiction at its finest?

Well, if there's anything we've learned from the recent "Tic Tac UFO" and other stories coming out from the U.S. Navy about encounters with UFOs, it's that sometimes the truth is far stranger than fiction. And in this book, you'll take a journey with Paul Blake Smith as he attempts to unravel a mystery steeped in lore, mysterious documents and files said to have been written at the highest levels of classification, and testimony from those who believe that not one, but an astounding three different meetings took place between Dwight D. Eisenhower and different species of aliens. Smith not only chronicles the complex and incredible history of Eisenhower's life and presidency but gives us small clues as to why Eisenhower might have been the perfect leader to make these meetings happen.

Perhaps more surprisingly, Smith also gives us insight into a UFO crash in New Mexico that may have been connected to the Eisenhower meeting(s) in a very interesting way; no, not *that* UFO crash. We have to look one year past Roswell when in 1948 another flying saucer was said to have landed in the New Mexico desert. While this event remains highly contentious, Smith lays out why the event may have actually occurred, and how one president had seemingly handed over the keys to cosmic dealings to his successor. We also dig deep into the myths and realities of the so-called Majestic Twelve documents, and how Truman and Eisenhower would become entangled in one of the biggest stories of half-truths, lies, and revelations in dealing with the UFO issue in America.

As mentioned above, there wasn't just *one* meeting between the alleged aliens and Eisenhower. Perhaps there was a Holloman Air Force Base meeting, where video footage is said to exist of a craft landing at the base and beings emerging to meet with military officials and Mr. Eisenhower himself. Smith runs us through each meeting by supplying testimony from actual witnesses, genuine government documentation, and quotes from those involved. While many writers would choose to fill the gaps with wild conspiracy and speculation, Paul Blake Smith carefully lays out for us why these stories may hold water, and a timeline of events that takes a very messy puzzle and begins to reveal a clearer picture of intrigue, educated theory, and just plain good storytelling.

As a UFO researcher, it's easy to dismiss sensational claims and stories handed down through second, third, and fourth hand-claims. Time is rarely on the side of anyone who chooses to dive into the rabbit hole of interviewing witnesses and recording stories of UFOs and extraterrestrial visitation. Memory is easily replaced by influence and sheer varying perceptions of events. But it's authors and researchers like Paul Blake Smith who keep their heads down, do the hard work, and record and preserve those stories as accurately and as truthful as possible. It's so easy to get caught up in the cloak and dagger aspects of secret meetings, government cover-ups, and conspiracy theories. But what if even a fraction of these stories did involve such meetings, cover-ups, and strategic negotiations across worlds? Smith asks these very questions in both an objective and open-minded approach, posing theories but never demanding acceptance by his readers.

When it comes to writing responsibly on the topic of UFOs, those who have a relationship to the phenomenon, and those who study and research it, one thing must always be kept in mind; it's not about exploiting those involved for a good story or the limelight. It's about digging deep, reading between the lines, and coming out on the other side with a clearer picture of what we may be dealing with when it comes to America or even the world's place in the cosmic agenda.

We now live in a new era of possible disclosures by our military and government on the UFO issue like never before. But we must always remain cautious of the narrative being laid out for us. We must look at the bigger picture of what we are truly searching for; the truth. And by looking at events like that which have been laid out in this exciting book, we can separate the signal from the noise, and find the truth, the whole truth, and nothing but the truth... whether we like that truth or not.

So enjoy this fascinating new book. It's a must-read!

Ryan Sprague
March 15th , 2020 - "World Contact Day"
New York City
Ryan Sprague:
Co-host of CW television's "Mysteries Decoded" (www.cwseed.com)

Host of the paranormal podcast "Somewhere in the Skies" (www.somewhereintheskies.com)

Contributor to The Travel Channel's "Mysteries at the Museum"

Author of *Somewhere in the Skies: A Human Approach to an Alien Phenomenon*"

PROLOGUE

The Greatest Story Never Told

"This really is a great story!" A podcast host recently blurted this out during an otherwise calm conversation, recorded live, on the air, and currently available as an internet video.

"It *is!*" the broadcast program's guest, a UFO author, replied enthusiastically. Listening to this, I could practically *hear* the excited grins and childlike wonder from these two mature adults when talking for a few minutes about the near-legendary allegation. The out-of-this-world legend about the late American President Dwight David Eisenhower (1890-1969) secretly meeting with landed, friendly alien beings in seemingly sleepy 1954.

I had to agree with the two men on the podcast. I first heard of the mind-blowing claim in 1985. To me, it's like "the greatest story never told," in a sense. Why? *Because no one has ever really put the tale together properly in a sane, sober, complete nonfiction book,* separating the wheat from the chaff, so to speak. When you remove the exaggerated fiction and keep the firm facts, it ends up being, well, the most amazing and electrifying historical drama, *ever*. After years of researching the story, I have discovered there was much more to it than just Eisenhower being surprised to hear aliens had suddenly landed not far away and wanting to chat. It's past time this staggering, well-planned, classified event was told in an even-handed, *non*-hysterical manner, all while jettisoning inaccurate conspiracy theories that have recently larded it down.

When searching in the early part of the new century for full-length books about the amazing UFO crash recovery by the U.S. Army in 1941, just outside my hometown of Cape Girardeau, Missouri, I was stunned to find there wasn't a single one published. So by 2011 I decided to do something about it – by researching and writing it myself. I collected all of the available data, did my own investigating, and began piecing together the seventy-year-old tale as best I could. "**MO41, The Bombshell Before Roswell**: *The Case for a Missouri 1941 UFO Crash*" took me over four years to research, write, edit, and rewrite, resulting in so much material I created a second book that same year (2016), "**3 Presidents, 2 Accidents: More MO41 UFO Data and Surprises.**"

During that book research, I kept stumbling into this scant but very exciting rumor about the United States president and aliens huddling on a desert airbase runway under the cover of darkness. The extraterrestrials allegedly put on quite a thrill-show. But that may well have *not* been the end of such contact, nor the start of it. More direct communication might have been going on, with or without President Eisenhower, as we shall see. Again, I was so intrigued I naturally wanted to find and read a full-length book about it. I started searching around but once again I couldn't find any such publication – so I decided once more to research and write one myself. I had started to piece together the tale in the mid-1990s, then stopped, but kept my data in a file. Then in early 2017 I got started once more, but stopped now and then during the next two years, to tend to other writing projects.

Just like the "MO41" case, I found that almost every adult from the staggering '54 UFO human-alien "summit" saga was long since deceased, and in some cases so were their children. Not good, but I'd dealt with that hurdle before.

To make matters worse, I noticed that some UFO/ET websites which aired thumbnail sketches on Eisenhower and the landed aliens often seemed to get carried away with frightening claims of evil, scheming "grays;" brutal kidnappings and spaceship examinations; and an imminent otherworldly invasion, with "read more here." Pure "click-bait," as it is dubbed. Plus, several sources just seemed to simply parrot what they had heard third-hand elsewhere, perhaps adding a few scary creative touches of their own. A mild-mannered, diligent UFO researcher from Canada, Grant Cameron, put it into perspective when he stated in 2012: "Most of the Eisenhower contact stories seem a little far-fetched and may well be the creations of the minds" of those who passed them along, with personal agendas affecting the story (negatively). I tried to avoid falling into such traps, clinging often to actual leaked government document quotes on extraterrestrials to guide me. And along the way, I did my best to relate everything honestly and fairly, with no intention of misleading or influencing anyone down the wrong path.

From 2017 to the first three months of Corona Virus-plagued 2020, I scoured web pages; magazines; TV shows on videotape; various book chapters; historical biographies; digitized Oval Office logs; online old newspapers; modern paranormal online message forums; and *YouTube* documentaries for more clues and claims. I placed some calls and sent some e-mails. I became aware that in

2004 – the 50th anniversary of the Eisenhower-ET event - the normally-complacent U.S. media e-mailed the late president's surviving son (a virtual lookalike for his father) for a comment. A fine military historian and author in his own right, he simply replied "*no*" at the time to the alien allegation, which he was likely never fully explained to him in the first place, not even by his dad, having no "need to know." John Sheldon Doud Eisenhower (1922-2013) passed away years later without further comment. Knowing that his father allegedly somberly swore all present to strict secrecy on the night of the event, this negative response didn't bother me.

A few contemporary sources touched briefly upon the tale. A fictional novel was crafted in 2013 by author John Romero, creatively turning the ET contact saga into a kind of sci-fi world war with a psychic's help, apparently, but I still haven't found a copy of "*The Eisenhower Enigma*" to read. In early 2020, a well-reviewed independent film written and directed by Christopher Munch, called "The 11th Green," explored Dwight's interest in aliens and the "urban legend" that he "had one or more face-to-face interactions" with them. "The History Channel's "*Ancient Aliens*" has aired the presidential-extraterrestrial tale, not once, but twice, yet in scant detail, the most recent in a spring 2020 episode. Somewhat the same can be said of the syndicated television program "*Unsealed: Alien Files*" when reporting the tale (featuring very tall humanoids) in 2013. The Mutual UFO Network's series on the History Channel, "*MUFON, Hangar 1*," mentioned in 2014's premiere episode that in their headquarters - filled with "70,000 files" - there existed "numerous eyewitness accounts" which told of the Eisenhower event. But the problem is that MUFON does not open its files to the public, and I was not a member of the club. I began to realize why no one had ever really produced a solid book on the topic; it was tough going for any writer with no first-hand eyewitness accounts, the trail having gone cold for decades now.

I dutifully kept writing and polishing (albeit somewhat part-time), adding more and more information from various resources, cramming it all full of checkable facts, and fleshing out thirteen total chapters (plus two chapters I ended up eliminating). Along the way, I added a little eye-catching new data to the fairly well-known Richard Nixon-Jackie Gleason UFO encounter at an American airbase in 1973 (Chapter Eleven). Stunningly, that famous duo's amazing experience took place, allegedly, *on the exact 19th anniversary of the Eisenhower ET encounter.* Were the two tales somehow related? In a special "Top Ten List," I show that it's very possible.

Another question kept nagging: *is there a smoking gun, any paperwork around today to help prove the 1954 encounter case?* It turns out that rumors have been floating about for decades that President Eisenhower – and likely an aide – put pen to paper that year and drew up a special agreement with the extraterrestrial visitors. At some point, this secret treaty was signed and handed over, without the notice or approval of the United States Congress (which would make it constitutionally illegal and unenforceable). To find out more, into a computer search engine I entered the words "Eisenhower alien treaty." One of the phrases that came back read *"ten-year agreement."* Then I read the mentions of Dwight's so-called "Greada Treaty," or "Plato Pact," or "Alien Accords," and when that was Googled the computer came back with *"1954 to 1964."* In clicking on various sites listed for that time-frame, none of them seemed to give any real replies or details, however. No genuine explanation for this specific timing. *What was this ten-year accord?* Why did someone feel that a *decade* was the length of a contract resulting from the shocking alien encounter? Frustratingly, I could not find any direct answers. However, when I did some further online snooping for the year 1964, a startling new piece of the puzzle revealed itself. I uncovered something other UFO researchers had not, that is if my hunch is correct. Interesting data about another

American president, a powerful politico who knew, liked, and worked with President Eisenhower in the 1950s (see Chapter Eleven). After all, they were both born and raised on poor rural Texas farms (before Eisenhower's family moved to Kansas).

Additionally, I found that back in February of 1954, a very famous world leader suddenly developed a tremendous urge to meet with the American president – just the two of them, with no aides nearby – to discuss something so explosive it has never been revealed to this day (see Chapter Nine). I also learned that a very dogged and intrepid UFO researcher (now deceased) discovered that President Eisenhower had more than *one* airbase encounter, with another taking place in 1955. Dwight quietly flew to New Mexico for more direct communications with landed extraterrestrials that "year after contact" (see Chapter Ten). I additionally came to understand that the dashing but doomed American president immediately following Eisenhower also made a trek to still smallish Palm Springs, to Dwight's door, in 1962 (see Chapter Eleven).

Helping me out was a remarkable digitized document from early 1989, leaked in mid-2017, sparking debate on its authenticity but seemingly revealing fresh clues as to yet *another* presidential alien situation, one that I was not familiar with. An amazing claim from within this controversial report mentioning President Harry Truman in 1948-'49 could seemingly have set the foundation for the '54-'55 Eisenhower encounters with his hush-hush ET meeting (see Chapter Three). *Was this the very first presidential live alien encounter?*

In my research, I also relied at times on advice and sometimes data from three smart, perceptive ladies: author Patricia Baker, host of the "Supernatural Girlz" podcast; researcher/author Linda Moulton Howe, host of "Earthfiles;" and Heather Wade, host of "The Kingdom of Nye." A great big *"thank you!"* to these three dedicated seekers of truth, and also to the congenial and dedicated Ryan Sprague, for his fitting Foreword.

In March of 2020, I watched a unique video for the first time, just posted to the internet. It was of Linda, recently speaking to a group about a 2015-'16 case of an American who claimed to received messages from an alien race in binary code, translated by a Ph.D. geneticist. One stunning section of it read as follows: *"Ike's embedded citizens are ready. Disclose. Evolve."* Howe interpreted this puzzler as a reference to President Eisenhower and noted the next line mentioned "Emerther," an alleged ET race supposedly known to Eisenhower (as explained a bit further in Chapter Eleven). It is all certainly up for debate, but... *was this a prophetic reference to this very book?*

To be candid and clear, I fully admit that the 2/19/54 case I lay out herein relies on a good deal of second-hand (or even *third*) claims and overall *faith*, not hard, tangible evidence. Anecdotal allegations, speculation, and hearsay are collected herein, yes, but much of it is fairly corroborative and very enticing. Strong supportive proof may well exist but remains still sadly elusive as of 2020, buried under mountains (and decades) of government secrecy and classification regulations. Hence, I put together as best I could this detailed "compendium" utilizing as many named sources and authors as reasonably possible, so now the reader can decide on the mind-numbing tale's merit. And yes, in summation I must candidly point out that although my case presented herein is a circumstantial one, many a court trial is won on this sort of circumstantial evidence alone. By the end of the book, I am confident you'll be swayed by the case I put forward; it was enough to convince *me* and I'm a fairly cynical, skeptical sort.

"President Eisenhower's Close Encounters" is now presented for your approval, airing a fresh perspective on the most amazing and exciting sagas ever – if true (and I think it is). Please keep an open mind and judge for yourselves...

Paul Blake Smith

southern Missouri

March 17, 2020 – St. Patrick's Day
(final revisions on September 7, 2020 – Labor Day)

INTRODUCTION

Setting the Stage

On January 21, 1953, Americans watched (or listened via radio) as its military-minded new president was sworn into office, their 34th, vowing somberly "to preserve, protect, and defend the constitution of the United States." Dwight David Eisenhower settled into the business of governing while ending America's involvement in the distant, frustrating Korean War. It was a fairly quiet, slow-paced, but effective start by the new administration, that first year. Eisenhower's military efforts in southeast Asia were coming around nicely, and peace was established in war-torn Korea. The troops were coming home. The economy stabilized, relatively. Union strikes and social unrest were nearly nonexistent. In retrospect, things seemed pretty peaceful, on the surface.

According to UFO researchers, the first year of the Eisenhower administration also saw a quartet of alleged ET crashes that the American military rushed to cover up. Although hushed at the time, some eyewitnesses spoke up decades later. One particular instance from 1953 occurred in New Mexico, near the White Sands, New Mexico, "proving grounds" for the first atom bomb detonation ("Trinity") in the summer of '45. "Four bodies were recovered" from the alien disc in the sandy soil, supposedly. In May of 1953, investigators allege, a UFO crash-landed outside of Kingman, Arizona, with at least one four-foot-tall, brownish dead alien found with the wreckage. In Utah that same year, an alien spacecraft allegedly crashed near government property and has proven difficult to research to this day. Yet another under-investigated but tantalizing claim in 1953 pinpoints an area "some miles northwest of Great Falls, Montana," involving a swift government/Air Force cover-up with at least one dead alien body recovered from the debris, possibly more. {Some sourcing from *"Majik Eyes Only,"* by author Ryan S. Wood.}

Perhaps understandably, by December of 1953, a new rule was put into place thanks to the protective Pentagon and new president's input. It was a hideously restrictive law that would have an impact to this day. The U.S. Joint Chiefs of Staff issued *"Army-Navy-Air Force Publication #146"* which stated that anyone who allowed the unauthorized release of information concerning UFOs was committing a grave crime covered within the Espionage Act, which could result in ten years in prison and a substantial fine. American servicemen of all ranks were likely made aware of this action and might have been understandably reluctant to discuss or disclose extraterrestrial crash recovery facts. It could cost them just about *everything.*

We can thus see that government secrecy at most any cost - on ETs and UFOs especially - was going to continue under the new, button-down Eisenhower administration. Authoritarian Dwight was used to army discipline and no back-talk. Private citizens were likely not generally aware of the new rules in effect for silence on UFOs and ETs, but were any alien visitors themselves? All we know is that in theory, an extraterrestrial spaceship's controlled landing on a secure American military base or a secluded government facility would have been ideal – and that is just what has been alleged, taking place less than two months after the new extraterrestrial rule went into place. Coincidence? Or part of an overall, developing strategy for an eventual, well-planned, sustained "First Contact," as some may call it?

Keeping this strict clamp-down in mind... to understand the main Eisenhower-extraterrestrial encounter saga from February of 1954, we'll set the scene by mentioning that after a full year in power, Chief Executive Eisenhower was oddly ready for not one, but two sporting vacations in that cold, dreary winter month. The first was to travel with the First Lady to sleepy Thomasville, Georgia, to hunt quail with some friends, including Dwight's remarkably wealthy Secretary of the Treasury, who owned the out-of-the-way plantation famous for game-birding. They were likely protected by a familiar and trusted special unit of Georgia State troopers (see in Chapter Ten), a low-key team of six men that might have played a significant security role a week later. President Eisenhower happily posed for news photographers with his host and Georgia farm staffers, holding up his downed game birds. The trip had been fun and worthwhile to him, seemingly, but was there another, hidden purpose for going?

Soon after those chilly, damp days in Georgia, Dwight Eisenhower returned to his White House duties while also readying for a very different vacation: a long-planned golfing trip to warmer, drier climes. The First Couple had been plotting for over a year with old friends to visit golf-crazy Palm Springs in southern California. But it sure seemed like a long, long way to go just to hit the links and shoot some birdies, not actual birds, and loaf at taxpayers' expense.

So it was that President Dwight D. Eisenhower and his wife; a few personal and professional aides; and some Secret Service guards were packed and ready to go on February 17, 1954, departing Washington D.C. that chilly afternoon aboard a shiny, silver aircraft, headed west, into the wild blue yonder, looking forward to a relaxing and seemingly uneventful Golden State getaway.

CHAPTER ONE

Airbase Air Space

"Five different spaceships landed on the base runway."

— "Sergeant X"

It seems ridiculous and far-fetched at first, does it not, the whole idea that a United States president could secretly take off one night while on vacation and go meet extraterrestrials – and keep it a secret for several decades? Before we dig into the juicy details of this mind-boggling allegation, let's first consider a story that came bursting out in the international media in 2010, having its seed planted in 1999, but originating from way back in 1940s' Europe.

It seems that in September of 1999, a scientist wishing to remain anonymous wrote a letter to the United Kingdom's Defense Minister, describing what his grandfather once related, regarding a World War II experience that his surviving family desired more information. Over a decade later the missive was leaked to the press. It seems the grandparent had allegedly said that during his World War II experience while acting as a trusted R.A.F. bodyguard, he overheard nearby British Prime Minister Winston Churchill (1874-1965) discuss a most remarkable topic. The great allied leader was conferring in England with five-star American General Dwight D. Eisenhower about a strange, metallic "Unidentified Flying Object" that had been recently buzzing a Royal Air Force reconnaissance plane, flying over the British coastline, allegedly on August 5, 1944. The "UFO" was buzzing about at speeds greater than any man-made airplane, accelerating and darting around in the sky unlike anything seen before. It was undoubtedly otherworldly since not even the Americans or Germans had unveiled any sort of super-advanced aerial craft like this. The R.A.F. airplane's crew supposedly photographed the foreign, active craft, which "hovered noiselessly" over their vehicle for a while before soaring into the wild, blue yonder. Churchill and Eisenhower exchanged private comments on the bizarre "foo-fighter," as UFOs were often dubbed in the 1940s. Then the bodyguard heard Mr. Churchill make a rather chilling statement: "*This event should be immediately classified as it would create mass panic amongst the general population, and destroy one's belief in the church.*" Supposedly Churchill wanted the topic kept secret for at least fifty years, and then "have its status reviewed by a future prime minister." And Eisenhower agreed.

It would seem this secrecy-at-all-costs approach stuck with the very *un*-progressive, play-it-safe Dwight Eisenhower. He never discussed the startling WWII UFO case with anyone further. Dwight had very likely heard still other tales of "daylight discs" and phantom "Foo Fighters" during the war. He kept it all under his hat, so to speak, as to not upset the apple-cart. It was just plain unacceptable to admit that allied forces didn't control even friendly *home* airspace, let alone the rest of the planet.

Unfortunately, the British government near the turn of the twenty-first century claimed it was unable to find any supporting evidence for this particular wartime UFO incident. The R.A.F. bodyguard near the famous duo had supposedly told his daughter, then age nine, some of the high-level conversation around the time of the incident, so she would remember the tale and keep it secret until some point after the war (in case her father didn't survive). The young woman did hold the allegation private initially but discussed it with family members decades later, and thus it was brought up (in letter form) by her son, the curious astrophysicist – the R.A.F. man's highly educated grandson. The unfinished tale appears lost to history unless secret files are someday officially released or leaked. However, it should be noted that on December 13, 1944, Supreme Headquarters Allied Powers Europe – with "Ike" overall in charge – issued a press release mentioning some similar strange aerial sightings but dubbed them "a new German weapon." The data was published in the *New York Times* the next day, but busy General Eisenhower likely had no input on this statement and the topic was not again mentioned by Allied Powers in the slightest.

So bearing this long-hushed tale in mind, let's now review a kind of "Top Ten List" of admittedly sketchy but riveting clues and claims that say the greatest presidential adventure of all time happened and was effectively covered up for many decades - just like what Dwight Eisenhower conspired to do with Winston Churchill in 1945. Here we go, in no particular order...

#1.) Gabriel Green (1924-2001) made a minor name for himself in southern California during the 1950s as an open-minded UFO investigator who publicly alleged to have experienced contact of his own with landed, friendly extraterrestrial beings. This made Gabe an early "contactee," or to some Americans, a "kook." Mr. Green hailed from Whittier, the hometown of Richard Nixon, who was of course

Dwight Eisenhower's vice president and later a chief executive on his own. In day-to-day reality, Gabriel was a simple Los Angeles-area school photographer and a college-educated World War II veteran.

Green claimed that one day – probably in 1954 – a U.S. serviceman contact him and requested anonymity for his tale of something quite unusual recently while stationed at Edwards Air Force Base, about ninety miles northeast of Los Angeles.

"Sergeant X" - as we'll call him - claimed he was working with a platoon at the Edwards gunnery range one afternoon. The specific drill consisted of firing artillery shells at distant targets set up in the wide-open desert. The sergeant's squad that day was under the personal command of a general, one we'll call "General Z." Suddenly, five highly unusual spacecraft floated down out of the sky and moved over the artillery field, much to the busy soldiers' shock. Shiny and silver, glinting in the sun, these different-sized crafts. *This was no drill.*

General Z coldly ordered the men to turn their guns on the unidentified flying objects, and they promptly did so despite being quite alarmed and amazed. All watched flabbergasted as the exploding shells had *no* impact on the UFO squadron whatsoever. These were highly dangerous and effective weapons normally, but in the case of the odd spaceships that descended that day, they were completely useless, not leaving a mark. Deeply impressed, General Z eventually ordered a cease-fire, the entire outfit probably standing there stunned and speechless, like never before in their lives. As the slack-jawed unit watched, the unexpected squadron of strange airships - two cigar-shaped and three rounded or saucer-like in design, the sarge said - moved quietly through the airbase air space and landed on a runway near a large aircraft hangar.

The men were hustled from the scene and sworn to silence, and that was all Sergeant X knew. But he was bursting to tell someone who knew about such supernatural things, thus his unauthorized and likely covert contact with Gabriel Green.

All during the 1950s, President Eisenhower kept his lips tightly sealed on aliens possibly visiting here. Officially, "UFOs" and "flying saucers" were just silly, easily-dismissed mistaken identities, or so the U.S. government alleged. So disgusted was Gabriel Green that he decided to run for president to replace Eisenhower in 1960!

In his 1960 campaign flier, entitled "Independent Non-Partisan Write-In Candidate for President," Green issued the following party statement: *"We affirm that flying saucers are real, that in reality, they are true spacecraft manned by people from other planets, who are visiting and making contact with various persons on our planet to impart information which can be used for the benefit of all men of earth. We deplore the actions of our government in withholding information on this subject."* This certainly sounds like a direct shot by Mr. Green at the Eisenhower administration regarding the Edwards Airbase landing event. "They're here to help us help ourselves," Gabriel told a radio interview in August of 1960. He called upon — expressed in his write-in presidential campaign fliers and posters - the creation of a special panel of newsmen to declassify and release governmental secrets on ETs to the public. {Green's other proposed policies included the abolishing of taxes, free college educations, and creating spaceship missions to Mars. He also ran for president again in 1972 — against incumbent Richard Nixon - with these themes in mind.}

Overall Gabriel Green may have sounded a bit wacky in his day, but he might have been onto something and quite "ahead of his time," as we'll see...

#2.) Desmond Arthur Peter Leslie (1921-2001) spoke at length in mid-1954 to a reporter for the military magazine *Valor*. Mr. Leslie was a UFO investigator and writer, an English gentleman who toured America in '54, including Southern California. But Desmond Leslie was no ordinary probing overseas journalist. Desmond was a second cousin to Winston Churchill and a former Royal Air Force pilot who loyally and expertly flew fighter jets in World War II.

In their October 9, 1954 issue, Mr. Leslie is quoted by *Valor*'s reporter as having visited the Edwards AFB vicinity that summer, speaking to some of the soldiers stationed there. An Air Force officer – we'll call "Lieutenant Y" - told Desmond that he had been at the airbase during the previous winter and witnessed *a round spaceship coming down out of the sky and landing on a runway not too far away!* The lieutenant said it was about one hundred feet in diameter, and that the base was quickly put on high alert and suddenly sealed off. No one was allowed to leave for any reason, Y alleged, and those soldiers who were already off the grounds on a pass or approved leave were stopped at the front gate upon their return, given their possessions, and told to "beat it." Mr. Leslie stated that he began questioning others discreetly at Edwards and learned to his satisfaction that an ET event did indeed occur, and that the spacecraft was placed under guard inside Hangar #27. Desmond's main source said he had even briefly "seen the craft" resting in the hangar. Possibly *multiple sources* leaked the startling secret to the visiting British writer, perhaps many doing so anonymously. {Source: *"Alien Contact"* by Timothy Good.}

It could be that Mr. Leslie was trusted with the interplanetary summit information as he was already somewhat of an expert on UFOs and ETs. He had, after all, just co-authored a book with Polish-American alleged "contactee" George Adamski (1891-1965), published in 1953. It was entitled – most presciently – *"Flying Saucers Have Landed."* Part of this book was about Adamski encountering a pair of friendly, human-like aliens who supposedly landed their spaceship outside of Los Angeles, in the Mojave Desert, for contact and communication!

At any rate, the upshot from the autumn '54 military magazine article is Desmond Leslie's foremost finding: *President Eisenhower was notified of the landed alien presence at Edwards and arrived straightaway that very night,* from his nearby vacation in Palm Springs. Supposedly the popular president got a good look at everything otherworldly in hushed, secure conditions.

It is worth noting that Mr. Leslie once co-wrote a B-movie screenplay, *"Stranger From Venus,"* which was about a human-looking alien emerging from a crashed ET flying saucer. The script was produced in mid-1954 and premiered in the United Kingdom in late December that year, but had no U.S. release, suspiciously. The extraterrestrial character in the film comes to warn people about the dangers of the atomic bomb and continued nuclear testing, and that if mankind were to put an end to these weapons of mass destruction and wars in general, it would receive great scientific insight from his fellow advanced extraterrestrials. This (fictional?) plot appears to contain amazing insight into the Eisenhower "secret summit," as we shall later see.

#3.) Harold T. Wilkins (1891-1960) was a Cambridge-educated journalist and author who said he too learned the story of five different otherworldly crafts coming down for a landing at Edwards AFB with an Eisenhower covert inspection. The tale was received from a letter sent to him "from a friend in California" in April of '54 (probably Mr. Gerald Light; see Chapter Nine). Wilkins wrote a bit about the Eisenhower-ET assertion within his book, *"Flying Saucers*

Uncensored," released in 1955. It was probably the very first book to bring up the astounding topic. "These five saucers landed voluntarily at this Edwards Air Force Base. They were discs of different types and their entities invited technicians and scientists to inspect" the advanced alien aerial technology, Wilkins claimed in print. Harold's Golden State pal alleged that *he* gathered data from three different sources at Edwards Airbase, none of which he named, perhaps fearing harsh repercussions for all when violating U.S. military secrecy oaths.

The problem with Wilkins' believability was his perpetual public passion for peculiar paranormal pablum, such as an innocent belief in the lost continent of Atlantis; the hollow-Earth theory; and a vanished race of white people in South America, none of which were ever proven true. Still, Mr. Wilkins was a fairly respected pioneer in his day in seriously relating UFO sightings and stories and bringing the idea of ET interaction to the public consciousness, through his entertaining books.

#4.) Francis "Frank" Scully (1892-1964) was a 1950s supernatural-theme author and columnist for *Variety* magazine. Having a passion for UFOs, Frank penned *"Behind the Flying Saucers"* in 1950. He wrote in his folksy column the astonishing allegation that the American military secretly recovered dead alien bodies from crashed spaceships, twice in Arizona and once near Aztec, New Mexico, in March of 1948. Mr. Scully might well have been quite correct on that one, as we'll see later, although some of his information may have been hoaxed, or muddied, through a pair of alleged con artists, or a deliberate hack job by a paid-off "journalist" seeking to undermine his credibility (it's a long story).

To get to the point, Frank's widow Alice Scully (1909-1996) once claimed that she and Frank learned back in June of 1954 that

President Eisenhower had indeed made a secret visit to Edwards Airbase earlier that year for a covert UFO inspection. Their information was related via a carpenter whom they had employed at the time, one who said he had been working on the desert military base around the time of the amazing incident. Yet Scully didn't have enough backup data to go on and chose not to print the story, not wishing to incur the wrath of the military or the government. Patient Alice survived hubby Frank by 32 years and only told the tale to later investigators. Frank Scully died in, of all places, Palm Springs, just four months after another unusual Eisenhower summit there (see Chapter Eleven).

Now for three brief, anonymous-sourced tales that certainly need more details and supportive sources, but are most fascinating. They were originally produced by Australian researcher/author Dr. Michael Emin Salla (1958-), who wrote a long essay on the "exopolitics" of the Eisenhower-extraterrestrial encounter in 2004, timed to the event's 50th anniversary...

#5.) Supposedly the unnamed wife of a deceased military policeman who was once stationed at Edwards Airbase said her hubby was on duty there one night and ordered to guard a "flying disc" resting just inside a large airplane hangar. The MP said he was quite aware that President Eisenhower had visited the base for his own look-see at the off-world craft, although apparently, the military husband had not been around to witness that actual event.

#6.) Another surviving widow in the twenty-first century alleged that her late husband had once informed her that he perused top secret images at the Pentagon, including ones showing President Dwight Eisenhower meeting some extraterrestrial beings at Edwards Airbase.

#7.) Still another unidentified source has stated that he was part of a medical team told to stand by at an airfield not far from Palm Springs, waiting for President Eisenhower, who was taken there by automobile one February '54 night. The informant claimed Dwight then boarded a military transport, to fly hush-hush to another area airfield, Edwards Airbase most likely.

More recently, a retired USAF man reinforced this by stating he learned that an ambulance and its medicos were ordered to hustle from nearby George Air Force Base in southern California to stand by at Norton Air Force Base, just in case... all while Eisenhower utilized Norton AFB briefly to board a C-45 twin-engine Beechcraft airplane, regularly used in the past to ferry officers on short trips. He was flown to Palmdale, very near Edwards AFB, and from there could have been flown or driven with security to the proper Edwards hangar, to personally greet the landed ETs.

#8.) William Brophy is the son of a lieutenant-colonel of the same name who served as a B-29 Bomber pilot, originally stationed out of Alamogordo, New Mexico. The father had heard plenty of stories from his fellow pilots and servicemen. He had a sensational peacetime story to share with his offspring. President Eisenhower, it seems, was called one night on a golf vacation and urged to come out to Edwards Air Force Base. Dwight was in Palm Springs, California, and was requested to meet on a base runway with friendly, tall, blonde-haired "Nords." Those were tall, Nordic-looking, humanoid aliens who landed there one February afternoon and conversed with Air Force officials and later the president, the Brophy family narrative asserted. Two early-model F-102 jets were on the runway nearby, ready to be tested, when courageous Eisenhower exchanged greetings and opinions with the friendly off-world astronauts. {Source: George A. Filer III, New Jersey State Director of MUFON Eastern Region and editor at www.nationalUFOcenter.com.}

In a 2019 message to this author, Mr. Brophy provided a little more detail, claiming the '54 encounter was carefully set up in advance as the alien beings were inquiring about a cigar-shaped spacecraft of theirs that had been "lost" (wrecked) while "near Dutton, Montana, on October 12, 1953." Brophy explained that "two tall "Blondes" were killed "on Highway 91" in that tragic Montana event when their craft crash-landed "after exploding due to radar-jamming of their controls." Did the alleged "Nords" want their twisted, ruined spaceship back? It was in pieces, William explained but being held in Nevada for scrutiny. If so, then why did the beings present themselves at Edwards Air Force Base in southern California? Because this high-tech testing site was as close as the aliens were going to get in finding a remote, controlled setting to entice nearby President Eisenhower, who would be the ultimate "decider" of such classified issues. Dwight never went to Montana as president, but the Nords wanted their fallen comrades back, presumably, and took a bold step for retrieval in southern California.

#9.) Charles L. Suggs II is a former U.S. Marine sergeant who stated in 1991 that his father - Naval Commander Charles L. Suggs I (1909-1987) – once confessed to being one of the six men guarding Eisenhower when aliens arrived at Edwards AFB in February of 1954. Nordic-like humanoid ETs with "pale blue eyes and colorless lips" and white/blonde hair communicated peacefully with the nervous but enthralled president and his small entourage. The elder Suggs allegedly told his son that the president was protected by alerted base officers and a squadron of B-58 Hustlers, cutting-edge military aircraft that would not become officially operational for another two years. The human-like "Nords" were also on their guard, sending just one bipedal representative down a ramp from a quiet, settled spacecraft, keeping several feet from Eisenhower while being protected from behind by another cautious "space brother." The alien craft involved was allegedly "a bi-convex saucer" in design, sturdily standing on the runway via "tripod landing gear." Supposedly this race of high-tech space ambassadors declared they were from a planet in another solar system. They came in peace and meant no one any harm, but were curious about the human race and the American president's plans for atomic bomb testing. They asked "detailed questions" about the subject, showing they knew quite well more dangerous detonations were being planned.

#10.) Contemporary UFO author and lecturer Richard M. Dolan (1962-) of New York City (an Oxford University grad) has collected enough information to convince him that Dwight Eisenhower truly did meet in private with ETs in '54. Mr. Dolan included the story within one of his popular books and appeared in the 2014 *"MUFON, Hangar 1"* program on the History Channel, an episode that expostulated on the staggering subject, and how it was to be kept secret from the populace. The president "disappeared for ten hours" one night, to pull off the secret summit. The arriving aliens offered President Eisenhower advanced technology, Dolan said he too learned from his sources, and in return asked for a private permanent base with which to operate out of. "Rumors came out within a week that Eisenhower had a meeting with aliens," Richard told *Hangar 1* viewers, mostly because "this leaked out on a radio show" hosted by a reporter named "Frank Edwards."

Author/journalist/broadcaster Frank Allyn Edwards (1908-1967) was that popular '54 radio show pioneer in question, and yes, he did speak and write often about "UFOs and other paranormal phenomena," according to online biographies. Dolan asserted that "millions of people listened in" to the revealing '54 paranormal program's declaration, via the old Mutual Radio network. Perhaps so, for host Edwards' national radio audience was once estimated at 13 million fans per show! Edwards was an open-minded American journalist/commentator who was "really into UFOs and flying saucers," author Dolan noted.

According to investigator Grant Cameron, about a month before Eisenhower's trip to Palm Springs, Frank Edwards reported on his radio show that a UFO had crashed near the California-Oregon border. Mr. Edwards told his large radio audience that it was his information that the crash-landed spaceship had been covertly moved "to a West Coast U.S. airfield." As the months passed, more UFO reports were relayed on Frank Edwards' program, likely upsetting the powers that be. From his broadcasting station in Washington D.C., Frank Edwards even spoke of the now-famous unidentified craft sightings going on in the nation's capital that May of '54.

Frank Edwards was abruptly fired from his radio program in mid-1954 "for reasons that remain uncertain. His interest in UFOs was said to be a factor," a biographer summed up. Could it have had something to do with mentioning over the airwaves the likely highly-classified Eisenhower encounter? What were Frank's specific sources for that staggering story? Military men from the airbase, even direct eyewitnesses to the event? Certainly, no copy of this particular program exists now, or Frank's notes, but happily the canned Mr. Edwards went on to rebound in other radio positions and writing jobs as time progressed.

Just recently, today's so-called "UFO community" was stunned — and thrilled — to air a photograph relayed by Frank Edwards' family. In it, he is shown posing in 1964 with none other than *former President Harry Truman*, who even took the time to *sign* the picture. Was Truman (in office from April 1945 to January 1953) a source for Edwards in the spring of 1954? Surely not... but perhaps through a third party? Conjecture, purely, but as we'll see, Mr. Truman *might* have been hovering on the fringes of the Eisenhower-ET saga. Another possible source is USAF Captain Edward J. Ruppelt (1923-1960), who directed "Project Blue Book" until September of 1953, all about Air Force UFO investigations. Ruppelt typed up a cogent memo (unearthed decades later) on the red-hot rumors of Eisenhower's secret base visit for cosmic reasons, wanting firm answers just like reporter Frank Edwards, or anyone else.

{Speaking of progressive media reporting at the time – often a rarity – take the case of respected newspaper columnist Dorothy Mae Kilgallen (1913-1965). In February of 1954, Dorothy informed her daily readership that "flying saucers are regarded of such importance" by the U.S. military behind the scenes that "a special hush-hush meeting of world military heads" was being planned in private "for next summer." Was such a confab the result of the hushed Eisenhower affair at Edwards? She also wrote a May 1955 newspaper column about a British cabinet source who told her about recovered UFOs "which originate on another planet," adding, "We believe, based on our inquiries thus far, that the saucers were staffed by small men – probably under four feet tall."}

Even though that's *more* than ten different sources... we'll toss in an extra little "bonus story" that also helps support the amazing Eisenhower allegation. An obscure *Los Angeles Times* newspaper employee named Donald Johnson, age 48, and his pal, businessman Paul Umbrello, said they were driving south near the Mojave Desert on one side, the Pacific Ocean on the other that late afternoon. They were "about one hundred miles" from Edwards AFB when they spotted something unusual in the sky. A great light, at first, but it seemingly grew in size as it got closer. It was a silvery disc! The two stopped the car and got out to take a closer look, very pleased and excited by their "flying saucer" sighting. The weird aerial object was headed west, from the mountains and desert towards the sea. "It was silver with an outer surface of dark metal, the most brilliant I have ever seen," Don recalled. "We observed it for twenty minutes." The floating airship was silent and quite vibrant in the darkening sky. Johnson reached back into the car and grabbed a camera. He focused and "started taking pictures." Umbrello added, "It flew in a strange way" for it to be ever confused with a man-made aircraft, making it tough to capture in an exposure. The spacecraft was definitely unlike anything they'd ever seen before. As discussed in an article in a 1999 edition of *"Flying Saucer Review"* magazine, the two men watched the disc waft in the air over the Pacific and then fade out of sight. It was on or near February 19, the 50th day in the Gregorian calendar. For their '99 article's interview, the two men were given a polygraph test, and passed with "flying colors."

Once the spaceship finally moved on, out of sight, the two men continued their journey, babbling away over their sudden sighting. So thrilled by this unusual event, they recorded their memories on audiotape, and placed it and the resulting photographs in a file in Don's house. Years went by and the memories faded a bit, but later Mr. Johnson went back to look it up after a UFO investigator caught wind of their tale. They noticed Donald had scribbled the date of when the aging, dust-covered folder was sealed and labeled: *"21 February 1954."* If this was truly the same aerial craft that was controlled by aliens and peacefully landed at Edwards Airbase for eventual inspection by Dwight Eisenhower, Johnson stated, "then we saw something historic."

Obviously, all of these aging tales desperately need further examination and explanation, details, and dissertation. But as the years fly by, it is admittedly likely too late to find out more. Overall however we can see a very intriguing circumstantial evidence case accumulating. But is there any possible foundation to the notion that Dwight David Eisenhower was ever interested in the topic of extraterrestrials? Had he ever experienced his own first-person encounters *before* becoming America's 34th president?

CHAPTER TWO

The Ike We Liked

"Eisenhower did indeed meet with extraterrestrial, off-world astronauts."

— Congressman Henry McElroy

Historic ET involvement or not, Dwight David Eisenhower was unquestionably one of the greatest American heroes of the twentieth century. Born in Texas in October of 1890, Dwight (as one of seven sons) grew into an active, athletic young man in the American Midwest, but mostly on a Kansas farm. He was nicknamed "Little Ike" (later shortened) by his brothers while developing a keen passion for the military, which he joined at the age of twenty-one, entering the U.S. Army's West Point Military Academy. His subsequent decades in the service of his country paid off as "Ike" rose steadily in army ranks with insightful ideas on developing a more efficient and effective U.S. fighting force. Working his way up to a *five*-star general in the second world war, Eisenhower was a natural-born military strategist, utilizing clever subterfuge and secrecy in his plans to help fool and foil the enemy in wartime.

Dwight married once, for life, and fathered two children, although one died young. For the most part, he managed to keep his rather notorious temper in check as he worked his way up to Major-General by 1942, specializing in war and spy strategies. Quietly clever Eisenhower - a fearsome chain-smoker – was liked (and specially selected) by liberal President Franklin Delano Roosevelt (1882-1945) as the U.S. military's Supreme Allied Commander in the European theater during the critical WWII effort. FDR passed over one hundred other candidates of greater rank, familiarity, and notoriety to promote him.

In his youth, Dwight delivered and read newspapers. He would later make his own news in these same publications, and even write his own book. As a boy, he loved to read books on wars, specific battles, and brave, armed soldiers, causing him to doodle and daydream of combat. His mother, a devout pacifist and Jehovah's Witness, learned of her son's growing fascination for military life and grew dismayed. She took away her son's army books and locked them in the family home's attic. Thus, at an early age Dwight learned first-hand about squelching facts and locking up data.

{One quick amazing fact: Dwight Eisenhower never once saw battle or experienced active combat. He never once even physically hurt, shot, or killed anyone, thus pleasing his mom.}

After his great success as in the global war, feisty President Harry S Truman (1884-1972) picked trusty Dwight in 1945 to be his new Army Chief of Staff and later, "Presiding Officer of the Joint Chiefs of Staff," as American troops were slowly brought home to an increasingly troubled U.S. economy. So popular in opinion polls that

Mr. Truman offered, incredibly, to step back into the *vice* presidency role in order to make Dwight the Democratic Party's presidential nominee in 1948, Eisenhower could punch his own ticket for future planning. He rejected Truman's notion in favor of a little rest, memoir-writing, and a virtual part-time job at Columbia University in New York City, pumping up the family coffers first before entering the political arena as a Republican, all at his own leisurely pace. He could also engage more freely in some of his favorite pastimes: fly-fishing, hunting, playing poker and bridge, and most of all, golfing. {Only later did he take up painting but did wisely ditch smoking.}

Intimates said they knew the older Dwight D. Eisenhower as a very respectable, confident, shrewd, ethical, and open-minded man in private. On the negative side, Dwight could be a bit cold and aloof at times. "Not a warm person," as his granddaughter-in-law recalled. At his very worst, Dwight could be cranky and resistant to change, as are many older men who have been through an active life in an ever-evolving society. He won the Republican Party nomination in mid-1952 and then the up-for-grabs presidency, all while an irritated President Truman sniped at him from time to time during the campaign. Before long, the two former friends and co-workers were barely on speaking terms.

American voters so liked Ike and his agreeable wife, Mamie Geneva Doud Eisenhower (1896-1979) they put them in the White House by large victory margins in both the '52 and '56 campaigns. Republicans and Democrats alike respected and cared about the deeply Christian, low-key Eisenhower's. For some reason, which seems a bit odd now in hindsight, Dwight was often beloved just for his then-famously "crooked grin."

In a nearly unprecedented move, outgoing President Truman set up a special meeting with the new president-elect in early November

'52, just after the national election. At that time, Harry gave victorious Dwight special access to the comprehensive "National Intelligence Digest" which was produced by the newfangled Central Intelligence Agency. There were some classified subjects the two men needed to chat about in the privacy of the Oval Office, away from the press, which took initial meeting photos, then were escorted out. What exactly the famous duo managed to discuss behind those closed doors has never been fully revealed.

Few folks to this day realize that Dwight Eisenhower was the first American president to hold a pilot's license (since 1939) and possess a thorough knowledge of aircraft and high-speed flight. In July of 1957, he became the first sitting president to fly as a passenger in a helicopter, , taking off from the South Lawn, and since then the standard procedure for presidential families. Dwight extensively used chauffeurs and did not even drive his own car, preferring limos to take him places without fanfare. In fact, the new First Couple were so modest they drew criticism by settling into a "cozy suburbia" in the White House, choosing to play cards, watch television, and go to bed just after 11:00 p.m. at the latest.

Mamie loved TV soap operas while Dwight preferred cowboy westerns and the "Sergeant Bilko" comedy show, according to biographers. Dinner was almost always served promptly at 8:00 after a half-hour of mingling before that with assembled guests, about fifteen at most. Scintillating artists and innovative entertainers were generally not invited to perform, or even dine in the presidential mansion. Dwight and Mamie's only son was off in the service and the couple did not own any pets. It was a remarkably quiet – some say *humdrum* – older man's existence, approaching an age when most folks consider residence in retirement communities.

As president, Dwight had dutifully spent much of his time reading a lot of briefing documents, intelligence reports, and news stories in order to keep up with the changing world. By the late 1940s and much of the '50s, "UFO" and "flying saucer" reports — and even motion pictures — were seen often in newspaper headlines and on movie theater screens, whether he liked it or not.

As incredible as it seems, a letter published in the *New York Post* in June of 1997 stated back in early 1952, Dwight Eisenhower had experienced his *own* UFO sighting...

What was printed in that New York City paper was an anonymous letter from "a crew member" of a United States aircraft carrier stationed to cruise across the Atlantic Ocean, experienced in early '52. The U.S.S. Franklin D. Roosevelt - part of the American Sixth Fleet - was steaming off the British coast when it was boarded by an admiral and retired Mr. Eisenhower, during Dwight's final tour of special duty in Europe just before he hunkered down to campaign for president. A storm set in that evening, featuring thunder, lightning, and substantial rain. The soaked ship — rumored to be carrying nuclear weapons - rocked Eisenhower to sleep, but only for so long. He reportedly wandered up to the bridge at about 1:30 a.m. in his pajamas and bathrobe, looking for a cup of coffee. Then four servicemen on the bridge, ably commanding the huge ship in the storm, chatted amiably with the famous ex-general until something caught their eye. It was a bluish-white UFO, a well-lit object that came down out of the rainy skies and hovered about one hundred feet over the water, "right off the starboard bow." The five military men stared at it, nearly wordless and incredulous, then exchanged stunned glances at each other. "Flashes of lightning helped to more clearly illuminate the strange craft," the retired sailor recalled in '97. The commander steamed the huge carrier right past the hovering disc, getting a good look. Finally, after the UFO zipped away,

Eisenhower calmly told the crew he would "go check on this." Before he left, he cautioned the startled servicemen to simply "forget about this for now." The subject was not brought up again, not in the hours, days, weeks, or even *years* afterward.

The writer of this amazing tale wanted the truth told before he died, thus the letter to the *Post*. If the story is genuinely nonfiction, it certainly shows that Dwight Eisenhower was mentally and emotionally piqued and readied for more visits from alien beings *before* he assumed the office of the presidency. If the letter was a work of fiction, then, well, it provides amusing entertainment for the masses and has no impact on allegations to come in this book. The popular *New York Post* did enough research to confirm the author's story before they went to print in 1997. The alien spaceship didn't just quickly buzz the giant sea-ship and take off; it hovered in place over it for *"nearly ten minutes"* that the five men saw, perhaps longer before being noticed hanging there in the stormy sky. There could be no doubt it was not of this earth.

Was this extraordinary event part of an overall plan by extraterrestrials, to purposely prepare Dwight D. Eisenhower for eventual face-to-face contact? Or could it even have been a gentle "reminder" for him of something otherworldly he took part in from a few years *earlier?*

Back in the summer of 1947, as popular legend tells us over and over, something quite otherworldly came hurtling down to earth on rough, rural New Mexico soil, outside a small town (and army airbase) called Roswell. Later-leaked and quite authentic-looking government documents (majesticdocuments.com) reveal that as President Truman's Army Chief of Staff, General Dwight Eisenhower was made fully aware of the jolting ET situation, and in fact, on 7/8/47 was even in charge of authorizing military personnel - like stern-looking Air Force General Nathan Farragut Twining (1897-198–) - to go to the desert crash sites and investigate and to make a full report for Truman and his top military brass, plus some trusted advisers. Leaked in the mid-1990s, an Army Counter Intelligence Corps "Intelligence Assessment" from 7/22/47 mentioned the following two remarkable sentences, regarding the twin New Mexico desert UFO crashes, one of which produced five deceased "grayish-pink" alien bodies: *"General Twining and staff is preparing a detailed report of both incidents and briefings later to follow. Likewise, the belief of CIC that General Eisenhower will see a showing of recoveries sometime in late August this year. The president was given a limited briefing at the Pentagon."*

Did General Eisenhower indeed go view dead alien bodies and ship debris? According to a 2009 "Coast to Coast A.M." radio show call-in source, once-secret film footage exists of Dwight privately observing the New Mexico-recovered ET bodies and UFO debris alongside famed aviator/industrialist Howard Robard Hughes (1905-1976), in a warehouse-type setting back in mid-1947. The nervous call-in source said he had viewed only *some* of the film he inherited and chillingly reported, "Wha' I've seen scares me to death." Most disappointingly, such images have yet to surface as of 2020, however.

Meanwhile another later-leaked military memo – from the Majestic Documents site - mentions General Eisenhower permitting an airbase-touring Catholic bishop to have access to sensitive matters in New Mexico during the now-controversial summer of '47. (For more, see Chapter Nine).

So was Dwight Eisenhower involved in any military assessment of the Roswell crash? It's difficult to say firmly, but to this day "Eisenhower Road" runs through that desert city. Of all the street names in America to pick from...

Despite fine investigative efforts by the likes of Dr. Stanton Terry Friedman (1934-2019) and Ryan S. Wood, plus hardworking journalist Linda Moulton Howe, some skeptics have not entirely embraced the so-called "Eisenhower Briefing Documents," possible blockbuster government evidence that was discovered in 1984. The alleged secret papers were photographic images of a supposedly top-secret report about the covert study committee "Majestic-12," dated November 18, 1952. The still controversial and contested "MJ-12" document was supposedly written up and supplied by the Truman White House, shown to newly-elected Mr. Eisenhower before he took office, as a "preliminary briefing" on the secretive subject on what was known by the United States government regarding alien visitation. Much of the Military/Academic Joint Intelligence Committee material concentrates on the '47 Roswell crash, but some detractors feel the documents are fakes. To be sure, the "Eisenhower Briefing Documents" were never produced as actual, tangible papers to be tested by reliable and unbiased sources, only shown within a roll of developed snapshot film sent in the mail to a researcher by an anonymous source, postmarked in Albuquerque, New Mexico, home of Kirtland Air Force Base and the long-rumored site of some secretly-recovered UFO crash examinations. But *if* real, the 1952 summary was likely a type of "refresher course" for knowledgeable President-Elect Eisenhower. Some even feel he had little regard or interest in the report as *he already knew* the information contained within it.

We must bear in mind that no government document is perfect, especially in a pre-computer program era like the 1950s, where typewriters were used and their ribbons often locked up at night, to keep government secrets. Secretaries and stenographers made mistakes, as did the sources who dictated the information, and *multiple* tries, or versions, were created to knock out the kinks, plus add or subtract data. Any of these drafts could have been smuggled out at some point by a courageous source, who later passed them along and/or leaked them, the data was so explosive. This author believes the "Eisenhower Briefing Documents" are likely genuine, perhaps a bit flawed for reasons stated, and urges readers to view a 2002 documentary currently online entitled *"UFO Secret MJ12: Do You Believe in Majic?"* to help decide the controversial report's merits. Or read Linda Moulton Howe's groundbreaking 1989 book, *"An Alien Harvest,"* or better yet, access her marvelous "Earthfiles.com" site. One important factor to remember: the U.S. government printing press in those days had a dust-altered "raised" letter Z in their issued documents — and so did the Eisenhower briefing papers.

Many UFO authors and skeptics also debate the merits of the so-called "Cutler-Twining memo," a rather famous Eisenhower White House document(s), allegedly, dated Tuesday, July 13, 1954 — then amended and sent on Wednesday the 14th. In it, USAF General Nathan Twining is notified to attend an "extraordinary meeting" at the executive mansion on "Thursday the 16th" (mistaken dating, Thursday was the 15th) by the "NSC/MJ-12 Special Studies Project." Top secret *UFO/ET stuff*, in other words. The twin directives were dictated by "special assistant to the president" Robert Cutler (1895-1974), the trusty National Security Adviser from 1953 to 1955. But why all the memo secrecy about which White House entrance for General Twining to utilize at 8:45 a.m. for the big meeting? Very few subjects could cause such restrictions, but a hush-hush confab regarding recently landed, friendly aliens would certainly make the grade. Presidential appointment records show that a National Security Council meeting *was* held at the Eisenhower White House on July 15, and yet General Twining was not officially listed as present. However, logs reveal Nathan *was* around Dwight that Thursday, attending a White House luncheon with him with about twenty others present, something Twining was alerted to do by Cutler in the original memo of the 13th. So, was the whole memorandum valid but with a dating error? Or clumsily hoaxed? The debate rages on.

The Cutler memorandum to General Twining was discovered in 1984 by two researchers, digging within the National Archives. Some say it was planted there (but does that make it fake?) but if genuine, might give us a strong clue as to the officials who later dealt with the 2/19/54 Eisenhower-ET encounter and put a stop to any public announcement of it. It seems the National Security Council was a deep influence on the matter, along with the ongoing, always-secretive "MJ-12" committee, which UFO investigators began to learn more about in the mid-to-late 1980s. By that point, there was no one left alive from it to comment on the issue; the last member of the listed original alien studies committee had died two weeks before the discovery of the "Cutler-Twining Memo."

To help buttress support for the reality of the special, secretive UFO study group, a November 4, 1953, memo - obviously leaked decades later - from President Eisenhower to the head of the CIA mentions "the MJ12 Operations Plan" and also "the MJ-12/Special Studies Project." It also makes clear the president had issued specific directives on UFOs on January 23, 1953 (just after taking office), and Sunday, March 22, and some "expenditures for UFO Intelligence programs" back on June 16, of '53. Official appointments logs reveal the usual high-level Oval Office meetings for Eisenhower that 6/16/53, then an abrupt, unusual end to recorded events at 3:30 p.m. What was going on so red hot that it 'could not be recorded? The November memo to the 'IA's director also recalled a "Classified Basic Authorization" of something important issued on 3/22/53, and existing records reveal that President Eisenhower called up and invited over that quiet afternoon a close friend named "the Honorable Paul Hoffman." More on him later.

Still other leaked and trusted U.S. government documents over the years refer to "MJ-12" and its mind-blowing committee activities/opinions on understanding alien visitation. They can be seen within www.MajesticDocuments.com. One UFO researcher has claimed that Mr. Eisenhower was also briefed on the ET situation by an "MJ-12" member "in Atlanta on November 15, 1952, and had a further meeting on November 18th at the Pentagon" with two MJ-12 Committee members present. Intriguing if true. Since the controversial '52 briefing papers have nothing to do with the events of February of 1954,'we'll move on...

No one can argue that President Dwight D. Eisenhower calmly ruled his peace-loving country in one of the quietest eras ever. Some historians call 1954 the most peaceful, *dull* year in all of United States history. The year was noteworthy in hindsight for its many "UFO" and "flying saucer" sightings around the world, often making the news. France in particular experienced a large wave of odd ET sightings in '54 (and supposedly, Eisenhower asked an aide about it). According to eyewitness reports, "dwarfish creatures" were being seen, at times besides landed shiny, silver discs, triggering some small amount of paranoia and fear among the French citizenry.

"When I go back far enough," President Eisenhower told the assembled media that December of '54, "the last time I heard this talked to me, a man whom I trust from the Air Force {sic} said that it was, as far as he knew, completely inaccurate to believe that they come from any outside planet or otherwise." Any citizen could look at that statement — printed on the front page of the esteemed *New York Times* - as a denial of otherworldly happenings, but 'let us examine it carefully. Eisenhower did not say *he* did not believe in aliens or their "UFO" spaceships in our skies, visiting our world. He simply passed along the negative opinion of an Air Force adviser. Dwight was, in fact, legendary for his double-talk to the press, done to purposely mislead them; he had proudly done so since his early army days to remain closemouthed about sensitive military operations. He said he *enjoyed* throwing off the press to keep projects secret.

Historians also note that President Eisenhower was supportive of Vice President Richard Nixon, so "Tricky Dick," but they were not particularly close on a daily basis. Young Mr. Nixon most likely had no idea what was going on with the president in southern California that February of '54. News accounts show that Dick Nixon was back in Washington during Dwight's "golf vacation," trying to soothe old political rivalries, mostly within the Republican Party on Capitol Hill. Eisenhower spent most of his mid-February Palm Springs trip calmly golfing, while his aging but trusted Secretary of State John Foster Dulles (1888-1959) was in Europe, attending conferences and laying the groundwork for foreign policies. Chief Executive Dwight knew how to delegate authority to those he respected. But as we know now, something shocking and otherworldly was going on behind the scenes, effectively kept from the public.

In his post-1961 retirement ex-President Eisenhower certainly never mentioned extraterrestrials when penning his presidential memoirs while living (part-time) in laid-back Palm Springs. He obviously could not reveal classified, top-secret information, however, so this discrepancy is a no-brainer. Similarly, a few decades after Dwight's presidency his White House "diary," or logbook of events, was published in book form. The six days of his So-Cal golf idyll were either scarcely noted or just left *blank*. When one is lounging on vacation, one has the free leisure time to fill in diary or notebook entries at some length.

Doodling by the president on White House stationary revealed decades later a rather odd, almost-alien-looking male human standing in the foreground, bald and stoic. It seems to have Dwight's face. A saucer-like object appears to hover in the sky over this eye-catching figure! The phrase *"internal security"* was scrawled, near warships like the kind Dwight traveled on in '52 when he saw a UFO. A bored President Eisenhower created this drawing at a dull cabinet meeting. Some other similar "Dwight doodles" show flying triangular-shaped objects, plus cylindrical and long V-shaped images, as if odd alien spaceships. But interpretations can differ, of course.

A mere sergeant in the late 1950s – but an Army Signal Corps. specialist - Stephen L. Lovekin (1940-2009) went on to become a respected U.S. Brigadier General. Near the end of his life, Lovekin said he was present at Maryland's Camp David in 1959 with a relaxed Commander-in-Chief Eisenhower seated nearby, drawing UFOs on a sheet of paper while waiting for an important telephone call. Lovekin said that while Dwight was in the presence of a few trusted military aides, the president began talking about "UFOs in 1952, shortly before he took office." Was this the memorable U.S.S. Roosevelt incident? Whatever the case, it wasn't the first time the unusual subject affected and intrigued the president, Lovekin noted. Also, President Eisenhower "was a doodler" and drew "various forms of UFOs . . . he was interested in shapes and sizes," Lovekin recalled to a documentary film interviewer. Alien visitation was real, Lovekin stressed, and Eisenhower *"was fully aware of the facts."* Stephen added in another interview: "It was a very, very important concern of his.... He was very much into it. He believed in them." So much so, "he realized the concern of the American people" also on the presence of aliens observing life on earth but felt he could not act as "his hands were tied."

Retired Stephen Lovekin additionally said he was aware that President Eisenhower frequently received and read UFO reports behind the scenes, issued mostly by military sources. "Without him knowing it, he lost control of the entire UFO situation," Lovekin explained, by way of the military-industrial complex taking over the physical evidence and its application in hushed corporate projects, mainly in aircraft/arms development. {An excellent site for more on this topic: www.roswellproof.com.}

During all of this in the 1950s, were advanced alien beings somehow, someway making some sort of *contact* with a government agency or at least some military operatives, perhaps by the airwaves? Perhaps in order to relay their desire for a special summit with newly installed Eisenhower? That was admittedly a wild-sounding allegation, but one that a former New Hampshire state legislator publicly confirmed via a special video produced on May 8, 2010.

It seems that on that date while living in Virginia, ex-congressman Henry W. McElroy, Jr. (1941-) stated on camera that he once read a shocking government report from 1953. It explained that a certain congenial race of ETs was in radio communication with American military scientists, asking to meet their top leader in private, in a peaceful, protected setting. This friendly race of otherworldly beings - humanoid ambassadors if you will – wanted to open a historic dialogue. This would help create good relations between humans and their peaceful alien brethren... which Mr. McElroy further stated he felt President Eisenhower *did*.

Wow! It was a thought-provoking, historic notion (if true). Why would a very conservative politician in 2010 risk his reputation and any further career in any chosen field by coming forward with a silly hoax? Why set yourself up for ridicule from the skeptics... unless you really *did* read some shocking but genuine government secrets? Congressman McElroy would have been a total fool to take part in a prank, or a fool to have openly fallen for fakes. It was all-important enough to him to chance possible unpleasant repercussions or retribution from the U.S. military or government.

The New Hampshire former state representative said that one briefing document for newly-sworn-in President Eisenhower "was pervaded with a sense of hope" that historic contact and communication between one "benevolent" extraterrestrial race and the human race could soon be established, should American leadership find it desirable to set up a summit between the two parties. Mr. McElroy further said that although he 'could not name specifically where or when the impressive face-to-face contact with aliens occurred but asserted confidently that he believed that *"Eisenhower did indeed meet with extraterrestrial, off-world astronauts."*

For his credibility, it should be noted that the unassuming, publicity-shy Henry W. McElroy in his governmental employee days worked on the "State-Federal Relations and Veterans Affairs Committee," where he read the 1950s document and learned of the exciting tale. He also served on various other committees in New Hampshire's legislature, for many years. Henry was no attention-seeking clown seeking higher office or a pundit's job on television, just an aging American who wanted the full truth out now, for the world to consider, while he was out of office, not seeking a new political position requiring votes, but before he passed away.

There have been claims in past decades from UFO researchers that "Project Sign" and/or "Project Sigma" were secret ongoing military-based scientific operations attempting to contact through very high-frequency radio signals any orbiting extraterrestrials in space. And that this covert process - involving early computer binary language to communicate without detection by average citizens with ham radios - eventually set up the Eisenhower-ET summit time, place, and date. There 'has not been any smoking-gun proof of this over the years, however, but such allegations seem reasonable enough, placed in context with the actions of presidents Truman and Eisenhower, as we shall see.

Was the Eisenhower-ET Edwards Airbase meeting premeditated, set up well in advance? The data collected herein seems to conclude that it was. For instance, research shows that on February 13th, '54, Jim C. Lucas of Scripps-Howard News Service wrote that "representatives of major airlines" were planning to meet in Los Angeles (of all places) "with Military Air Transport Service Intelligence officers to discuss speeding up UFO reporting procedures." This would include airline pilots being asked, "Not to discuss their sightings publicly or give them to newspapers."

The high-level confab did indeed take place, on February 17th, the day Eisenhower left the White House for California, and two days before the otherworldly Mojave Desert landing. U.S. Air Force officials met in private with representatives of America's biggest commercial airliners. A news organization's published story on the military confab summed up sources as having stated that said airline pilots would from that day forward be forced to *report all UFO sightings directly to the USAF at the nearest military airbase* (even while still in flight) *and then to keep their lips sealed*. So disgruntled were the hundreds of civilian passenger plane pilots involved in this strict governmental control that they signed a petition to *protest* this strict new policy, but it failed to have any impact at all on the unusual situation.

Adding to the notion of a predesignated time and place comes a detail from the contemporary *"MUFON Hangar 1"* television show. One of their episodes claimed that "documents show that Edwards Airbase was shut down to incoming air traffic and all nonessential personnel from February 19th to February 21st." Should this report be true it strongly indicates clear communication was set up by American intelligence officers and friendly extraterrestrials to lay out in advance the possibility of a peaceful alien landing during those three days, while the president vacationed nearly 130 highway miles away, or "about two and a half hours' drive," the MUFON television show asserted in 2014. *Flying* directly from the Palm Springs area to Edwards AFB would have been close to ninety miles in about a half-hour's time or less, we'll say (depending upon airspeed).

By January of 1953 - likely even before taking office in November of '52 - the new chief executive felt he needed a warm, uncluttered place to relax and play yet more golf... in order to give himself an effective cover story as he awaited a possible friendly alien landing not far away, in a controllable remote setting - like Edwards Air Force Base. If the communicative ETs showed, they showed. If not, Dwight could happily golf his heart out and no one would know the difference. It was an ideal plan.

At the nice-but-not-ritzy home where the Eisenhower's were to stay in Palm Springs, rooms had been added during 1953 construction and special telephone lines were installed in advance of the visit, too. Also included were acceptable quarters for ever-present Secret Service agents in this "Western White House," according to an article looking back on that era. "Times" - these low-profile agents who worked for the U.S. Treasury Department - would have worked in shifts, some relaxing while others patrolled the president's temporary vacation living arrangement inside and out. At least two federal agents would have accompanied Dwight on his automobile trips into town, mostly to local country club golf courses. It was rare, but not unheard of, for a president to ditch his agents and go off alone, mostly at night in that era.

Keeping an eye on the physical and mental/emotional well-being of a president was of substantial importance to federal agents assigned to protect him 24 hours a day, 7 days a week. It is a bit lost to history today how ill Dwight Eisenhower was at times during his eight-year presidential tenure. He would not suffer his rather famous heart attack for more than a full year after his '54 encounter, but in addition to that Dwight bravely soldiered through Crohn's Disease; a ventricular aneurysm; dental pain; a mild stroke; stomach and gallbladder problems; and an adrenal tumor (not discovered until after his death). Capping this off in the spring of 1969, Mr. Eisenhower died of congestive heart failure, following more heart attacks suffered in his retirement. Needless to say, he was often not a well man.

Dwight Eisenhower and his impishly-charming wife Mamie, their personal valets and secretaries, a small handful of White House aides, a Secret Service contingent, and the president's mother-in-law flew on 2/17/54 from D.C. to the West Coast aboard "Columbine II," the new official large airplane for the commander-in-chief in those days, just before the advent of the now well-known moniker "Air Force One" (although that *was* its official designation even then). Sleepy, upscale Palm Springs was the only destination listed. In 1954 the southern California city "boasted" a population of only around 8,000 residents, although its sprawling community was linked by other similar desert towns as word spread over the decades – often via wealthy Hollywood stars – about how warm and dry, peaceful, and pleasant it was most of the year in this scenic, mountain-ringed, palm-tree-studded area. {Today Palm Springs' population consists of over 45,000 residents, plus many visiting tourists from all over the world.} Frankly, there wasn't a whole lot to do in town in '54, making it a pretty strange presidential destination, minus the golf courses, which were frankly nicer and more plentiful back on the East Coast.

State, county, and local dignitaries, excited citizenry, the local and West Coast media, and the traveling White House press corps were well-prepared for the arrival of the Eisenhower's when they touched down at the modest Palm Springs Public Airport that mid-winter, seemingly looking only for a restful escape from the pressures of national and global leadership. Dwight was to be joined on the links by his old business executive friends, plus accomplished professional golf star William Ben Hogan (1912-1997).

It was on a Wednesday evening that President and First Lady Eisenhower's plane touched down at 9:02 p.m., Pacific Time. Republican Governor Goodwin Jess Knight (1896-1970) and Palm Springs Mayor Florian Gillar Boyd (1928-2013) were on hand to proudly greet the First Couple on the tarmac, watched closely and cheered on by some soldiers and several thousand enthusiastic citizens who gawked from the sidelines, snapping pictures, according to news reports. None of the greeters knew there was a bit of a loose, top-secret agenda to the vacation, not even Mamie. The president and only a couple of advisers who accompanied him knew it was at least possible history was about to be made – maybe – in a carefully prepared, covert operation.

But when it came to meeting congenial extraterrestrial beings face-to-face in private, was new President Eisenhower at least *partially* just trying to "even the score," or even "do one better," with his former boss, ex-President Harry Truman? Did Harry and Ike's recent past play a role in the stunning contact of 1954?

CHAPTER THREE

The Vermont Key?

"What I've heard was that Truman was at the first meeting, not Eisenhower."

— a MUFON source

Two middle-aged men named "Paul H." were old friends and well-funded campaign supporters of Dwight Eisenhower, residing at times within a somewhat-upscale resort in Palm Springs called "The Smoke Tree Ranch." For fully understanding the overall preparation for the 1954 Eisenhower summit with aliens, we must examine how Dwight came to hang out with these two specific businessmen on the outskirts of the peaceful desert community.

Paul Hoy Helms, Jr. (1889-1957) was a Kansas-born, wealthy president of his own baking company and has been described as "a local sports philanthropist." He hosted the First Couple at his place, but likely knew nothing of any sort of ulterior motive for the president's visit.

Paul Gray Hoffman (1891-1974), of Pasadena, California, was an Illinois-born Army soldier in WWI; a past president of the Ford Foundation; and the then-current chairman of the struggling Studebaker Corporation. Mr. Hoffman is a key name in this affair, and he was no innocent babe in the government woods. According to According to the now defunct website, smokershistory, the elite corporate exec once served as an OSS officer during WWII. The long-defunct "Office of Strategic Services" was the precursor to the Central Intelligence Agency, meaning Hoffman was once a *spy*, to put it simply. Sneaky subterfuge could, at times, be his business.

Paul G. Hoffman served President Truman as an economic administrator of the Marshall Plan from 1948 to 1950. He once headed up "Democrats and Independents for Eisenhower" in the 1952 presidential campaign, which upset his old boss Harry. Just a week after Dwight's big November '52 electoral victory, the Palm Springs newspaper *Desert Sun* reported that Hoffman "has rented a home at Smoke Tree, and plans to spend most of the winter here," and was part of rumors "that the president-elect is planning to stop over here," even before he took office, possibly. Evidently that pre-inaugural visit 'did not happen, although a December edition of that same local newspaper reported Eisenhower's appointed new White House chief of staff, Llewelyn Sherman Adams (1899-1986) personally visited and inspected Smoke Tree. Such a long, long way from D.C., when critical preparations for the new presidency were of prime importance in that limited timeframe.

It is obvious that via Hoffman and perhaps Vermont-born Adams, setting up President Eisenhower to idyll in Palm Springs, not too terribly far from Edwards Airbase, was imperative, right from the start. It was supposedly to go *golfing*, right? Why couldn't the president stay at Hoffman's Pasadena home, and hit the links in the L.A. area? Or, say, warm-weather Florida, or Augusta, Georgia? Dwight was a member of the Augusta Golf Club, site of perhaps the finest course in the world, where "The Masters" tournament is annually played. A much shorter, less taxing trip from D.C. Dwight loved to golf, hunt, and fish in that rural area and did so repeatedly. He went there so often a house was built *on* the Augusta course, just for him!

President Eisenhower would never have just allowed Paul Hoffman to foster this "Visit Beautiful Palm Springs" idea on his own; it would seem much more likely Dwight instigated the plan and his close friend Paul agreed to help, quickly renting a Smoke Tree Ranch home to create the pretext of the president's "just happening" to stop by on a visit out in the desert, all while ET radio wave space communication was apparently going on in private in 1953, with extraterrestrials and U.S. military brass both supposedly searching for a sound, specific date and remote setting for a historic "first contact" landing. It would be a special private event filmed and become "one for the history books," sure to get Ike re-elected in '56.

{In the aftermath of the 2/19/54 Eisenhower-ET encounter, global-minded Hoffman was named by the president as a delegate to the United Nations, 1956-'57, and managing director of the special United Nations Development Program from '59 to '72. He had the free time to pal around with Eisenhower; in 1954, Hoffman's Studebaker Company merged with Packard, then both cars quickly went out of style and business. But sturdy metallic vehicles with complex engines, the ability to comfortably hold passengers, and travel long distances was Paul's expertise. Was it to be applied in assessing landed UFOs?}

Hoffman's Smoke Tree rental house was eventually dumped as the host site, however, and Paul Helms' renovated home was selected for "security reasons," something that happened to a famous friend of Ike's successor when planning his presidential visit to Palm Springs in 1962 (see Chapter Eleven).

To get a better grip on the true ulterior reason for President Eisenhower's suspicious Palm Springs trip and ET adventure, we have to backtrack first by zeroing in on the mid-summer of 1949 - by way of 2017...

Its authenticity is debated, but in June of 2017, an anonymous source leaked a shocking 47-page briefing document to syndicated radio podcast host Heather Wade. The congenial and candid Miss Wade soon went public with the report and it initially drew a few skeptical detractors, while many researchers feel it was/is authentic, deserving of great, serious scrutiny. It's a detailed January 1989 Defense Intelligence Agency summary of the extraterrestrial situation in America, likely drawn up during the Ronald Reagan administration, likely intended for the incoming new team of President-Elect George H. W. Bush (the Vice President) and his top advisers. {See Appendix.} One date on an early page of the DIA report is January 1, 1989, when President Reagan was vacationing in – of all places – *Palm Springs*. A second date, listed for an "Operation Majestic-12 preliminary briefing" with the data enclosed, was for Sunday, January 8, when Reagan had just returned from this southern California trip (and recent ring finger surgery). He then received a National Security briefing promptly at 9:30 a.m. in the Oval Office on Monday the 9. Within an hour, Vice President Bush met with the affable chief executive, for an hour's discussion, digitized records currently reveal. Was it about the shocking, top-secret DIA report?

A key part of the dazzling government document explains in amazing detail that March 1948 UFO crash in Aztec, New Mexico, where almost all ETs on board were killed. However, a still-living alien being - named "Setimus" - was pulled from the damaged craft, deeply asleep in a kind of pod. He was revived and given a home within Los Alamos National Laboratories in that southwestern state. Human-like Setimus allegedly spoke English surprisingly well and was versed in homo sapien behavior, modern geopolitics, and the planet earth's troubled environment. He gave interviews to scientists at Los Alamos, portions of which were included in the '89 DIA report. The captured ET was said to be so peaceful and helpful, he was eventually granted diplomatic status! But here's the document's upshot: *Setimus and his advanced ET species had "decided on a long-term program of carefully calculated" contact with certain humans, including those in the highest levels of American government - like President Dwight D. Eisenhower.*

The shocking '89 report added: *"With the advent of the Atomic Age, this program escalated to include eventual diplomatic contact with many of Earth's governments."* So the USA was not alone in receiving the alien representatives, allegedly. Thanks to the recent *"explosion of technical progress"* by humanity, it was now evidently important enough to risk injury or even death to establish critical sustained communications with humans at this point in history. This mind-boggling advent was of course kept hushed up by the U.S. government and military. America was/is a world leader in every sense, especially when creating and test-detonating vastly devastating atomic weaponry, first under the dictates of the recent Roosevelt and Truman administrations, so apparently, the United States government was the first to be contacted. But historical facts show us that Dwight Eisenhower was not only stepping up the testing but also sending nuclear weapons out to installations around the world, arming it and imperiling the globe at an alarming, astounding rate. Did that alone draw in concerned alien observers?

So, back in 1948 (when Ike was still a top general), agreeable Setimus remained at Los Alamos Labs for a full year, then was moved, and during this time gave interviews and allowed himself to be examined by military scientists and doctors. It's quite a blockbuster story if true. Certainly, nothing stands out today to make one believe it is a hoaxed fantasy.

We must remember that no government document is perfect, as no writer or secretarial employee is perfect, nor completely in the know on the subject of extraterrestrial visitation, which is quite compartmentalized and top-secret at the highest levels of the federal government. Sources dictating material are of course only human and make mistakes, too. Thus, criticism of the 1989 report for a few mistakes or changes in normal DIA style — such as front cover dates and "Top Secret" stamps - seems a bit unfair. The '89 DIA report was mostly on the findings of the secretive "Majestic Twelve" covert UFO study group, and may well have been a first or second draft, with small errors remaining to be corrected in a later re-typing. No one expected it to be leaked and exposed publicly decades later, instead, it was probably to have been polished after proofing, to remove errors. Someone evidently smuggled out a first draft or second-run copy. *It is this author's belief we can take its content as authentic.*

Anyway... in 1948, cooperative visitor Setimus was said to have been an "adult, Earth-like humanoid male" who "spoke perfect English with a slight and untraceable accent and exhibited many telepathic and psychic skills as well." The closely-examined alien was "in his general appearance, completely human. Internally there were slight differences." Setimus's landing debacle near Aztec, and his subsequent induced awakening, it should be noted, took place just a few weeks before the first of three major atomic bomb tests in the South Pacific, approved of by President Truman and his then-Army Chief of Staff Eisenhower.

According to the 1989 report, the kindly alien survived his Los Alamos captivity just fine, but in March of 1949, he was taken away for some reason and placed in an obscure *"rural Vermont safe house,"* operated by U.S. Army Intelligence.

Vermont? Of all the new places to go for six months, what was in Vermont that was so appealing? And out in the woods?

As it turned out, that mid-summer of 1949, Dwight Eisenhower was out *somewhere,* away from work, and facts are that at times in his life he used to go fly-fishing in... *rural Vermont!* So much so, the state's fishing museum later created its own exhibit of Eisenhower fishing gear, and in 2009, changed the title of a specific Vermont installation and re-dubbed it "The Dwight D. Eisenhower National Fish Hatchery" after the man who so enjoyed fishing in the state's chilly waters. Also, a Vermont mountain-top hotel has named a room after the Eisenhower's, following their stay there in 1955, if not earlier.

In August of '49, diplomat Setimus was finally returned to New Mexico, via Kirtland Air Force Base in Albuquerque, where he was picked up on some remote desert property nearby, on the 21st by an extraterrestrial craft. Setimus was quietly returned to his kind. Before leaving our planet, the '89 report claimed, *leading administration figures and President Truman himself were said to have visited the peaceful spaceman in secret that summer in Vermont!*

Is this incredible blockbuster true? And if it so, was ex-Chief of Staff of the Army for Truman — General Dwight Eisenhower —

involved with sustaining, questioning, and examining the Vermont-based humanoid?

In August of 2019, an older male caller to a Heather Wade podcast that this author took part in - discussing the crashed UFO recovered in Cape Girardeau, Missouri in late April of 1941 - wanted to pass along his first-hand information on the late March 1948 crashed alien ship in Aztec, New Mexico, and its revived lone survivor. The surprise anonymous caller stated that he worked for the U.S. government in that era, and learned that the "guest" humanoid was quite intelligent and considered to be "a mechanic on board the ship." The ET was able to fashion a communications device from some of the wreckage of the craft over the following year, and sometime in 1949 contact the members of his race to set a time and date for some of them to come back to Earth and pick him up. The caller said he would like to tell more about the remarkable saga, but he was still afraid of violating national security codes and what repercussions it might bring him, even to this day. In what he relayed the anonymous caller perfectly backed up data in the 1989 briefing document, which Wade assured was sent to her by a completely separate source.

Speculation: as 1948 and '49 went by, cooperative Setimus conversed privately with U.S. scientists in sizzling New Mexico and gave them information as he saw fit, and was rewarded. He was moved to cooler, more open spaces in shady Vermont, surrounded by the rich, full trees and lush nature that he professed to love (mentioned within the '89 summary). "Green things must be respected above all else," Setimus once declared, according to transcripts.

According to the DIA report, Setimus needed a special diet as he was "less able to process the wide range of foods that earthmen are *used to.*" So it is logical to assume special food and drink was at times trucked to the ETs shady Vermont compound along with anything else he needed. Special Army Intelligence forces were likely active in and out of rural Vermont, raising some eyebrows, no doubt.

Here is where the plot thickens, or at least jells...

Harry Truman's White House appointment logs for Monday, August 1, 1949, reveal that the Republican Governor of Vermont, of all people, had called Vermont's Republican Senator George David Aiken (1892-1984) the previous week and asked Aiken to set up an appointment with the president for 12:15 p.m. that day in the Oval Office. It had to have been about something pretty darn important, considering these circumstances. Calling or writing Truman wouldn't do. Conservative Governor Ernest William Gibson, Jr. (1901-1969) – a former decorated Army infantryman from rural, small-town Vermont – traveled a long way to chat in private with liberal Harry "off the record," which means no notes were taken due to the highly sensitive nature of their secretive conversation. This confab was unusual, although Governor Gibson also asked to see (and did) Harry back on May 18th. The August man-to-man meeting was only for fifteen minutes, but *something big was up,* it is logical to assume.

In late July of '49, records show a U.S. congressman from Vermont also huddled with Harry in the Oval Office.

In a Thursday, August 4th press conference in his Oval Office, President Truman was asked a question by a reporter about something Paul G. Hoffman and Secretary of Commerce Charles W. Sawyer (1887-1979) were up to together. Truman told the assembled press corps that Sawyer "has reported to me on his visit to New England." Certainly, Vermont is part of that region. Later that same Thursday afternoon, Truman's Secretary of State and his Defense

Secretary took up Oval Office time, and then they took off somewhere, unusually not appearing at a cabinet meeting the next morning, and in fact, not showing up at the White House West Wing until August 9th. One can certainly argue that the Setimus situation was both a matter of "foreign affairs" and for Defense (Army Intelligence), which set up the alien's move to Vermont.

In his daily West Wing routine, President Truman was close to his correspondence secretary, former newspaper reporter William D. Hassett (1880-1965), who hailed from a small town in rural Vermont, naturally. Amazingly, Mr. Hassett had taken *more than forty* "secret trips with the president" - Franklin D. Roosevelt – in the late '30s and 1940s! He and the Roosevelts would quietly travel north to rural Hyde Park, New York, usually leaving on Friday and coming back Monday morning, according to a female associate (who was friends with Mrs. Edwin G. Nourse, a name we'll see later). Could Bill have done the same with the Truman's, heading north this time to his beloved rural Vermont? He would have been the perfect, experienced shepherd for such an elicit trip. {Source: Harry S Truman Library archives interviews.}

By the mid-summer of 1949 Vermont was within a day trip for the D.C.-based liberal president, who seemed to enjoy travel and did so quite often. Long auto and train trips were par for Mr. Truman's course, never better shown than via his cross-country automobile road trip he undertook with only wife Bess, starting from Independence, Missouri, to New York City, in the summer of 1953, made into a popular 2009 book.

Keeping that in mind... on Friday, August 5, 1949, Harry and Bess Truman supposedly *"motored (the President driving) to Shangri-La for the weekend,"* Oval Office logs declared.

Say *what* now? First, the president *drove himself* seventy miles in summer traffic, often on dangerous two-lane rural roads?! This was nearly unheard of. He *should* have been chauffeured by the protective Secret Service, with treasury agents in follow-up cars. And secondly, Harry Truman had told friends that the un-air-conditioned, rustic Shangri-La was "boring, and needed more work inside and out," and that he "didn't want to spend time there," having nothing to do or see. {Source: Camp David's website.} And third, Harry had supposedly just gone alone to Shangri-La on Friday, July 29th, with no visitors noted in his logs. He did not surface again for the record until Sunday, July 31st, when he picked up arriving Bess Truman at a train station in Silver Springs, Maryland. Something sure seems fishy here...

"Shangri-La" was of course the original name for rural Maryland's "Camp David" - officially it was titled "Naval Support Facility at Thurmont" - but was the whole notation of Harry traveling there – on either recent weekend - a bit of a ruse? *Did the president briefly go there... then actually take off for Vermont in secret, instead?* No appointments were listed for Harry's Saturday or Sunday, no notes at all for both critical summer weekends. What would restless Mr. Truman be doing at the hot, undeveloped presidential retreat for nearly *three* days with no one to talk to? He didn't even like to fish, not in cold streams. Such a described trip seems ludicrous. Rural Vermont was about five-hundred driving or train-trip miles away, or more likely, just a short plane flight. But another thought: could Setimus have been imported for a spell, from Vermont *to* Camp David? It was a very similar, shaded, secure atmosphere for talks between presidents and world leaders, and the captive alien humanoid was now that, in a sense, was he not? A de facto ambassador. The United States was locked in a Cold War with the ruthless Soviet Union and recently-communist China; good relations with diplomatic ETs possessing superior technology was likely *critical*, to keep them "on our side." A smart president couldn't just ignore advanced, off-world visitors — a policy President Eisenhower adopted, as we will see.

In 2013, an online forum source posted this gem: *"I spent a little time of my life as a MUFON Field Investigator, and in that time, I've heard of these {presidential-ET} meetings. What I've heard was that Truman was at the first meeting, not Eisenhower."* Later, another poster chimed in: *"From what I was told, though, it was Truman that met with the visitors."*

All we know for certain is that ol' Harry was back in his Oval Office on Monday morning, both August 1st and 8th, for business as usual. Truman's chosen head of Economic Cooperation Administration, Mr. Paul G. Hoffman, was a Tuesday, August 9th, 1949, visitor to Harry's Oval Office for a private fifteen-minute meeting. And we must recall, Hoffman and Eisenhower were *very* close friends.

To be sure, there's no hard proof or smoking gun here, at least within President Truman's White House appointments records, of any trip to Vermont. However, if genuinely undertaken, it would naturally have been kept off the books, a hushed state secret, as one would reasonably guess of such a classified journey. And one thing is for certain: Truman White House logs show various visits by Hoffman and George Allen, two figures who strangely latched onto Eisenhower during this extraterrestrial plotting, as we will see.

{Truman's complete office/home telephone records and full access to his mail for this period are not available, and visitors to his Blair House residence in '48 and '49 could well have gone unrecorded, it should be noted. Thus *much more contact* by those individuals involved, mentioned herein, during the period of noisy White House reconstruction, seems very possible.}

Elsewhere in the '89 DIA briefing report, it was stated about Setimus at Kirtland AFB on 8/21/49: *"...arrangements were made for a future meeting at the same location, to open diplomatic relations."* Another shocking statement, leading to more questions. First, the author of the DIA briefing document mistakenly placed Kirtland Airbase in "Texas" when it was/is located in central New Mexico, but are we not all human and prone to the occasional miscue? Is *every* detail of *every* government report *always* immaculately correct? {A typed April 1966 White House letter to President Lyndon Johnson's close aide mistakenly called the base *"Kirk*land," as a classic example.} And secondly, how did humans – or Setimus - communicate with other ETs to decide the proper site for picking him up, at a specific earth time and date? The document didn't specify. Thirdly, how did the U.S. government "open diplomatic relations" with alien humanoids, exactly? Certainly, Kirtland AFB has built up its reputation over the decades of having hosted some very strange-sounding UFO affairs; did the U.S. government conduct secret back-channel communications there as of 1949 utilizing the Aztec crashed disc's recovered ET communications device? Even with congenial Setimus gone, and then Truman out of office, was sustained secret U.S.-alien contact ongoing, with this technology now understood by our top scientists, leading to the optimistic document that Congressman McElroy read? {See previous chapter.} And lastly, if so, did it all eventually lead to Eisenhower's carefully prearranged southern California alien contact in February of '54?

{All of this may sound pretty speculative at first, but the clues seem to add up nicely. And it all dovetails almost perfectly with the names and dates accumulated by dogged research of UFO investigator William S. Steinman, who had privately published an obscure 1987 book on the hotly-debated '48 New Mexico canyon UFO "crash," before being dreadfully harassed right out of "the UFO business." Since then, other investigative authors have also confirmed with impressive details the authenticity of the Aztec case.}

In focusing on August of 1949, a visit on the 9th by Paul Hoffman with President Truman is noteworthy also for the other guests that showed up at that West Wing office that day, according to the president's daily appointment logs. Dr. Edwin Griswold Nourse, Ph.D. (1883-1974) visited Harry at 11:00 a.m. (along with two others); Nourse is a name we'll see later as allegedly visiting aliens in California in the aftermath of the '54 Eisenhower-ET summit.

At 11:30 a.m. on 8/9/49, the New Hampshire-based former Navy Secretary also dropped by the Oval Office, likely still having a family home not far from neighboring Vermont. At 12:20 p.m., another key figure in the later Eisenhower-ET saga makes his first appearance. Multi-millionaire businessman George Edward Allen (1896-1973), officially a counselor at a D.C. firm and an oil company executive as well. He arrived around lunchtime to meet with his old pal Harry; humorous and heavyset Mr. Allen would later "just happen" to show up with President Eisenhower repeatedly during his February '54 Palm Springs vacation. Liberal George was supposedly a jovial friend of conservative Dwight, whom we must remember was President Truman's "Presiding Officer of the Joint Chiefs of Staff" at the Pentagon in much of 1949, albeit somewhat a part-time job. Mr. Allen was so close to Eisenhower he bought a home in Gettysburg, Pennsylvania, to be Ike's next-door neighbor. {Trusty George eventually died in Palm Desert, California, of a heart attack, in 1973, having been a good friend to widow Mamie in his last four years.} Mr. Allen was intrigued by flight; after the 1940s, he joined the executive board of some successful companies, including two aviation ventures. Like his good friend Hoffman, Allen was patriotic, intelligent, educated, helpful, wealthy, and had the free time available to answer a presidential call to pitch in on various projects, behind the scenes. Discreet Hoffman and Allen were like two well-to-do peas in a pod, good and trusted men who got along well with figures in both political parties.

In returning to that early 8/9/49 afternoon, Secretary of the Army Gordon Gray (1909-1982) arrived to see Truman as well, bringing along the Secretary of Defense and another adviser. Gray was listed in both the leaked 1952 and 1989 UFO briefing papers as a member of a presidential advisory committee on ongoing ET studies, called "Majestic-12." He went on to be named National Security Adviser to President Eisenhower. Obviously, something cosmic was up.

Oval Office appointment records show that on the morning of August 11th, Harry Truman stopped what he was doing to dictate a special letter to his former Army Chief of Staff, Mr. Eisenhower, "thanking him for his services." Truman dictated: "*I appreciate all that you have done, as well as that you will do in the future as a consultant and adviser... The nation is extremely fortunate to have had the benefit of this most recent service by you.*"

So we know that Dwight Eisenhower loved rural Vermont; was an immensely popular, powerful, and respected figure in the late '40s; had access to Army Intelligence files, and could write his own ticket on *any* exciting-sounding project. The '89 DIA document explained that "*top government and military administrators*" visited the alien Setimus. Reliable "Ike" would certainly be all that. He handled very sensitive military intelligence matters regularly as part of his jobs for Truman in the late 1940s.

Officially, Mr. Eisenhower was away from his Columbia University presidency post in July and August of 1949 for "a two-month vacation out of state." To take off for two whole months was a bit unusual, even for Eisenhower, who cited unspecified "health problems" he needed to recover from – somewhere else. If he *did* go to Vermont to relax – as he had done in the past – and monitor or visit Setimus, was this the foundation to future alien contact, *the whole key to fully unlocking a greater understanding of the eventual February 1954 ET encounter in California?*

Yes, admittedly, it seems comical on the surface, rich for satire, the idea that Dwight Eisenhower secretly went fishing and foraging in the thick Vermont woods in 1949 with a tree-hugging alien, chatting the lazy days away in the shade and beating the mid-summer heat, far from the nearest town. That probably didn't happen. But it doesn't mean that General Eisenhower wasn't a helpful part in setting up the rewarded humanoid ET and perhaps communicating with him personally – possibly even at the same time his old boss, President Truman, did too?

Speculation: the U.S. Army might have used troops – local one–? - to quarantine the "sequestered" alien's countryside "safe-house" and escort any American visitors, perhaps under Eisenhower's supervision. Maybe the Vermont National Guard? This would pique the interest of Governor Gibson, who then called and met with President Truman on 8/1/49 as Oval Office logs show. A governor is in charge of his state's National Guard reserve, and such mysterious road-blocking, house-guarding, perimeter-patrolling procedures would have taken up manpower and money.

Before we go any further, let's also bear in mind this nonfiction oddity: Vermont's Glastenbury Mountain and its surrounding property has been subject to mysterious disappearances for centuries, with a specific round of citizen vanishings between 1945 and 1950, when six people strangely disappeared without a trace in six different cases. The general locale is called "The Bennington Triangle," since it covers the Bennington, Vermont, surrounding area.

Vermont paranormal researcher/author Joseph A. Citro feels this large triangular patch features "special energy that attracts outer space visitors" (source: *Reader's Digest*). Other UFO buffs who have spoken to locals have also wondered if the disappearances are part of ET abductions since there are often sightings of unexplained lights in the unique area's skies around the same time as the vanishings. 2018 national statistics allegedly show that "California alone has reported more than 23,400 UFO sightings since 1940, though the odds of seeing a strange flying object are highest in Wyoming and *Vermont*." Thus overall, it now seems that rural Vermont was – and still is - a most fascinating yet fitting locale for an alien to reside in.

At last, Sunday, August 21, 1949, arrived. This was the DIA document's specific day of assigned transfer. Setimus was set free, supposedly. Vermont was a distant memory. The ET left planet Earth entirely, it was said, from a New Mexico airbase... just days after New Mexico Senator Clinton Presba Anderson (1895-1975), of all people, visited President Truman in the Oval Office. Anderson would befriend another Democrat president in 1962, showing him around some classified parts of Los Alamos National Labs – yes, Setimus's old home, allegedly - and Kirtland Air Force Base (see Chapter Eleven). And what is more, records show that Senator Anderson met with Eisenhower at 12:15, alone in Oval Office, the day before the president left for Palm Springs in February of '54.

Just eight days after the "diplomat" Setimus departed the planet, the Soviet Union detonated their first atomic bomb, although they did so in relative secrecy with no public announcement, despite its enormity. On September 3rd, 1949, startled American scientists picked up the resulting radiation in the atmosphere, and Truman was informed. He kept it quiet until a speech on September 23rd. In between Harry referred to the Soviet secret by a special code name: "Vermont." The American public was stunned and frightened in response, to put it lightly. Was the Soviet atomic test controversy warned about by Setimus the friendly alien in Vermont with supposed "psychic" or "clairvoyant" abilities?

To back up a bit, White House logs show that on Friday, 8/19/49, President Truman left his office at 4:45 p.m. to go to the D.C. Naval Shipyards to take a cruise with George E. Allen and seven listed friends, aboard the S.S. Williamsburg, where the chief executive stayed out of the public eye all weekend. Among those friends going along with Harry and George was the Secretary of the Air Force and Senator Anderson from New Mexico (who was also an Albuquerque insurance company owner). Perhaps with USAF help, Setimus was to have been scooped up by his alien brethren at Kirtland Airbase in Albuquerque on that Sunday, as mentioned.

No official White House notations were recorded on Saturday and Sunday. All we know is that Harry was seen publicly next giving a speech in Miami on Monday, August 22nd. And on Thursday, August 25th, two members of the "Majestic-12" UFO group came to see Harry for a confidential "off the record" Oval Office meeting: CIA Director Admiral Roscoe Henry Hillenkoetter (1897-1982) and his CIA predecessor, Admiral Sidney William Souers (1892-1973). And added to that, the next day, Dr. Edwin Nourse returned for a presidential chat. We'll examine him more closely in Chapter Nine.

Existing appointment logs show that Paul G. Hoffman *again* returned to visit Harry S Truman at 3:00 p.m. in D.C., at Blair House, on a quiet Saturday, August 27, 1949, regarding a private matter not explained within the appointments diary, just six days after the alleged time of the alien Setimus was "returned" while in New Mexico. On August 31st the *other* senator from New Mexico, Dennis Chavez (1888-1962), got a sit-down, face-to-face with Harry for over half an hour in the Oval Office, which was rather unusual. This same senator called President Truman, according to records, *on the very day of the UFO crash near Aztec, New Mexico,* the one that the military reached and pulled survivor Setimus from (March 25, 1948), and *then he met with Harry at 12:15 p.m.* in the Oval Office the very next day then, something was so important. *Senator Chavez met again with Truman on a quiet Saturday, 3/27/48, for ninety minutes.* Dennis was also familiar with the 1947 Roswell, New Mexico, UFO crash – according to researchers - and may have participated in its cover-up. Records also show that Chavez had also met with Truman in the Oval Office on July 25, 1949, just a few minutes after another visitor huddled with Harry: *a congressman from Vermont!*

Again, *is all of this* mere *coincidence?* It hardly seems possible now, in light of all that has been unearthed and chained together herein. *Thus it seems like we can put real faith in the contents of the 1989 DIA briefing document*, even if its cover page has some errors or changes in format that might upset some so-called "experts" today.

Let's quickly review what earthy President Harry S Truman had to say about alien visitation on the afternoon of July 20, 1952 - during a famous Washington D.C. "UFO flap" - when a reporter asked him: "Do the Joint Chiefs of Staff talk to you or concern you about the unknown...unidentified flying objects?" Harry replied on camera: "Oh yes. We discussed it at every conference we had with the military... There are always things like that going on. Ah, flying saucers and we've had other things, if I'm not mistaken." It was an astonishing, often-overlooked admission, one that can be seen on *YouTube* to this day. Truman knew he had only six months left in his presidency, but rather carelessly let slip that the ET issue was actually being taken seriously and carefully examined behind the scenes, for why else would a president bother his top military staff with such an

President Eisenhower's Close Encounters

issue? And again: who was his top military adviser overall? *General Dwight Eisenhower.*

Thus the '48 alien crash and mysterious humanoid Setimus almost assuredly *had* to have been well known to Eisenhower, who was likely already familiar with the '47 Roswell affair and now busy readying his campaign for Truman's job at the time of the recorded television interview that summer of '52. Dwight said he felt in his heart he was the only man in the country who could handle the job; now we may understand that seemingly arrogant sentiment more fully, at last.

For what it is worth, the controversial former U.S. Air Force "Office of Special Investigations" member, Richard C. Doty (1950-) said he once worked for the government in smearing and sabotaging civilian claims about UFOs and ETs, including hoaxing documents to preserve and protect ongoing secret classified secret American alien recovery/contact programs. After a few years following his retirement from the service, Doty has supposedly "come clean," repeatedly confessing his sins. He has stated that the American military/government does indeed possess recovered alien spaceships and dead ET bodies they have examined in military base labs... *and that also a few living humanoid extraterrestrials have been kept in covert conditions at Los Alamos National Laboratories, as far back as the 1940s,* since they proved to be peaceful and communicative. Just what was mentioned about the Setimus claim in the 1989 document, leaked in 2017. However, some in the so-called "UFO community" still don't trust ex-Sergeant Doty – who was often based out of Kirtland AFB in Albuquerque.

Again, let's reference the 1989 DIA briefing document, which described the increase of UFO sightings since 1947: *"A long-term program of carefully calculated contact"* was undertaken by

- 83 -

intelligent otherworldly beings, *"with the eventual goal of raising of awareness of our place in the galactic community."* This included the U.S. presidency: *"This program was escalated to include diplomatic contact with many of Earth's governments,"* a startling sentence later mentioning *"the case of the United States of America."* Once more: *first* Truman, *then* Eisenhower?

Just after June of 1952, when President Truman gave General Eisenhower an award at the White House, Democrat Harry and Republican Dwight became grumpy rivals. The Eisenhower National Historic Site put it this way online: "Eisenhower had begun to regard Truman as an inept, undignified leader who had surrounded himself with crooks and cronies. Truman, in turn, was furious with Eisenhower's claim there was a "mess" in Washington. He was incensed that Eisenhower would undermine Harry's efforts to end the Korean War by promising to go there himself. And he certainly was not pleased with the candidate's criticism of his foreign policy, particularly since Eisenhower appeared to be in total accord with it before the campaign. Eisenhower even refused Truman's invitation to join him for coffee in the White House on Inauguration Day." There was an ongoing feud by the early 1950s, and the competitive spirit within Eisenhower might well have played a part in his decision to meet with ETs on a much grander scale than Truman.

In just one example of subterfuge and scheming (if not outright lying) Mr. Eisenhower was capable of, albeit for a noble cause, he directed his staff to tell the press in mid-November of '52, after his election win, that he was holed up in a New York City residence, interviewing candidates for his cabinet. In front of dazzled reporters on the front stoop, appointed new cabinet officials and political big-shots paraded past the cameras. Instead, Dwight had taken off on a secret trip halfway across the world, to Korea, to inspect the ground situation there, in person, as he promised during the fall campaign.

Everyone around him in New York stayed mum for days to help pull off the ruse. The world's media had been distracted and duped. But this was ever-planning Dwight's way of doing things, meeting folks in-person to resolve issues. A late 1953 dinner speech, found online today, has President Eisenhower addressing a group with a story of how his hometown of Abilene, Kansas, had a "code" that people lived by: *always resolve your differences with people "face to face."* Meet them head-on, look them in the eye, and talk out your problems or disputes, he said. Korea got a small taste of that.

So we can see that after he was sworn in, new-President Eisenhower likely covertly encouraged and shaped a year of private, ongoing ET communications, negotiations, deliberations, and Smoke Tree home construction. Remarkably remote Edwards Airbase in the arid desert of southern California was chosen as the most ideal, secure locale for such a private "summit conference." Dwight needed a cover story in which to attend the distant event without the press or the public getting wise. So a "much-need golf vacation" was the concocted ruse, the excuse or premise needed to make history - perhaps much like Truman telling the press he was off to Shangri-La?

Yes, the transcontinental trip was rather tiring, aboard sleek Columbine II that February 17, 1954, but the public airport greeting on Wednesday night for the First Couple in Palm Springs was refreshing and energizing. Dwight and Mamie were quickly met on the runway at the plane's steps by Paul Hoffman (and Paul Helms), then whisked away to their 400-acre "Smoke Tree Ranch," located just outside city limits at 1850 Smoke Tree Lane. Life there seemed pretty guarded, remote, and sedate. Since its early days the place featured a community clubhouse and dining hall, a swimming pool and sun deck, tennis courts, riding stables, trails, a dude ranch, guest cottages, and seventy-five homes, added in number over the years.

Five low-key days total, leaving Monday for the return flight to D.C.—that was the plan, originally.

By all reckoning for extraordinary, otherworldly, "first *landing* contact" the right man was now in the right place – well, *close* - at the right time, with everything going to plan. Perhaps that was also because a *second* Dwight Eisenhower had arrived in town as well.

CHAPTER FOUR

Palm Springs, not Warm Springs

"Ike broke off a porcelain cap from a tooth."

— Press Secretary James Haggerty

By the first vacation morning in Palm Springs - Thursday, February the 18th , golf-greedy Dwight was out a Smoke Tree Ranch door to a chauffeured car, to go play a brisk round at 9:30 with Paul Hoffman and Paul Helms at the Tamarisk Country Club. George E. Allen joined them for lunch in the clubhouse. Tourists, locals, and the press weren't exactly encouraged to go along, although the exclusive site wasn't walled or well-fenced, nor lined with tremendous security. A new rule was put in place, however: *no one was allowed to film or photograph the president while golfing,* supposedly because he was so worried about an errant shot on the links. The Secret Service grimly enforced this policy, along with course officials, by snatching cameras out of the hands of gawking fans. Very few photos overall were permitted taken during the president's desert golf excursions that week. As the media reported, during the president's vacation, the assembled treasury men – "casing Palm Springs for three months ahead of time," according to one newspaper account - were not just tough, serious, and armed under their suit jackets, they also kept machine guns in their golf bags, as if expecting possible big trouble.

But there were more than just hidden weapons going on below the surface of this southern California vacation. Let's take a look at some more fascinating facts regarding the president's northeast-of-Los Angeles visit...

Popular journalist Walter Winchell (1879-1972) wrote in the local papers that he flew with industrialist Howard Hughes, on Tuesday the 16th, from Beverly Hills to Palm Springs. Did Hughes and Eisenhower hook up in any way during the visit? Intriguing! But Winchell made another interesting discovery, revealed in the *Desert Sun* on Monday, February 22nd: "*President Eisenhower's dead-ringer look-alike is in town. New Yorker Chester Miller. Same balding pate, height, and grin.*" Huh! Now why in the world would the president need to bring in a doppelganger? This was an innocent "golf vacation," remember?

If body-double Chet Miller was there quite innocently, what are the odds he "just happened" to fly from New York City to show up in the exact remote town precisely when Eisenhower did? Knowing what we know now about the possibility of aliens arriving nearby in great secrecy... and Ike's penchant for secret planning... the double's presence simply couldn't have been an accidental twist of fate. Was cunning, strategy-loving Dwight plotting some possible subterfuge while visiting Edwards Airbase, or while staying in Palm Springs? Mr. Miller was spotted with his wife on Sunday night the 21st at a supper club in town, as reported in another local newspaper article, and he was described as "an independent filmmaker." It is unknown how long Chester Miller had been in town, or when he finally left. But something fishy sure seems to have been up.

Various Treasury Department agents had been in the Palm Springs area "for more than a week" leading up to the February 17th arrival of the president, a San Bernardino newspaper noted. "Secret Service agents have been combing the desert resort region for signs of danger," such as checking out members of the exclusive ranch community (including servants) and the places Dwight was planning on going (mainly two clubs and a church). The region was swarming with federal agents, it would seem in hindsight.

Paul Gray Hoffman seemed to hover around Dwight now just like a T-man, every day on this vacation, media stories revealed. One syndicated newspaper columnist even wondered if their closeness, and Hoffman's influence, was good for the nation. And of course, the ubiquitous George Edward Allen was often orbiting the president, too. Perhaps reporters were growing jealous. No one, however, seemed to question why low-key "Ike" needed another vacation, so soon after his last, and why he had to travel thousands of miles at taxpayers' expense just to do so. There was no campaign event involved, no fundraisers or special dinners on the Palm Springs presidential schedule, despite the wealthy local residents and visitors, many from Hollywood.

By 9:00 that Thursday morning, February the 18th, the president's press secretary - crusty James Campbell Hagerty (1909-1981) - held a press conference at the Spanish-Colonial-style "El Mirador Hotel." That's where the media was bivouacked, far from Smoke Tree. The confab was designed to brief local, national, and international news reporters and photographers on the planned vacation schedule for the chief executive and his wife, and it certainly lured the press away from the president, allegedly golfing across town. There was little of substance to report at El Mirador (which means "watchtower"). Big Jim Hagerty was an imposing former *New York Times* reporter who knew how to manipulate the press and shape issues Eisenhower's way. Therefore, in theory, Hagerty could have told the assembled media that Eisenhower was out golfing and would be out of contact with the press for some time, while Chet Miller could have then stood in for him, taking his swings on the exclusive country club courses, freeing the famous president for something else far away. Remember, no photographs or film allowed, at least after that first morning's outing — with Helms, Hoffman, and pro Ben Hogan - at Tamarisk. Some media and public photographs *were* taken for a while that day, to get that pesky curiosity factor out of the way. Don't bother good ol' Ike on his vacation, was the general theme for the remainder of the desert idyll.

And there was something else unusual going on at this time: Columbine II was noticed missing at the airport! Hagerty explained to reporters that the president's plane had been flown to Burbank, for servicing at a factory there. A cover story? Or the simple truth?

As always in matters of covering the activities of a sitting president, competing reporters, photographers, and newsreel cameramen - estimated to be around 120 in total - kept up the best coverage they were allowed, again usually at arm's length. In this case, the press - which arrived in a separate plane Wednesday night - likely got bored with El Mirador, which was in town. {The hotel closed in 1973 and some of it was sold off. What remained burned to the ground in 1989. Since the structure's bell tower was a local landmark, in 1991 it was rebuilt as part of a medical center and remains in place to this day.}

A large ballroom in the hotel was specially prepared and decorated in advance, with tables and chairs set up for reporters working on stories, and at least one telegraph, for sending out information deemed important or urgent. A teletype machine was also hooked up, in addition to plenty of El Mirador ashtrays, cigarettes, drinks, and snacks. The media's hotel rooms were reserved well in advance at first by Paul Helms, who originally told management it was for a baker's convention coming up, keeping the president's visit a secret for as long as possible.

Around 5:00 p.m. that Thursday afternoon, James Hagerty returned at El Mirador, this time to the assembled media that Dwight's vacation would likely be extended beyond the original planned four-and-a-half days. Was this deliberately done to give aliens an extended chance to show at Edwards Airbase? Had someone glimpsed or heard about a "sneak preview" UFO in the area? In the Burbank/Los Angeles area that very day – the 18th – an astronomer reported spotting "a huge ellipsoidal object that was first seen flying towards the west." Abruptly, the spindle-shaped UFO made a quick turn "to the north at an estimated speed of 120 m.p.h.," and disappeared from view. {Source: Loren Gross, *UFOs: A History, 1954: January-May*.}

On Friday the 19th , James Hagerty held yet another press conference at the El Mirador at 9:00 a.m. and encouraged media attendance at the planned party that night. And Eisenhower again supposedly played golf, this time at the restricted Thunderbird Country Club, opened in 1951 in the Rancho Mirage part of town. The aging president used an electric golf cart for the back nine, the Secret Service walking fast nearby to keep up. Dwight played with three locals, unknown to the rest of the nation; it was a joy to feel the warm sun, as opposed to the cold, damp, bird-hunting vacation outside of Thomasville, Georgia, the previous week. Again, "press photographers were denied the privilege of taking pictures," a local newspaper reported of the golf outing.

Records show that at 1:00 on that Friday, Dwight enjoyed lunch at the Thunderbird Club with several friends, including arriving Paul G. Hoffman and George E. Allen. Evidently, it was the real Eisenhower, too, chatting with folks in the clubhouse dining hall. But that wasn't enough time with Mr. Allen; records show that the president motored to George's attractive home in La Quinta for a visit there between 4:00 and 6:15 p.m.

Now then... guess who else *might* have arrived on the scene as well? They weren't even on good terms, but *ex-President Harry S Truman*. Citizen Harry just *might* have been lurking in the 'hood, but the clues for this are admittedly scant. The *Desert Sun* newspaper once reported ex-President Truman visited Palm Springs in 1959 (true) and that he also arrived in town sometime earlier in the 1950s to stay at La Quinta, right where his close friend Mr. Allen had a home. In recalling the Eisenhower's ballyhooed February 1954 visit decades later in his 1987 memoirs, the former "cowboy mayor" of Palm Springs - Frank Mitchell Bogert (1910-2009) – wrote something most intriguing: *"Harry Truman also spent considerable time in the village during this period."* {Then the author promptly named the Palm Springs house Harry stayed at in 1959, instead. Memory merge?} While there is admittedly no smoking gun record of Truman's presence in La Quinta, to this day there is an elementary school in town named after him (and a public park named for Eisenhower).

Theory: *if* ex-President Truman *was* in the sprawling desert community, separated by twenty miles from Eisenhower's Smoke Tree guest quarters, it raises the chances that something *really* big was up. And that Dwight secretly met with Harry at George Edward

Allen's estate at this time, *the very day of the prearranged alien landing,* far from the public eye. {The official record says Eisenhower was driven back to Smoke Tree at 6:45, then that's it for the day — was this part fudged? Or is that when "Ike" *truly* took off for Edwards AFB?} Perhaps just as Eisenhower was a supporting player to Truman's ET visit to Vermont (or Camp David) in August of '49, perhaps now Truman was playing that smaller part to Eisenhower's starring role in California in February of '54. That's purely conjecture, however.

If mildly cantankerous Harry Truman truly was bunking with George Allen in La Quinta, he could simply say to any prying busybody he was in town to raise funds from the local well-heeled residents for his planned presidential library. If something went wrong with the "runway summit" — like Dwight's possible death, incapacitation, or kidnapping by suddenly-sinister aliens — then Harry's presence was a very viable contingency plan. Truman in La Quinta could quickly step in and act as a very informed, experienced president to handle the reins of government. That certainly wasn't constitutional, but possible in such a 1950s emergency as youthful Vice President Nixon, back in D.C., likely had no clue what was going on in the California desert, and perhaps even knew *nothing* about *any* alien visitation in general at this point. {Veeps were traditionally told very little of secret government ops in those days; V.P. Truman didn't even know about FDR's atomic bomb development, not told until just after President Roosevelt's death.}

Assuredly, if human-like, peaceable aliens *had* landed at Edwards Airbase that Friday afternoon, some telephone calls were doubtlessly made to and from the sprawling desert air facility, to find out exactly what was going on, and how safe it was for a president — or two. Going to George E. Allen's house was frankly the perfect place with complete privacy to take care of just such classified calls and commands. No suspicious press; no prying Palm Springs dignitaries; no curious citizens visiting; and no wives or hangers-on were around.

We know that *if* Paul Hoffman was still with Eisenhower at this point, he inevitably left to head over to El Mirador to co-host a party for the idle media, held inside and out, on their Starlight Patio as nighttime set in. The Helms/Hoffman cocktail party officially started at 6:00 p.m. and was considered "an outstanding event," as the area papers later raved. James Hagerty was there, bantering with the large crowd of reporters, who were focused on the hotel goings-on, allowing the president to operate in complete secrecy that Friday night. This deliberate ploy to distract the press was effectively utilized again by Dwight in February of 1955, as we'll see in a later chapter. Reports say even members of the First Couple's entourage were partying there on 2/19/54, like Mamie's personal secretary, making one wonder if Mrs. Eisenhower also dropped by at one point. Therefore, Dwight's Smoke Tree set-up was left virtually vacant that critical evening. Reporters had no clue what was *really* going on.

Remember Eisenhower's Korean trip secrecy? *Distract the press*, that was key to letting Dwight undertake his secret mission by plane.

Theory: while at George Allen's place that late Friday afternoon, the president finalized by phone his plans to be driven to an intermediate airbase, and then flown under the cover of darkness for Edwards AFB. Bermuda Dunes Airfield or Thermal Airport might have been utilized for this covert flight, at least during daylight hours, to discretely aid Mr. Eisenhower in strict silence, no one the wiser. Perhaps Dwight even sent lookalike Chet Miller in a dark sedan at 6:15 back to his Smoke Tree ranch guest house or office, where there were nearly no eyewitnesses, everyone out socializing. Then, some hours later, the same small airfield handled Dwight's hushed arrival back in the Coachella Valley and the *real* president was hustled straight home.

To flash forward a bit: after dawn, Saturday the 20th, the president reportedly arrived at 7:45 a.m. at a special office set up for him at Smoke Tree, a block or so from the Helms residence. Had he even slept a wink that night? What was so important that he needed to get to his secure ranch office, with its special phone lines, away from everyone else as soon as the sun fully came up? He knew he had to be there, bright and early as the media was scheduled to arrive soon. During the Cold War, America's leaders had to appear calm and in control, which was also helpful for the stock market.

In privacy, the president scribbled a quick letter that Saturday morning to his son, John, describing his previous two days of golf. He swiftly signed some 19 minor bills into law, then smilingly spoke to the press pool, which had arrived by bus from El Mirador. "Sixty camera and newsmen" covered this "event," held outdoors, where the president was awkwardly but comically locked out of his small office for a while. Later, keeping up scheduled appearances, he played golf at Thunderbird yet again with pals Helms, Hoffman, and Allen. The familiar foursome had lunch at the club. The president almost *had* to do this; *golf was the whole public reason he came to Palm Springs.* If he *didn't* hit the links as scheduled, the bored press would get antsy and curious, if not suspicious. Meanwhile, Mamie socialized with some wives and guests, keeping an eye on her elderly mother Elivera, both likely without an extraterrestrial clue.

Dwight was recorded as having gone back to Smoke Tree from Thunderbird on Saturday at 2:45 p.m., the rest of his day strangely left wide open. From 3:00 to 7:00 was undescribed downtime; likely the aging chief executive took a nap to catch up on his likely sleeplessness from the night before, and handled more phone calls, monitoring any ensuing Edwards AFB matters from a distance. He'd get up and attend a scrumptious dinner, though, with a handful of excited guests, around 7:00 p.m. This meal was held within the Smoke Tree Ranch's cozy, rustic banquet hall that evening when some dental woes occurred. This is the point where many Ike-ET story-tellers go a little off track, feeling Eisenhower "disappeared" from his vacation to secretly head to Edwards Airbase; he did not as *his tooth emergency was real.*

To explain further: a few invited guests showed up in the Saturday sunset's glow for supper with the Eisenhower's, hosted by Smoke Tree's Bailey family, founding members of the colony. According to some rather loose secretarial notes of the president's daily appointment calendar, the meal was supposed to start around 8:00 p.m. and was likely scheduled to last for an hour or two at the most. Mrs. Bailey was basically in charge of preparing and doling out the big meal utilizing some ranch staffers.

{According to author and "MJ-12" document investigator Ryan S. Wood, the 1952 Eisenhower briefing documents and a later-leaked 1954 *"Special Operations Manual 1-01"* were viewed by three different military sources for confirmation as authentic, including a Navy man named "Dale Bailey." This man worked in the mid-1970s for an admiral who operated a weapons facility at Kirtland AFB in 1954. An online check of this name turns up "W. Dale Bailey," with previous addresses listed at *Palm Springs* and *Palm Desert, California.* Coincidence? Or a blood relative of the Smoke Tree brood hosting Ike's dinner on Saturday?}

All were served a slice of duck meat and scrumptious side dishes. Almost certainly there was cake ready for dessert and various breads doled out here and there, in slices and in rolls, provided by Paul Helms, the bakery executive who helped fund and promote Palm

Springs civic programs and L.A.-area sports endeavors. Mr. Helms was bald and somewhat stocky but may have been ill at the time whether he knew it or not; he died of cancer at age 67 less than three years later.

According to this author's source, the hostess for the evening meal proudly informed the assembled guests that the tasty tan fowl on the dinner table before them had been shot that very morning by hunters within her own family. The scene likely resembled Norman Rockwell's "Home for Thanksgiving" painting as all ages smiled around the table. President Eisenhower cut off a sizable portion of his roasted bird meat, stabbed it with a fork, and placed it in his mouth for chewing as likely many watched.

Dwight Eisenhower's right hand let go of his fork and quickly shot up to his jaw as he stopped chewing and grimaced in pain. Asked what the problem was, the president replied that he had just bitten down on something quite unexpectedly hard, and hurt one of his teeth. All were taken aback, watching anxiously as "Ike" rubbed his jaw and likely spit out – as delicately as possible - his food and his incisor's busted crown into a napkin, the pain growing worse.

"What's in this duck?" Eisenhower grumpily demanded to know.

The nervous, apologetic hostess, Mrs. Bailey, replied, "Oh, I'm so sorry, Mr. President! The boys used buckshot to bring them down," explaining that perhaps bits of the small metallic balls – or "grapeshot" - were still within the roasted meat.

"What kind of a sportsman uses *buckshot* to bring down a duck?!" the wincing president groused, pulling away from the table. The concerned chief executive described his dental dilemma briefly to the startled gathered guests, the hostess, and her kin mortified.

Later that night the president's spokesman calmly explained that Dwight sought treatment via host Paul Helms' dentist, so the chief executive likely left the room with Mr. Helms sometime after the meal, searching for a telephone and an address book to call this specific oral medical professional.

Various employees of the ranch, the small number of presidential aides scattered around Palm Springs, the media, Secret Service agents outside Smoke Tree, and residents of the local desert city were all somewhat - if not completely - in the dark as to the true nature of what was going on from this point forward. All *some* people knew was that President Eisenhower had left his dinner rather abruptly, and word slowly began to spread (accurately) that it was due to a "sudden medical emergency."

Somehow, during the course of the evening, word of the sudden departure filtered back to a few bored members of the fourth estate at El Mirador, and as one could expect, press speculation and gossip began to incubate in the fertile soil of utter boredom. Phone calls were placed by some reporters to a contact or two at Smoke Tree, and they were told "everything's fine." Then a bit later it was learned that the president was now mysteriously "missing." One witness's account described seeing Mr. Eisenhower grimacing in pain and leaving in a hurry to receive "immediate medical help" - so *wow, what a story!* Was the beloved president having a serious health crisis... perhaps even a heart attack? The media promptly rolled a snowball down a slippery slope; more rumors began to take shape and gather speed, growing outrageously out-sized and out of hand. While experienced reporters assembled at El Mirador excitedly postulated as to the true nature of the problem, many likely recalled that President Franklin Roosevelt abruptly died while on a quiet idyll in Warm Springs, Georgia, just nine years before. Since FDR died

President Eisenhower's Close Encounters

vacationing in Warm Springs... maybe Ike had just done the same while quietly vacationing in *Palm* Springs?

One of the more respected dentists in the desert area in those days was indeed phoned at his home Saturday night, but according to one source looking back on the event for this author from the 1990s, the dentist in question answered his telephone, listened to his caller, gave a surly "Yeah, right, sure," and then went right back to sleep. We can thus speculate reasonably President Eisenhower tried to carry on eating his meal and relaxing afterward for a couple of hours, but by nine or ten o'clock his affected tooth was throbbing and it was time to make a call for emergency dental assistance.

It would seem likely that a Palm Springs area dentist being called and summoned to his office would include the phone requester's phrase: "In order to work on the damaged tooth of the president." Feeling he was being pranked, the disbelieving dentist allegedly went back to what he was doing, it can be safely stated... but if it was *sleeping*, then this indicates the dentist was probably not aroused until sometime after, say, 10:00 or 11:00 p.m. - perhaps even in the middle of the night/early morning. A Palm Springs source for this anecdote recalled to this author that the president's dental treatment "took practically half the night." Temporary crown repair - for "tooth #9," Ike's upper left central incisor, according to records - on any human being should take a competent dentist about an hour to undertake the preparation work, and after a break, require perhaps an hour or so to repair with a new crown. And this after the dentist was finally called back and urged to hurry up, the president was waiting at his Palm Springs office. Thus Dwight didn't get home from all of this delayed treatment until sometime around midnight (rather like the night before). It had to have been a rather humbling, frustrating way to spend the evening after the monumental ET summit just 24 hours before.

Press secretary Jim Hagerty was finally contacted by someone (a presidential aide?) at the steak fry across town Saturday night. Scuttlebutt circulated that Mr. Hagerty abruptly left his dinner party tight-lipped. Further chin-wagging established he was heading to Smoke Tree, then to El Mirador to make an official statement on the president's enigmatic condition and mysterious whereabouts. To the unrestrained press, the electrifying inside scoop of the decade seemed forthcoming.

A writer for *Time* magazine reporting a week later felt that odd Saturday night was extraordinary, all right, but for the wrong reasons. He labeled the increasing media frenzy that night "a demonstration of journalistic mob hysteria." It seems another reporter at the time – aggressive Merriman Smith (1913-1970) - had phoned in an official United Press International story, back to New York headquarters, boldly (and foolishly) asserting that President Eisenhower had suddenly died of a massive heart attack!

Just minutes later, the resulting, alarming UPI bulletin was duly retracted. Eisenhower was not dead after all (he suddenly got better, as the old joke goes). Mr. Hagerty had arrived, looking somewhat sour, irritated at having to set the record straight. "Folks, Ike bit into a chicken bone and broke a porcelain cap off a tooth," Hagerty briefed the eager media mob. {Obviously this opening statement was slightly inaccurate as it was *duck* meat served, not *chicken* meat.} The crowd collectively groaned.

The dour, dark-haired, gray-eyed press secretary further informed the assembled crestfallen journalists that the president had left the Smoke Tree Ranch simply to receive professional treatment in a Palm Springs dental office and would therefore be unavailable for comment as he recovered. All was well overall. "When the president goes to church tomorrow morning," Hagerty made sure to tell reporters – in a quote mentioned in the *New York Times* - "his grin will look the same as ever." Pencils went down fast.

The entire evening's pulse-quickening rumor-mongering was for *nothing*!

The imposing Mr. Hagerty, age 45, further told the now-tamed press that host Paul Helms personally took the president to see his local dentist, Dr. Francis A. "Frank" Purcell, "who replaced the cap." That was it, the whole honest story. The only hold-up - not told to the press - was that Dr. Purcell had ignored the first phone call and gone (back?) to bed; when he finally showed up the dental treatment simply took time. The president's official papers show genuine dental treatment from Dr. Purcell, left over to this day at his presidential library. End of story.

To show how innocent it was, Dwight would indeed attend church services the next morning, with his wife and mother-in-law, grinning famously just as Hagerty foretold.

Yes, this was Palm Springs, not Warm Springs. The vacationing president was fine, in general (pun intended). Records show his affected tooth's porcelain cap applied by Dr. Purcell was eventually replaced more permanently in July by the president's dentist. Dwight and Mamie enjoyed their church socializing Sunday, seated next to Mr. and Mrs. Paul Helms in their pew. Dwight "humbly prayed for divine guidance," one news account claimed. A Palm Springs *Desert Sun* report for March 1954 stated that the president and his entourage – including three Secret Service vehicles – then left the church and were then seen driving about the village "surrounded by Secret Service men."

{According to the U.S. Surgeon General's notes on President Eisenhower's dental treatment records (strangely not opened to the public until 1991), the leader of the free world *did* indeed receive dental treatment from a "Dr. Francis A. Purcell" on the Saturday night in question for a chipped porcelain cap on his "upper left incisor." One UFO researcher backed this up by discovering Eisenhower's secretary dutifully recorded the event in her diary. Dwight had experienced trouble with the same damaged tooth's crown in question, twice, two years before, the 1991 record-opening showed. For the past two decades, curators at the Eisenhower Presidential Library in Abilene, Kansas, laugh off the entire allegation as much ado about nothing, and on that particular Saturday, they are right.}

That mid-Sunday the 21st, the president's group enjoyed a private light lunch and a substantial break. The media was likely scattered about the region, traditionally having an off-day in Washington, on a Sunday. Meanwhile, back at the ranch... a "real cowboy cookout" Sunday evening created a homey, western feel for the First Couple, the press not invited, only finding out later. {Source: *Desert Sun* newspaper, which published twice a week in 1954.} But there over a hundred witnesses that Dwight was looking happy and healthy, saying he wanted to come back to the facility next year (but didn't). The dinner party was a major, innocent, long-planned event that included the mayor and his wife; Helms and Hoffman; eight people named "Bailey;" comedian Bob Hope's wife and daughter, a U.S. senator, publisher and TV personality Bennett Cerf, radio star Freeman Gosden, two noted Hollywood movie producers, and "Dr. and Mrs. Frank Purcell." Yup, Dwight's impromptu dentist from the night before. Dr. Purcell's widow June, some twenty-five years after the fact, *did* plainly remember attending the Smoke Tree Ranch steak fry on Sunday, February 21st, '54, and hearing her husband being introduced to all - including some reporters present - as the "dentist who had treated the president."

Author Larry Holcombe (1943-) in his popular 2015 book *"The Presidents and UFOs"* reinforced the notion that a U.S. president would not have been able to use his fairly busy Saturday and Sunday schedules in public with so many eyewitnesses for wedging in a vitally important, top-secret ET landing event. Hence, we can say that the entire Edwards Airbase alien affair was likely not pre-timed to definite standards, but if scheduled or at least deemed *possible* before the chief executive left Washington D.C. for California then it was probably rather loosely plotted to happen "some time Friday." Thus flights were restricted in advance to Edwards Airbase on that date, as mentioned earlier. And that the dental story is superfluous. Not relevant.

A reminder: a U.S. president doesn't have to make up any sudden "dental cover story" to leave for a few hours; he would simply tell his inner circle: *"I've just learned I've got some important business to attend to, I'll be back in a few hours, you guys just go ahead with your meal."* And then leave without further explanation, and all would understand, largely unruffled.

The desert weekend fun continued. But another noteworthy Palm Springs story *might* be important to highlight: a newspaper article (from 2/25/54) mentioned that retired Air Force Brigadier General Harold Arthur Bartron (1896-1975) was seen around town that weekend. One month after the July 1947 Roswell UFO crash, Harold was transferred to Wright Field's Air Materiel Command, near Dayton, Ohio, the home of so many rumors of recovered alien discs and wreckage, even bodies. It was not a shock to hear that Bartron and his wife were in a Palm Springs supper club that weekend, however; he once served at March Field in nearby Riverside (and eventually passed away two decades later there). Conjecture: Bartron might have been a very trusted, mature source who ferried Dwight by plane from the region, out to Edwards (or nearby

Palmdale) on 2/19/54. Or perhaps he merely arranged it, and some tight airfield security measures, with one of Eisenhower's regular Columbine II pilots tagging along to handle the extra aviation.

One employee of the Palm Springs airport reported to this author in the mid-'90s that there were "no side trips" from the city's public airfield for Eisenhower during his week-long vacation, confirming Dwight didn't utilize the airport in town Friday. Plus, we know Columbine II wasn't there anyway. This indicates once again his utilizing a smaller, more restricted military base in the immediate area, such as in Palm Desert (Thermal Airport), or one in Desert Hot Springs, or perhaps Bermuda Dunes. March, Norton, George... there were plenty of small local military airfields for a pilot to choose from. It's possible such a minor base or airport would be classified or "unofficial" and a covert military operation, not open or even *known* to the public.

At any rate, we can reasonably assume that perhaps just after sundown on Friday night, history was made. A sitting United States president found himself speaking candidly but politely with alien beings on a flat airplane runway, over ninety miles from "home." It was, in fact, the whole reason for traveling to Palm Springs in the first place, plotted since at least November of 1952. The president, his top, trusted advisers, and a handful of bodyguards brought it off and kept it hushed, largely, for the rest of their lives.

By sticking around afterward for four more days in Palm Springs, the president would be available to monitor and handle any alien-related complications at Edwards or in the general area, should it arise. And of course, he could *golf*, his daily obsession. It was good exercise and took his mind off his problems. He had to show the country – and any foreign agents around - that nothing was out of place, that all was right in his world. If there *was* a second possible suspicious time-gap in Dwight's schedule for something secretive, such as another trip to Edwards Airbase, it would have been on Monday evening, the 22nd. That was after President Eisenhower golfed around noon at the Tamarisk Country Club, with Paul Hoffman and George Allen. {That pair *again!* How often do two men like this remain close to first a president from one political party, then a second from the *other* party?} Golf was followed by lunch there and a few kindly remarks, likely until around 2:00. Dwight's daily schedule the rest of that day is oddly blank, while a second special party was staged for the distracted press, starting at 6:30 p.m. at the local Biltmore Hotel this time, hosted by someone named Sam Levin.

{Trivia: a curious tidbit to ponder: on February 21st, at 11:00 p.m. in the Van Nuys section of the Los Angeles region, a local retired USAF pilot and his wife and mother "observed an object described as a flying saucer." It disappeared to the west. Joined by neighbors, they "then saw another flying object coming out of the north." The soaring disc "made three circles over the area and disappeared to the east," likely in the general direction of Edwards Airbase. {Source: Loren Gross, *UFOs: A History, 1954: January-May.*} Coincidence?}

Tuesday the 23rd's schedule was fairly busy for the president, with more golf for the president at Tamarisk with Paul Hoffman, and by nightfall, the Eisenhower entourage packed and cheerfully blew town for D.C., surrounded by well-wishers and a dutiful press corps.

One strange story emerged back on Sunday afternoon, however. A news account stated that press secretary Hagerty arrived at the newspaper's offices and purchased "six copies of each issue which detailed the president's visit," which he claimed was "for the president." *Six* would be the number of men said to have protected Dwight Eisenhower at the alien meeting, coincidence or not. {Hagerty also ordered six copies apiece for the upcoming March 18th and 22nd editions, long after the vacationing Eisenhower's were to have left town. *Why?*} Also, a local newspaper article a few days *before* the First Couple landed on the 17th had James Hagerty admitting that Paul G. Hoffman was the key man behind arranging the presidential vacation in California. News accounts during the president's stay kept mentioning Hoffman's presence. Again, his influence, like Allen's, on events that week cannot be downplayed.

Looking back, one must now wonder candidly if lookalike Chester Miller was originally imported to bring along at the critical time, to step up at Edwards Airbase and present himself to landed ETs as the American president, at least if the landing situation was felt to be somewhat dangerous. How would aliens know the difference? If this "Plan B" speculation sounds a bit far-fetched, then remember again that Army man Dwight Eisenhower was a revered planner, and employed great subterfuge, trickery, and secret plots to aid the allied war effort in WWII Europe. Had Ike ever used a body double before? The answer is still uncertain and likely a military secret, but many world leaders have utilized them in the past, including Eisenhower's enemies Hitler and Stalin, and his allied friend, British General Bernard Montgomery, during the war. {In fact, the "Monty" double was so convincing that fooled Nazi spies were reportedly plotting to assassinate him!} If a body-double ruse was somehow detected by the media and called out in Palm Springs, the president could just say it was just a joke on the press corps, or perhaps a necessary security precaution.

The press and the public certainly got a good look at the First Couple Tuesday night the 23rd at 8:00 or so at Palm Springs Airport, when the presidential party boarded Columbine II, evidently back in time from Burbank's Lockheed plant from those supposed repairs, or wherever it disappeared to. This "Air Force One" took off at 8:24 p.m., headed east, and officially took until 7:15 the next morning to land in D.C.! A grueling 11-hour trip; were there any unrecorded stops along the way? Or some sort of secret trouble?

For all the world, Palm Springs appeared on the surface to be the most uneventful, even *bland* vacation a couple could take (although two intoxicated men were arrested with guns, attempting to get into the well-guarded ranch while the First Couple were packing to leave late Tuesday afternoon). Calm, dry weather and high temps in the eighties every day made for near-perfect conditions. But the planet didn't understand its very future was being secretly discussed that week, expostulated at some length with "foreigners" arrived from another world entirely. All of this took place on a vast dusty dry lakebed in the Mojave Desert, in front of a huge aircraft hangar.

It was the only place in the whole world to be on a Friday night.

CHAPTER FIVE

Sherlock on Muroc

"Encounters will take place at military installations."

— Army Special Manual 1-01

At this late date, we cannot dig up direct, tangible, indisputable proof, nor first-person eyewitness allegations covering every step of Dwight Eisenhower's excellent airbase adventure. Evidence left behind of the event, including typed reports, photos, and film footage, were all undoubtedly declared "classified" and "Top Secret," then tucked away in vaults. But... we can act as legendary fictional detective "Sherlock Holmes" in carefully reconstructing the event where some gaps exist, logically piecing together the Edwards Airbase mystery when information is lacking...

The scene: a dusty desert airbase, nestled between mountain ranges, baked dry in the relentless hot sun for a few decades. It actually began when a family of settlers with the last name "Corum" stopped and put down roots in the Mojave Desert in 1910, and soon others followed. A small town was somehow carved out of a dry former lake-bed, a very flat open area without much of a water source if it didn't rain. Taking their name and spelling it backwards as "Muroc," the settlement and its barren vicinity got its title. Muroc Dry Lakebed, it was officially dubbed, was soon on the map. In 1932, the Army bought some of the parched land and created a bombing range for test pilots to fly over in practice runs. Without laying down expensive pavement, pilots could easily take off and land, and taxi about, on the hard, flat, bare surface. More and more land was acquired by the military/government in the late '30s until a simple base was erected for the pilots and bombardiers living and working there nearly every day, alongside mechanics and flight technicians. Eventually, two parallel runways were paved. Test-piloting the very latest aerial technology became pretty hip, and to help pass the time, "hot-rodding" and souped-up car races across the desert floor also grew popular at Muroc. To take advantage of economic opportunities created by the growing number of macho aviators and auto-drivers (and their mechanics), bars and eateries; apartments and small homes; medical offices and stores popped up near the expanding military facility, and other nearby local communities began to take root, such as Palmdale, California, 37 miles away.

"Mojave Field" was the site's first military base title but this gave way to "Muroc Airfield" as 1940 neared; the site grew in stature and importance as it was able to stage large-scale maneuvers. More and more barracks, hangars, and offices were constructed, along with roads, fencing, and guarded gates. Again the small towns nearby also increased in size, with more sophisticated homes and motels and government structures, such as a post office and courthouse. After the outbreak of World War II in December of 1941, the desert site expanded even more so in size, scope, and importance. The very latest and greatest American airplanes; heavy bombers; high-tech fighter jets; and specialized aircraft were taken to Muroc for testing. Since more base buildings were constructed as the years flew by, some, like the enormous plane hangars, featured paved aprons and parking lots above the hard-packed, 46-square mile clay lakebed.

On February 10th, 1948, the camp title was officially changed to the more formal "Muroc Air Force Base." A year after the death of respected test pilot Glen Walter Edwards (1918-1948) in a terrible aerial accident at the base, the site changed the title again, this time picking up the official designation "Edwards Air Force Base." Yet old habits die hard and thus many in the American military or government in the 1950s would still often refer to the base by both its "Muroc" and "Edwards" titles.

From this point on, "Muroc" will refer to the huge, dry-lake-bed area, stretching for many miles, utilized for unpaved runways... and "Edwards" to the military base itself.

In today's world, "Edwards Air Force Base" is famous for its cutting-edge aviation and aerospace exploits, including the landing of the space shuttles. Going beyond the lower atmosphere, more and more flights were designed to soar through the upper atmosphere and even into what we commonly call "outer space," albeit briefly. Many types of high-tech, high-priced military aircraft were/are tested at stupefying speeds and refined, mostly at the special adjacent "Flight Research Center," which has been present there since *even before* the '54 Eisenhower encounter.

By the time 1954 ended, one online site mentions, "new facilities completed included a concrete runway 16,800 feet long, 3,000 feet wide, and 19 inches thick; 14 enormous hangars, tele-metering stations, computation laboratories, and technical facilities worth

$150 million constructed and in place. There were modern barracks for the airmen, 1,500 family homes, two churches, an officer's club, an airmen's club, an NCO club, and a civilian club. The airbase even boasted one of the sportiest green-grass golf courses in that section of California." {That detail alone might have attracted President Eisenhower.}

By February of 1954, "the best and the brightest" in their chosen fields were assembled at or near the Edwards base, just as they are to this day. It makes one ask: *what better remote place was there on the entire planet that an advanced and peaceful extraterrestrial race could select to set down on and be well-received by an educated, space flight-minded host in a remote setting?*

Thus, in perhaps years-long communications, Muroc/Edwards was likely settled upon by both aliens and humans as nearly perfect for secret face-to-face contact. It wasn't a sudden, impromptu selection. Remember, Dwight Eisenhower the lifelong military strategist was rather famous for saying, "Planning is everything." He added sagely, "If you haven't been planning, you can't start to work, intelligently at least." In a matter as important as this, plotting moves and counter-moves in advance was likely of great private concern to the soldier-statesman.

Yes, the Mojave Desert aerial installation, located so far from population centers, was a kind of "top gun" proving ground, testing the mettle of both advanced engineers and fliers, but also mechanics and technicians on the ground, in addition to the simple routine training practices going on above. The U.S. Air Force was naturally a large presence as there was no specific national "Air Force Academy" in those days (but soon would be).

So the agreed-upon setting was a distant Edwards Airbase runway near a large airplane hangar, not too close to the barracks and offices. The first detailed publishing breakthrough on the historic "summit conference" came from a pair of intrepid authors in the paranormal field, Charles Frambach Berlitz (1914-2003) and William Leonard Moore (1943-), back in 1980. The duo worked up a well-intentioned book *"The Roswell Incident"* on the '47 New Mexico spaceship crash by merging that tale with rumors of Eisenhower's '54 Edwards appearance, supposedly only for a mere covert inspection of stored inanimate ET crash debris. While this was a bit "off-base" (pun intended), Berlitz and Moore must be given great credit overall for their groundbreaking work. For instance, the duo described uncovering a yellowing typewritten memorandum by an Air Force captain that mentioned the president's furtive '54 journey to Edwards. They also tracked down a "high-level member in one of the departments under Eisenhower," then living in retirement in Arizona, a man who had been telling friends in private that Ike did indeed travel to the base (by helicopter) to see the extraterrestrial evidence. {Yet Eisenhower didn't utilize helicopters at the White House until 1957, making this small part of the claim a bit tenuous.} The tenacious 1980 co-authors even sniffed out and interviewed the widow of Dr. Purcell who treated the president's ailing tooth that Saturday night, as mentioned. The twosome also found out *many UFO sightings were reported in the Muroc-Edwards vicinity between 1947 and 1954* (plus perhaps more that were never officially called in to the authorities or the local newspapers). Startlingly fast and fluid flights of disc or cigar-shaped objects were spotted in the skies. Some of these UFO claims were pinpointed in specific times and locales where there were no scheduled U.S. aircraft in the area, while others reported seeing darting UFOs deliberately *buzzing military flights* as if the occupants were trying to get their attention. In military circles, these are known as "purposeful flyovers." The military and corporate-based civilian personnel at Edwards Airbase were being given repeated extraterrestrial "air shows" *quite intentionally*. In this careful manner, intelligent aliens were likely attempting to "break us in" on the reality of their presence, leading up to the big day of official contact. Ostensibly so that it all wouldn't be such a huge, sudden shock. It was as if an overall master plan had been set out in stages, taking years, for the eventual high-level interaction.

{For a specific example of these otherworldly sightings, check out the photo archives of the website "Open Minds," where a cigar-shaped craft was captured on camera from a higher airplane window's view while flying near another man-made aircraft over the Muroc area in that special year again, 1954. The plane in flight, seen in the black-and-white photograph, seems a good deal larger than the angled UFO clearly visible behind it. One can go to www.latest-ufos.com where the photo's owners proudly state it was snapped and presented to the public long before digital fakery was introduced decades later.}

It has been alleged – back in the late 1970s - that a metallic flying disc came down to earth at an astonishing rate of speed and crashed very near Edwards Airbase, sometime in 1952. This startling saga was written about only a quarter-century later by researcher Leonard Stringfield (1920-1994), a former U.S. Air Force Intelligence officer. Supposedly, a radar specialist was working in the tower at Edwards AFB in '52 when he noticed a strange, fast-moving blip on his screen. He looked up, out the windows, and witnessed for himself the dumbfounding desert floor UFO crash in person, from afar, of course. He soon received information from others on the base that a 50-foot-in-diameter alien airship had indeed crash-landed, with four dead otherworldly bodies on board, all measuring about four-and-a-half-feet in height. The alien airship was taken to a base hangar, despite considerable damage. In the scramble to make sense of the breathtaking accident, at some point an Air Force captain screamed at the specialist: *"You didn't see anything!"* And that was the abrupt end of that, he never found out anything more, or so the Stringfield story described. Unfortunately, any sort of backup evidence on this under-explored saga remains at large. {Source: *"Majik Eyes Only"* by Ryan Wood.}

Could this tale be true? A crash-recovered alien craft was stored inside an airbase hangar at Edwards *before* 1954? Could this be the *real* reason why ETs agreed to peacefully land there (allegedly) on 2/19/54, and then opened up communications? And why President Eisenhower would quietly sneak away from his vacation in Palm Springs to meet them and arrange a deal? It would seem logical, but speculative.

Could it be that at the time of the "showing off" - 1947 to 1954 - visiting ETs were keeping an eye on the ways of our U.S. military, government, population, education, culture, and behavior? They certainly needed to know what was going on with earthlings to find out precisely *when* and *how* to properly descend, disembark, and be received cordially someday. How precisely this ongoing alien study of United States culture and human reaction to UFOs was accomplished one can only speculate, but learning our American customs and the English language had to have been quite important. Perhaps an *extended* visit and *sustained* interaction with humans was prepared for by the aliens, not just for a few minutes. At least one eyewitness stated later that spaceships and alien entities were still around at Muroc/Edwards *over a month after* 2/19/54, as we'll see in a later chapter.

To reinforce our belief that alien airships arrived on that February day at Muroc/Edwards, let's consult a leaked, classified military pamphlet that's impressive in all ways. The amazing, authentic April

1954 *"Special Operations Manual 1-01."* This explosive, once-secret Army Intelligence booklet explained instructions for qualified military personnel on the proper handling of discovered alien hardware and included quite precise, noteworthy drawings of various sizes and shapes of ET spacecraft. It also described the different types of visiting aliens. Just how did the American military/government get this exact, mind-blowing level of detail on such a variety of intact, operable ET spaceships? Undoubtedly partly from the measurable contents of the Edwards Airbase hangars, after President Eisenhower gave the okay for an apparent exchange of technology, it would seem, for this would have been the first printed manual after Ike's ET summit (March 1954's edition was likely all set by the end of his visit).

Troubling today, within the special instructional manual, details were given on how the U.S. government was to undermine American citizens who claimed to have come in contact with aliens and their crafts and to muzzle the corporate-owned media on this issue. This was in order to have the people of the United States (and thus the world) believe that various tales of UFO sightings and alien visitors - "little green men" - were simply fantasies and/or untrustworthy hoaxes. That visiting extraterrestrials *do not exist.* Denial was of critical importance, due to issues of "national security." To keep a lid on things a while longer to quietly study the issue and accumulated tangible evidence behind the scenes, which was also to be denied.

The eye-popping *"SOM 1-01"* also issued a statement concerning our subject matter herein: *"Encounters will take place at military installations or other obscure locations selected by mutual agreement."* This strongly reinforces the notion of ongoing secret communication with aliens, likely by high-tech radio signals and binary code – and 1948-recovered alien communications equipment

- within the federal government's "Project Sigma," as discussed in Chapter Two.

"Section I, Living Organisms" of the '54 Army Intel manual features paragraph 23, entitled "Encounters," confirming the modus operandi of premeditated arrangements. This remarkable passage mentions how human-alien meetings might be *"initiated by"* the visitors *"as a result of overtures by the entities themselves,"* and *"set up by mutual agreement."* Again, this supports not just the Muroc/Edwards event but perhaps even the Setimus situation with President Truman (and Ike?) in the summer of 1949, for how else would aliens know the proper time and place to pick up diplomat Setimus? Evidently, the ET could somewhat "phone home," much as in a later famous Hollywood movie.

"Such a meeting would have the advantage of being limited to personnel with appropriate clearance." Once more, this sounds like our 2/19/54 desert runway conference. An ensuing paragraph in the training manual mentions how all alien beings who did show up should be *"detained by whatever means necessary and removed to a secure location"* if they weren't already, again likely to keep the civilian population and the cynical press in blissful ignorance.

The late science-fiction and nonfiction author Brad Steiger (1936-2018), along with his wife Sherry (1946-2020), were naturally fascinated with the Eisenhower-ET meeting and opted to write a few pages about it in a 2011 book on aliens. The wedded co-authors added that in April of 1991 they participated in a Bay Area radio call-in show called *"Right To Know,"* which featured three supposed eyewitnesses to secret goings-on at Edwards Airbase in the 1950s. The trio described in some detail how they knew some extraterrestrial beings had been quietly interacting with top intelligence agents within remote United States military installations, supposedly. What sounds initially like a far-out sci-fi novel or movie plot was quite possibly explosive, exciting, behind-the-scenes *reality*.

So now we understand that Edwards Airbase and its Flight Research Center (established in 1951) sit alone on over 300,000 acres in the desolate, fickle Mojave Desert, where it is often inhospitably burning hot during the day and freezing at night, but an ideal locale for the U.S. military to quietly test-fly their still-secret new planes - and apparently for aliens to import their own. All in relative privacy and safety - minus the unexpected opening salvo upon their arrival on 2/19/54, ordered by a powerful general (as described by "Sergeant X" in Chapter One). Thus we can say that *if* the February '54 meeting was indeed prearranged, *not everyone* got the memo in advance. Surely Dwight Eisenhower would not have given the order to attack; the president did not want the landing event to turn into the first violent step of a deadly interplanetary war. The five ships shrugged off the volatile shelling and peacefully set down near a hangar, unharmed... *Then what?*

Like smart detectives, we have to construct a fittingly reasonable scenario for what likely took place next...

The differing sophisticated, undamaged, shiny spacecraft sat in silence for a time on the smooth pavement, apparently with no wings, propellers, or noisy engines cooling down. The five silver "unidentified bogies" gleamed in the sunlight, likely resting on thin metallic legs, or perhaps just resting flatly upon the dusty ground. This was astoundingly advanced technology for 1954, found previously only in sci-fi movies. Surely such an incredible sight would have been cause for a remarkably diverse set of reactions in the highly-trained military men on the base, staring with dropped jaws and bugged eyes at the touch-down – *if* they had not been briefed ahead of time. Tremendous excitement flowed; a sense of wonder and adrenaline soared in most men, and anyone working inside the nearby hangar probably stepped forward bravely but with some hesitation, unsure what to think. Was this a drill? A strange test? Some advanced, man-made United States aircraft being tested that day, unscheduled?

Awed but unprepared soldiers, pilots, civilians, and even some decorated officers may well have reached defensively for the nearest weapons. Perhaps whispers at first, then shouts alerting others were in order. It seems safe to say that many a pulse quickened and knee trembled, for this was the Cold War era, when some Americans lived in genuine fear that the Soviets were someday going to attack, perhaps in mysterious advanced aerial craft, unknown to western nations. Was this the start of a commie invasion? Noticeable perspiration, white knuckles, and frantic observation undoubtedly began to greatly increase as word spread.

Likely an alternative thought emerged. Were these, in fact, *alien* outer space airships? Intergalactic visitors? Or as they often said in the 1950s, "Mars men" within "flying saucers"? Were they friendly, or hostile? Careful assessments needed to be made, and fast, by those who hadn't been briefed in advance.

What is the first order of business for trained military personnel, when faced with a new and important situation one is unsure how to deal with? *A typical soldier reports any news to his superior officer* and lets *him* handle the situation. The news would work its way up the chain of command. In February of 1954, the top dog, so to speak, was the Edwards base commander, who had been in charge since January of 1952. That man was Joseph Stanley Holtoner (1911-2010).

By contemporary online accounts reprinting articles on the good ol' days, Stan Holtoner was a very daring, courageous, and macho type, with a history of test-piloting airplanes, and even a rocket-plane, undertaken at amazing speeds. However, "he was all business" on the ground, as one Edwards AFB colleague recalled. Blunt and bossy, Stan held a Bachelor of Science degree in aeronautical engineering, graduating from college in 1932. In December of '52 swashbuckling Holtoner was promoted to the rank of Brigadier General.

"General Holtoner, Base Commander." Hmmm... Perhaps we now have a very strong candidate for "General Z," who supposedly directed some troops in the field that fateful day to fire artillery at the five descending alien craft. He certainly was the forward, daring sort, loving the thrill of flight. Stan's online bio declares: "J. S. Holtoner participated in the Thompson Trophy Race with the North American F-86D Sabre jet and on Sept. 2, 1953, he set a new 100-kilometer world speed record of 1,110.748 kilometers per hour and won the Thompson Trophy. During his tour at the Flight Test Center until May 1957, General Holtoner flew every test aircraft that was assigned to the center. For his contribution to the development of the new, all-jet Air Force, General Holtoner was awarded both the Distinguished Flying Cross and the Legion of Merit at the USAF Flight Test Center." But perhaps the New York City-bred Holtoner let his ego at times get the best of him. Upon his December 17, 2010, death in Goldsboro, North Carolina, an online forum contributor wrote: "I won't mourn his passing. Holtoner was universally disliked by most at Edwards. Whilst at Edwards the way he treated and talked about one of his 2nd in command's and his wife was nothing short of insulting and disgusting. No R.I.P. or Godspeed from me I'm afraid."

So as a rather notorious "Alpha Male" or aggressive daredevil type of a leader at Muroc/Edwards, base commander J. Stanley Holtoner was the man everyone would have been searching for that afternoon, to inform him of the ET landing. Or did he already know, again via ordering shells fired at the UFOs coming down, as "General Z" present? Would he really assault unfamiliar airships? Part of his 2010 obituary mentioned Stan's past work in the field of missile defense technology: "General Holtoner participated in the development effort of such major programs as the B-70, Minuteman, Ballistic Missile Early Warning System, and the tactical fighter." He worked at times "in the fields of strategic and tactical system, air defense, electronics, aeronautics, and the myriad of problems which constantly represent the research, development, and engineering part of the Department of Defense function." Attacking aerial objects seemed to have been his specialty. This begs the question: *if "General Z" ordered an attack on the incoming ships, did he know in advance the alien visitors were coming and set himself up in the field to deliberately attack them upon arrival?* If so, Eisenhower had to have been furious. He didn't go to the lengths of arranging the visit for over a year in advance only to try to *kill* the peaceful visitors and possibly trigger an interplanetary World War III.

On that particular Friday, February 19th, officers and enlisted personnel that weren't out on leave were likely scattered about the base in various buildings, likely unaware of what was going on outside, silently descended near the distant Muroc/Edwards hangar. All might have been pleased, however, that the noisy distant shelling at the artillery range had recently stopped, for some reason. Offices had to have been at some point alerted by telephone and two-way radio messages, and buzzing with all manner of manic reactions. "*Is this some sort of joke?*" was likely a common first response.

The very fact that the alien visitors brushed off exploding Army artillery shells and did not return fire from their ships, nor show any other act of violent aggression upon landing, was a very good sign to those stationed at Edwards. If this was an alien invasion or attack, by *whomever*, it was a very odd, passive one. The ETs seemed to merely brush it off. The relative calm had to have given impetus for those men nearing the five ships, perhaps with weapons drawn, curious with fear but also perhaps genuine hope and excitement. A military mindset was then – and is today – all about defending American soil, but also to work for peace if possible. Brace for the worst, hope for the best.

We can reasonably surmise that the ETs opened up some doorways or hatches on their ships and quietly set out ramps, probably metallic and automated. Then some brave bipedal beings slowly descended, feet and legs seen first down the ramps, hands held out clearly, clutching no weapons (or objects that could be misconstrued as weapons). Upon walking about the runway, they attempted to open an orderly communication with the first men on the scene.

It is *very* difficult to believe that President Eisenhower was summoned to the base by military officials, as the story alleges, if the arriving extraterrestrials had *not* managed to first openly declare their mission of peaceful contact while also showing no evil intent. And then sustained that stance for hours, showing no aggression. America's guarded chief executive could not and would not have been placed in any sort of danger by his soldiers, staffers, and military advisers, to be sure, without this assurance of passivity. Therefore, it is reasonable to conceive that the unexpected visitors had calmly communicated in English the message *"We come in peace"* during initial greetings, staring around the immediate locality, evidently bearing no grudge or firearms. The humanoids were possibly mustering warm smiles along with light hand-waving as they stood before some soldiers, empty-handed but hearts full of hope. Possibly they even allowed themselves to be searched, their ships included. Doubtlessly the space people issued repeated calm reassurances that they were unarmed and friendly, and eventually requested something along the lines of *"Take me to your leader."* Only in this case, that hackneyed phrase was inverted, as the leader (Eisenhower) was taken (after a few hours) *to* the strangers.

We can also surmise reasonably that this was all purposely done during broad daylight hours, maybe between 2:00 to 6:00 p.m. on Friday, so that the base personnel could clearly see the aliens and their ships and not feel this was part of some sort dastardly trick pulled off in the cover of darkness, with more beings lurking in the bleak night all around them, ready to attack.

Possibly soldiers, pilots, and mechanics surging with increased excitement, fear, and curiosity stepped closer, close enough to view the visitors and listen to any noises or words they may have emitted, or thoughts transmitted, perhaps with weapons nervously at the ready. However, what seems more plausible is that a mature, official United States military/government welcoming party was standing by – inside the hangar? - to diplomatically handle opening dialogue. These few men assessed the situation carefully with improvised protocol as still more phone calls were made to higher-ups, possibly to those high-ranking officers who were on leave in a nearby town, or even to the governor of California, Goodwin J. Knight, who was in charge of at least the state's Army national guard, and still hanging around the Palm Springs area that week. However, it seems more likely that President Eisenhower wanted the situation somewhat "self-contained", with as little outside participation as possible, to maintain maximum secrecy.

Precisely how many aliens were involved in disembarking? Who and what exactly *were* these celestial creatures now standing about near an open hangar at Edwards? While we cannot say for certain, it stands to reason they were a collection of pilots, along with possibly ambassadors and diplomats. Perhaps also on this journey were scientists, engineers, sociologists, zoologists, teachers, physicians, and important governmental figures. Or suitable combinations thereof.

It is quite possible the forgiving foreigners who landed *often* sent qualified members of their advanced race to other physical worlds to learn about foreign cultures and customs, almost like a kind of intergalactic "student visa program." The awkward opening of contact on 2/19/54 might have been something they were quite accustomed to, rather like the crew of the "Starship Enterprise" on the TV show "Star Trek," when "exploring new worlds, new civilizations." But they were also likely on their guard, braced to be assaulted (again) by someone overwrought with fear or hostility. What *did* they say to any base soldiers who had just tried to kill them upon arriving, minutes earlier?

Overall, the advanced ETs on 2/19/54 were a group of courageous astronauts and explorers, we can say that with assurance. They had smarts and guts. One can reasonably theorize that the unusual-looking space adventurers were already versed in the ways of our complicated world, having studied us well in advance, realizing the history of the specialized high-tech airbase they had arrived at. Maybe they "gave off good vibes" and exuded intangible, likable *thoughts and feelings*, as it were.

Perhaps *more* of the congenial visitors moved amiably from their ships down to the runway, looking around and breathing calmly, knowing the desert air was safe for their respiratory systems, thus indicating they had touched down on Earth before. Or at least they had previously run extensive studies in advance of our planet's lower atmosphere.

We can reasonably guess the aliens wore nothing too objectionable, unusual, or intimidating, appearing fairly normal in human-like forms and attire, perhaps charming their way in, so to speak. It was critical to appear friendly and noble, not clumsy or stupid, and certainly not disrespectful or arrogant. Slow steps, minor arm movements, and big smiles were the order of the day, perhaps from both sides at first.

Perhaps some Edwards AFB soldiers, fliers, officers, and on-site civilians — later sworn to silence - began to gather around the human-like visitors, wanting to know all about them. Maybe both sides even exchanged friendly banter. Someone fairly high up in the Army or Air Force — perhaps General Holtoner, the base commander - issued somewhat more formal greetings and introductions. One UFO researcher has claimed that he learned alien "communication that day was via mechanical translators" worn within spacesuits but offered no backing support for this.

At some point early on a wise, highest-ranking officer knew the ultimate proper course of action was to notify the commander-in-chief, President Eisenhower so that *he* could handle the situation, perhaps if merely via long distance. It is even quite possible some of the brass on the base was simply afraid to act in any substantial way *until* Ike was notified as they feared not being per Eisenhower's wishes.

Thus *more* telephone calls were patched through to Palm Springs, and likely the George E. Allen home, where President Eisenhower visited that mid-to-late 2/19/54 afternoon. Outside the estate, Secret Service agents prowled, keeping an eye out for spies, reporters, and nosy neighbors.

Speculation: as the minutes turned into more than an hour or two of polite but necessary opening conversation on the Edwards AFB dusty runway, the overall man in charge of the nation knew what was going on. It is possible President Eisenhower simply told the base officers over the phone: "Find out what they want, make sure it's not a trap, and keep me updated." And then he sat down with Mr. Allen — and Harry Truman? - for dinner. Humans need sustenance, even in unusual circumstances, especially older ones having just exerted themselves in the hot sun (golfing).

Later on, *the* call came in. It was go-time. All clear for a *presidential* base appearance. The breakthrough meeting was *on*.

The 63-year-old Eisenhower's heart and mind must have been whirring a mile a minute as he finally headed under the cover of encroaching darkness for Edwards, first by an unmarked car to a local airfield, then perhaps by a nondescript airplane, possibly civilian. It was time for the most historic and exciting summit conference of all time, and *Dwight* was needed to represent all of humanity in talks with friendly, advanced extraterrestrial beings.

What a freaky Friday!

CHAPTER SIX

The Visitors

"The aliens looked like humans, but not exactly."

— USAF test pilot

He went through life by several names, some legitimate, others mere insults. The 8th Earl of Clancarty (1911-1995) was a colorful member of the British House of Lords, for sure, so he commonly went by the name of "Lord Clancarty," which is what we shall refer to him as from here on, in respectful honor of his impressive dedication to finding truth in a sea of government deception on UFOs. To that end, the fascinating Irish-Dutch nobleman - whose birth name was the wordy "William Francis Brinsley Le Poer Trench" - personally investigated many an Unidentified Flying Object allegations as the 1950s, '60s, and '70s progressed, making quite a name for himself in the United Kingdom. That name by some cynical citizens, however, was at the least "eccentric," at worst "nuts," or "bonkers," sadly.

Despite being accused by some as a "gullible fool," university-educated Lord Clancarty courageously utilized an open-minded approach to researching the paranormal and put some remarkable resulting tales into several published books. He also headed a group of like-minded policy-making figures in the stuffy House of Lords who were demanding in the late 1970s that the British military/government open up its decidedly closed classified files on past reported UFO cases. Along the way, unfortunately, the earnest earl began to earn some of his eccentric esteem by also declaring his passionate belief that the earth was hollow and that aliens were able to access the center through a series of tunnels, plus a few other unproven theories that may have harmed his overall integrity and lofty goals as he grew older. So it was that Lord Clancarty's reputation was established, at least in Europe, and perhaps how he above all others was chosen sometime in the early 1980s by a "retired colonel" to hear about what went down at Edwards in '54. This secretive informant – said to have been a mature former "test pilot" - alleged to the earl that he knew the cold hard facts *because he was there, experiencing the shocking event while standing right next to President Eisenhower.*

The earl picked up the ball and ran with it in 1982, speaking out publicly on the '54 Eisenhower event. It may not help the overall credibility of the airbase allegation that it *finally* became a topic of conversation as a juicy nationwide story via the scandalous tabloid *The National Enquirer*, published on October 19, 1982. A full-page article by then-young writer Dary Matera (1955-) brazenly declared that the president one night quietly left Palm Springs, California, to hustle over to Edwards AFB to really and truly met with landed extraterrestrials, the article declared. An anonymous test pilot's recent confession to Lord Clancarty was then new supportive evidence, confirmed by at least three sources interviewed by Matera for the attention-getting story. {When contacted in 2019, Mr. Matera had no new information on the tale, but stood by it.} The *Toronto Star* was one of a small handful of newspapers at the time to pick up and run this seemingly-wild contention in the fall of 1982.

One reputable source that was quoted in *The National Enquirer* article confirmed that he too had heard the allegations about Eisenhower-at-Edwards: Dr. Josef Allen Hynek (1910-1986), college professor, author, lecturer, and astronomer, a man who earned much respect as a cautious, fair, dependable UFO investigator for three decades. Studious and now famous, Dr. Hynek said that he learned of the Eisenhower desert drama from various second-hand sources retelling what they had heard over the years, but was never able to dig up much more on his own. A retired American university educator (first at Ohio State, then at Northwestern) and one-time astronomy consultant to the rather infamous "Project Blue Book" governmental team that was appointed in 1952 to look into – and effectively whitewash - UFO sighting reports, Professor Hynek quit that controversial Air Force project to dedicate much of his life to privately tracking down the truth in the 1970s and early '80s, mostly as director of the new "Center For UFO Studies."

{Interesting side note: The USAF's "Project Blue Book" went through a sudden restructuring in March of 1954, just weeks after the Edwards UFO incident; was this change a direct result of learning that some aliens actually do exist?}

There is no question that Dwight D. Eisenhower would have surrounded himself with an entourage at Edwards Airbase, likely a test pilot and some security men, for "just in case." Going alone would have been risky, if not foolish. He likely "traveled light" to get there, however, perhaps with just one or two of his ever-present Secret Service agents on the flight from Palm Springs. But once at the base, did he include more experienced T-men or military policemen, or even cops, available to protect him from the unknown? A respected Canadian UFO researcher and writer of note, Grant Cameron, feels that Eisenhower had quite a large contingent either with him or stationed nearby when he met the cosmic visitors, perhaps as many as *250* men overall.

Additionally, another researcher's online description of the Eisenhower encounter has stated that "hundreds of soldiers present at Edwards AFB during the first contact" had experienced "psychological ailments as a result" of the otherworldly encounter, "ranging from dysfunctional behavior to pure psychosis, and even suicide." Where the author of this nerve-rattling allegation got his information was not explained. It seems pretty extreme, and speculative, but at least possible.

Lord Clancarty died at age 84 in 1995 without ever mentioning any "freak-out" by the humans at Edwards AFB, during or afterward, nor ever revealing the name of this mysterious pilot who related inside info. Since *The National Enquirer* article mentioning Clancarty's tale came out in October of 1982, and the earl gave a television interview regarding the Eisenhower assertion in England, airing in the fall of '82, it seems likely then that the talkative Clancarty had only just recently learned of the '54 Ike-ET summit. The unnamed American airbase source had privately told Lord Clancarty he was speaking out on the alien encounter because the other members of Eisenhower's immediate six-man protective unit were now all deceased, and he wanted the tale told before he too left this world.

It must be mentioned that several notable U.S. military figures *and* members of the Eisenhower administration did indeed pass away in the time-frame of 1978-'82, too many to recount here, seemingly leaving the ex-pilot genuinely free at last to talk indeed.

Plus, times had changed since 1954. Popular TV shows, motion pictures, magazine articles, and news stories featured alien life forms visiting earth, often for the sake of comedy or dramatic entertainment. Other-planetary aliens and their "flying saucers" had gone mainstream. "*E.T., The Extra-Terrestrial*" was a huge worldwide hit movie in the summer of '82. Thus the mysterious pilot source contacted Lord Clancarty, in mid-1982, evidently. While one possible candidate for this enigmatic insider is Brigadier General J. Stanley Holtoner himself – he used to be a colonel and a test pilot - from this point on he will simply be referred to as "Jerry Flier," a pseudonym since this is not an absolute known fact.

Why was it so necessary for "Jerry" the aging test pilot to remain so anonymously "undercover"? The retired aviator was undoubtedly surviving on a monthly military pension and healthcare plan, supporting himself and family members, and bearing a good personal reputation, so overall he was likely fearful of governmental recrimination for revealing classified data. Plus the old colonel felt tremendous faithfulness to General-turned-President Eisenhower. But why be afraid after nearly thirty years of loyalty, over a decade after Dwight's death? *Because Flier said he had been personally sworn to utter secrecy by the president himself* - perhaps under the threat of court-martial - and had dutifully lived up to that oath until finally talking to the famous Lord Clancarty a quarter-century later, risking everything, and only then under the cloak of assured anonymity.

The colorful but earnest earl had no wife or children, and died alone at his British seaside estate in 1995, leaving his UFO files and data to "Contact International," a research group he founded in 1967. If he ever told a relative or wrote down the identity of his ex-pilot identity in a report not destroyed or lost, it might lend the Ike-

ET saga some strongly supportive evidence, if uncovered today. But so far... nothing seems to have surfaced.

Lord Clancarty told one American researcher that he first read and heard of UFO or "Foo Fighter" stories during World War II, in Europe where Eisenhower was in charge, and such earnest paranormal tales greatly intrigued and influenced him. He began writing, printing, and mailing UFO newsletters in the 1950s, and by June of 1976 took his seat in parliament, still piqued by the topic. Soon the earl was leading a parliamentary committee in researching UFO/ET sightings, making waves and headlines in the United Kingdom and elsewhere. Base Commander Stan Holtoner, meanwhile, lived to the ripe old age of 99 and had even spent time in Clancarty's England. According to his obituary, in the spring of 1957, General Holtoner was transferred overseas to become deputy commander of the Third Air Force in the United Kingdom. Thus he could well have met the flight-obsessed earl at that time, and/or contacted him again in 1982, to finally spill the porridge on the riveting 1954 drama. But Holtoner might well be a miss since he wasn't a colonel when he retired – unless Lord Clancarty changed that detail to protect his source's identity.

{Before we leave this topic, one must ask: who are some likely military candidates for the elite group with President Eisenhower on 2/19/54 who died in the late 1970s/early '80s, freeing "Jerry" at last to talk? Well, a whopping *five* former Air Force generals died in 1979, an unparalleled total for one calendar year. And USAF General Orval Ray Cook passed away in March of 1980; he served as a deputy commander of the crashed UFO debris-related "Air Material Command" in the 1950s. Meaningful or not, Cook was transferred to Europe on April 1, 1954. Yet another prominent retired USAF general – Fred H. Smith - died in May of 1980, however, he was officially stationed in Colorado in 1954. Any of these trusted, respected Air

Force men could have been at Edwards Airbase on 2/19/54 if so ordered in advance by their commander-in-chief.}

The main USAF general in the know on alien visitation during the late 1940s and 1950s was Nathan F. Twining; he did not pass on until March 28, 1982. *Within months, Lord Clancarty had the story and excitedly went public with it. Was Twining personally involved?*

The late Texas journalist and conspiracy theorist James Farrell Marrs, Jr. (1943-2017) began his popular 1997 book *"Alien Agenda"* with a spine-tingling tale that sounds very much like our Ike-alien confab, one that first intrigued the author when he heard it in 1962. At that time, Jim Marrs explained, he was a college student, sharing a dormitory room with a young man named "Doug," who one day related a strange saga told to him by his father, a respected Air Force officer based out of the Pentagon in Washington D.C. Doug told Jim that his dad once took him camping, and over a few beers and a cozy campfire in a remote wooded setting the two discussed the idea of alien life beyond earth. Doug's dad was properly lubricated with enough alcohol to spill some beans on a shocking secret: *he was once part of a military contingent that made contact with friendly extraterrestrials "at a military installation on the West Coast."* The officer began to tell his son that during this incident some years before, alien spacecraft occupants stepped out of their landed ships to communicate with the assembled, nervous human delegation, and then...the Air Force man suddenly clammed up, likely realizing he was divulging state secrets his son was never supposed to be privy to in any way. Memories of his sworn national security oaths – and possible threats of court-martial and/or imprisonment for leaking - must have taken over, sadly.

"Doug" told Jim Marrs he pressed his serious, anxious father for more details on the high-level otherworldly encounter, but it was no use, the campfire revelation was cut frustratingly short, and never completed. Writer Marrs felt that the Pentagon father was *not* joking, nor the son in recalling the story. Jim expressed his regret at failing to illicit further information from his roomie during those college years and thus was never able to personally follow up on the shocking story in later decades. Was the unnamed high-ranking officer in the camping tale one of the aforementioned Air Force men who died in the early 1980s? Or perhaps N. F. Twining? Maybe J. S. Holtoner himself? Stan was transferred to the Pentagon in the spring of 1959. Holtoner retired from the service in 1967. However, his 2010 obituary did not mention his fathering any children.

{Author Marrs also passed along in his '97 book the tale of two psychic sources. First, a "remote viewer" who described seeing (in his mind's eye) the Eisenhower-ET runway summit, claiming it featured three alien ships and just a trio of "grays." They supposedly stepped out of one landed ship and met the president, then got into a black Cadillac with Ike to be chauffeured to a small airbase building for a friendly chat. Secondly, Marrs relayed the story of an alleged "channeler" named Richard T. Miller, who told him of receiving and writing down detailed mental messages from a concerned alien being named "Mon-Ka." The unseen ET asserted that his race had made direct contact with various earthly leaders in the past decades, including President Eisenhower, but Dwight greatly disappointed them by afterward failing to inform the public of the exciting face-to-face communication.}

At any rate, in returning to the heart of the Lord Clancarty narrative, as related by the mysterious confiding colonel, five separate and distinct alien spaceships came down and landed on the desert runway in '54, and afterward the stunned base brass tracked down by a series of phone calls President Eisenhower in the scramble to fully understand and contain the event. This data of course fits well with other known claims so far. The golfing chief executive was urged to the runway landing site as soon as it was felt safe that night, "Jerry Flier" confirmed, since it was ascertained that the humanoid visitors were friendly and unarmed.

That Eisenhower agreed to come all the way out to the airbase for a personal inspection, flying in from the Palm Springs region, would not be a surprise to those who knew him and spoke up after his death. He had a courageous and inquisitive nature. In a 2010 interview, grandson Dwight David Eisenhower II (1948-) stated that his grandmother Mamie once told him of her often-restless husband: "He has to poke his nose into everything."

Jerry told Lord Clancarty that three of the ET landed airships were "saucer-shaped" and two were "cigar-shaped"- again confirming precisely what "Sergeant X" told investigator Gabriel Green decades earlier. And of the aliens? They appeared human-like, "but there were some differences." This would have been tremendously fascinating to all the pilots and soldiers present, including Dwight Eisenhower; who *wouldn't* have wanted to go and meet them, if deemed safe?

Just exactly what did the landed ETs have for features? You know, for a face and a body? What did they sound like? How did they move about? How were they dressed? These questions and many others naturally come to mind. From the five slick aerial vehicles on the runway emerged entities that "looked like humans, but not exactly," aviator Jerry further explained to Clancarty. We can simply say today that the visitors were somewhat like humanity's "cousins," so to speak, proportionally similar but with slightly different features. They were "misshapen" in comparative appearance, the pilot told the earl. Thus we can conceive of the visitors as having two arms and hands, two legs and feet, one head, one torso, etc. But just, well... just a bit *different* and smaller than our body proportions.

Within the critical U.S. Army *"Special Operations Manual 1-01"* from April 7, 1954, detailed drawings and careful descriptions of various size-and-shaped aliens and their crafts were included in the startling manual, indicating that some of these descriptions could well have stemmed from 2/19/54. The Edwards AFB visitors almost *had* to have been filmed/photographed for this level of Army report detail: *"The humanoids might be mistaken for human beings of the Oriental race if seen from a distance. They are bipedal, five to five-feet-four-inches in height, and weigh 80 to 100 pounds. Proportionally they are similar to humans, although the cranium is somewhat larger and more rounded. The skin is a pale, chalky-yellow in color, thick and slightly pebbled in appearance. The eyes are small, wide-set, almond-shaped, with brownish-black irises, with very large pupils. The whites of their eyes are not like that of humans but have a pale gray cast. The ears are small set low on the skull. The nose is thin and long, and the mouth is wider than in humans and lipless. There is no apparent facial hair and very little body hair."* The *"SOM-1-01"* gave its qualified reader a general idea of how the otherworldly visitors looked in standing upright: *"The body is thin and without apparent body fat, but the muscles are well-developed. The legs are slightly but noticeably bowed, and the feet are somewhat splayed and proportionally large."*

In June of 2017 fuller details of the alien visitors to planet Earth *may* have emerged at last when the January 3, 1989, Defense Intelligence Agency's "Office of Counterintelligence" report was leaked to syndicated podcast/radio show host Heather Wade. The jaw-dropping 47-page briefing paper was dubbed *"Assessment of the Situation / Statement of Position"* on extraterrestrial visitation. Much of the alleged DIA report was an exciting "Classified Ultra Top Secret" history lesson, presumably generated for key, trusted members of the incoming new administration (1989-1993) for President George Herbert Walker Bush (1924-2018). The "MJ-12" group was confirmed as a very real entity, having been created in 1947 and kept going through the decades with different members (12 working figures and the president as the 13th). The mind-blowing *"Operation Majestic/MJ-1"* document featured many layers of details of past U.S. government interaction with landed – crashed or peacefully – ET crafts and their crew. In reviewing its many statements, let's take a look at the first classification of "EBE" listed ("Extraterrestrial Biological Entity") within the 1989 report:

"Earth-like Humanoids. There are several variations, more-or-less like ourselves. The majority of these are friendly and are the bulk of our EBE contacts. Most have a high degree of psychic ability and all use science and engineering of an advanced nature."

This frankly sounds like an apt description of what landed at Edwards AFB and asked to meet the president in February of '54, and again the following year in New Mexico (see Chapter Ten). The details resemble our pal Setimus, taken from this planet by his people in August of 1949. His "psychic powers" might have included an insightful view of mankind's future, including that General Dwight Eisenhower, was destined someday to become President of the United States, but that is merely speculative. Was peaceable Setimus now *back?* Why else would Eisenhower be cleared by security to go into a completely *alien* situation? Air Force officials would *never* put their beloved leader in harm's way, or injected into an unknown, possibly dangerous or vulnerable position like the Edwards encounter... *unless they knew in advance there was a trusted, old friend waiting for him.*

{*"Small humanoid "Grays"* - like those that died in 1941 Cape Girardeau, Missouri, and 1947 Roswell, New Mexico - and *"Non-humanoid EBEs"* were also listed in the 1989 report, but their descriptions don't match what was encountered on 2/19/54. Plus, *"Transmorphic Entities"* was a fourth known category listed that also does not align with anyone's understanding of the Edwards Airbase experience.}

"Their height and physique were more or less like those of a mid-sized earth man," was how pilot Jerry Flier allegedly described the sociable visitors to riveted Lord Clancarty.

The ETs were able to breathe the dry Mojave Desert atmosphere without any apparent problems, Jerry recalled. Presumably, therefore, the entities did not wear helmets or sport any sort of special respiratory gear, he added. How they were dressed overall remains a bit of a mystery; apparently in bland, simple flight-suits that didn't imprint on anyone's memory. Did they wear shoes? Headgear? Jewelry? Did they sport makeup, tattoos, or piercings? Or any particularly noteworthy fashion sense of any kind? Since nothing of the sort has been mentioned in any recovered or leaked government document, we can only assume not.

According to the Army *"Special Operations Manual"* of April 1954, *"The hands are small, with four long digits but no opposable thumb. The outside digit is joined in a manner as to be nearly opposable, and there is no webbing between the finger as in humans."*

That the visitors supposedly stepped down from their ships when President Eisenhower arrived, Jerry Flier recalled, indicates the visitors had gone back *inside* their awe-inspiring spacecrafts in the hours between originally touching down and greeting the first soldiers at the base, and then presenting themselves yet again, upon Dwight's dramatic night-time entrance at the selected hangar.

It seems reasonable to postulate that the bedazzled military men at the encounter wore their uniforms, with buttoned jackets, creased slacks, and perhaps hats on to ward off the rather chilly night air in February. Possibly Jerry Flier wore a leather bomber jacket, as many USAF pilots were fond of in those days. It was never stated but it also seems to reason that President Eisenhower had on his informal vacation attire, perhaps donning a light jacket or sports coat to warm himself too, along with his light sweater, baggy slacks, and headgear, likely his white golf cap worn on the links earlier in the day, to cover his famous bald pate. And he probably sported his wire-rimmed eyeglasses. At least one man not far from the president supposedly held and aimed either a home movie camera, or a larger, newsreel-type filming camera, so someday we might find out for sure. Possibly another took still photos with a big flash camera.

It is certainly not surprising, but count superstar Hollywood actress, author, and supernatural internet radio host Shirley MacLaine (1934-) as a believer in the Eisenhower-extraterrestrial allegation. The long-time movie star personally looked into the '54 story with a variety of sources over the past few decades, or so she claimed within the pages of her 2007 book *"Sage-ing While Age-ing."* Miss MacLaine mentioned how some well-briefed sources said they discovered the amazing tale from *viewing the actual film of the event.* Supposedly the footage was examined by some source's decades later, along with confidential files, and aging "insider contacts."

It is possible that actual military cameramen were utilized, already in place at the airbase which often needed to visually record test jet flights for later study; a serious-sounding 2009 online forum post suggested *three* film cameras were utilized that 2/19/54 (see Chapter Nine). Was a civilian film crew imported? Was this another reason why New York filmmaker Chester Miller was in the area?

Mysticism-loving MacLaine firmly believes there was at least one more celestial Eisenhower meeting, held a year later at Holloman Air Force Base, and she may well be correct (see Chapter Ten). In addition to all this, Shirley mentioned the opinion of Paul Theodore Hellyer (1923-), her personal friend and a former Secretary of Defense in Canada who has come out publicly in 2005 with his assertion that America and its neighbor to the north are long since fully aware of alien visitation (by at least four different species), and that the two nations work together in secret to cover this up, lest it starts a possible panic. Mr. Hellyer — a Member of Canadian Parliament in '54 - is quite aware of the Eisenhower-ET tale and believes that *it really did take place* as many have described, and further that it was indeed recorded for posterity.

Why would the president want to record his encounter? Perhaps if he truly were going to go public with the event someday, he'd need solid proof, so people didn't think he had flipped his lid in spoken claims. He could send copies of the footage to the TV networks for their news reports, and to movie theaters for their cinema short features. And have excerpts printed in newspapers and magazines. He could then cleverly leverage future trade deals and defense negotiations with other nations on earth to gain a better deal for America, pointing to his "inside track" with superior alien intelligence and firepower, in a sense. Who *wouldn't* want to do business with the USA and its ET-connected chief executive? This may have been Dwight's strongest motivation since before he took office, frankly. To achieve and maintain a position of American superiority and strength. Plus, the images would sure play well at re-election time... or would they?

Shirley MacLaine added that her brilliant Russian acquaintance, Dr. Roald Zinnurovich Sagdeev (1932-), the highly educated former head of the Soviet Union's space program, assured her in private that human-like extraterrestrials were quite real and visiting our planet, but he wouldn't elaborate further on the subject. Dr. Sagdeev is currently a Distinguished Physics Professor at the University of Maryland and shuns the limelight. It is with great intrigue that we must point out that Sagdeev *was once married to Dwight Eisenhower's granddaughter, Susan!*

At this point, let's recall the late president's great-granddaughter, Laura Magdalene Eisenhower (1951-). She puts real stock in the Edwards ET summit, but this daughter of Susan Eisenhower also endorses some other controversial otherworldly theories that have brought her criticism. "I've done lifelong research, with people who have information" on the 1954 incident, confident Laura assured in an interview in the spring of 2019. She's *sold.*

Any other Eisenhower relatives might know something? An online forum source reported this nugget in 2014: "*I asked Jean Eisenhower the real provable granddaughter of Dwight Eisenhower in an email whether she believed the story was true or fabricated. She said she believes it's true.*" In checking out this statement, it appears to be accurate, with Jean writing on her website: "*My inclination for the last few years has been to assume that alien beings are trans-dimensional (spiritual), some of them working in our best interests, and some of them seeming to work against us.*" She added, "*The evidence is strong that "aliens" exist in great diversity.*"

{To pause for a quick sidetrack: many American UFO eyewitnesses have stated that "Men in Black" come to visit them later, seemingly federal agents in dark suits who pressure them to keep silent about they have seen. In some of these reports, the imposing males who approach the UFO experiencers are clearly humans, and in other cases, the beings seem human-*like*. *Aliens*, who very much resemble human beings at first, but turn out not to be upon closer inspection. Are these MiB the same "humanoid extraterrestrials" described in the government documents, helping our American authorities keep otherworldly sightings silenced, to avoid panic or social upheaval? Just a thought.}

As mentioned on that Friday night, February 19th... after stepping out slowly, with no sidearms and hands held out empty, the visitors spoke in clear and understandable English. Expressing one's self carefully and courteously with the anxious, armed military men was quite essential. As was openness; the ETs deferentially asked Dwight and his entourage to freely examine, inside and out, their parked spaceships on the runway. A free, unfettered vehicular inspection, turned down, according to Jerry Flier. The aliens likely felt they had to swiftly show they were not backstabbers, no "Trojan horse," plotting to "pull a fast one."

Whether any of the visitors were distinguished as male or female entities was not stated, but we can at least be assured they were bipedal and moved about as any human would, one foot in front of the other, likely making certain not to make any abrupt or aggressive moves. Again, smiles, and compliments, were probably critical. The entities naturally wanted to speak to the most popular and powerful representative of the human race, and Eisenhower was the only one who fit the bill.

Yes, the desert night air cooled the open hangars down considerably, but the evening was just heating up. The atmosphere was, as they say, electric. Maybe even *fun*. After opening greetings and introductions, the newly-arrived president – surrounded by six special bodyguards - apparently asked the aliens just what they were doing at the airbase, as politely as possible. *What exactly did they want by this in-person meeting?*

Two main things, as it turned out. And they weren't souvenir t-shirts and caps!

Thus it was finally time for more detailed, specific talk. Serious negotiations. Each side desired something big... but *what*, exactly?

CHAPTER SEVEN

Chatting the Night Away

"How can we stop you? You are so advanced."

— Colonel Phillip Corso

The leader for the landed ETs spoke up. He wanted President Eisenhower to understand that his other-planetary group felt it was time to open a dialogue with the entire human race, to announce the presence of sentient beings from other worlds. To open earth-peoples' minds to the reality of remarkably diverse life beyond the planet. This was what "Jerry Flier" and another source claimed, of what kicked off and yet ticked off the runway summit conference.

The proposal went over like the proverbial lead balloon, or spaceship.

We must remember that Dwight D. Eisenhower was a deeply conservative, religious, button-down, older administrator. His cabinet consisted almost entirely of married, older, white Christian males. He approved of "Operation Wetback" in 1954, which was about to be implemented along the American border with Mexico, a cold-hearted process or rounding up and kicking out illegal aliens unlike any other deportation procedure in U.S. history. Eisenhower also authorized a troubling official purge of all homosexuals in government, with hundreds of federal employees tracked down, interrogated, and some ruthlessly booted out of any office if confessed as gay, no matter how low their level. *Extraterrestrial beings* among us? Gaining any potential position of influence? *Immediately unacceptable*, it would seem. Eisenhower made clear he wanted the aliens to keep their distance, if at all possible. Maybe they could come to a formal agreement on it?

"The preceding diplomatic treaty was drafted by the directorate of the Majestic-12 operation" - President Eisenhower - *"and a joint committee of extra-terrestrial visitors"* - perhaps meaning the alien landing party at Edwards AFB, along with *"representatives of the U.S. Diplomatic Corps."* The 1989 DIA briefing paper called the Eisenhower-drafted treaty *"a statement of intent."* Both sides had declared other things that they wanted from the heart-pounding "first contact" and future secretive interaction. But it took time, perhaps months, to hammer out the right wording. *"It was ratified and signed at Kirtland Air Force Base,"* the document read - and then mistakenly referred to the state for this airbase as *"Texas,"* when it is in fact in New Mexico. A glaring error, yes, but are *all* genuine Defense Intelligence Agency first or second-draft documents immaculate and error-free?

Anyway... the date for the human-alien treaty ratification was given as *"July the 18, 1954."* That was just two days after an alleged

"MJ-12" meeting at the White House (see Chapter Two). And the unique contract was a done deal *"by President Dwight D. Eisenhower and an individual on behalf of the EBE's."* Did this mean that Eisenhower personally flew into Kirtland AFB in New Mexico to hand over the document to an ET in hushed conditions on 7/18/54? Or did he send someone he trusted to represent him? Beyond that, did other presidents to come? Central to this book's Chapter Eleven, it was clearly stated in the '89 briefing: *"Each subsequent holder of the executive office has continued to uphold the intent of this policy towards the aliens,"* as *"the president is accepted to be the 13th member"* of "Operation Majestic-12." Meaning, he had to be a leader who oversaw the ET/UFO board and took action at times on issues it produced, as well. And getting the new humanoid visitors to agree to "keep off the grass," so to speak, was most imperative and needed to inked and stamped by both sides, even if it was technically unenforceable and unconstitutional.

It was truly a "Close Encounter of the Third Kind," as the common ET expression goes, that cool Friday night on the edge of the Edwards base hangar. But the opening notion of open contact between races soured Dwight fast. Whether any member of his presidential entourage also took an active, vocal part in the alleged discussion is not known, but unlikely. Nor is anyone aware of whether a *number* of the unearthly visitors joined in the chit-chat, or if they simply had one or two representatives do all the talking. It is likely that *no* physical exchange such as a handshake was permitted as the troubling notion of transacting germs and bacteria likely entered the minds of greeters on both sides. It is also not known if the visitors ever gave their specific names or relayed their title or their race's general name. But we can tell from the start the skeptical, tradition-loving president urgently wanted the strangers to establish an aloof attitude from the entire planet.

Openly declaring the aliens' presence and their ability to traverse time and space to arrive on our planet whenever they liked was doubtlessly going to throw much of the civilized world into an uproar, Dwight Eisenhower doubtlessly felt. Americans alone might cease believing in, and taking part in, their normal social structure; their military protection; their religious beliefs; their usual past-times; and even their occupations. {Remember the thinking behind Ike and Winnie's reaction to a UFO event in WWII, from Chapter One?} Everyday working society might thus ground to a virtual halt, killing productivity. The stock market and investment/bond world would go into a steep decline, and thus the global economy would be in ruins, potentially. Many citizens in 1954 – like the 63-year-old Eisenhower – recalled well Wall Street's 1929 market crash and resulting Great Depression; would it happen again if aliens openly paraded about, sharing startling new foreign concepts on business, technology, employment, and society?

Also, what if the aliens just popped up unannounced in most any major city or small town, and set off a wild response in *any* country? Would there be a virtual *stampede* by thousands (or even *millions?*) of very emotional people to either view the alien beings wherever they were... or to fearfully flee from them, believing them to be "of the devil," or at least somehow sinister? What if the ET spaceships dotting our future skies caused accidents and disruptions to our air traffic, and even to cause distraction to people in cars and on foot on the ground? Life on earth would be thrown into daily chaos.

Even darker thoughts had to be racing through the president's world-weary mind. What if the ETs were only kindly in mien upon first arriving, establishing a kind of "beach-head" for when they would later run rampant across our globe, either through superior physical force or perhaps merely through dangerous radical teachings that would turn our societies upside-down in countless ways? And what if this smiling group of courtly space ambassadors were representing a small slice of a whole onslaught of various *other* alien races to arrive soon, also expecting to be greeted warmly, without proper assessment, and then virtually take over the planet? Even if these landed humanoids were truly friendly and wise if President Eisenhower let one class of extraterrestrials in to communicate openly with the people of the earth, wouldn't that open the door to *more*, including possibly *hostile* creatures who would have a field day here with unacceptably anti-social actions and ideas to convey? Just one initial acceptance to this particular human-like ET race could conceivably open a veritable "can of worms," a "Pandora's Box" of miseries. Plus, an old West-Pointer like Ike had to have been mulling the concept of a possible "alien invasion" someday. He knew his history of warfare and sneaky spy strategies, of scouting missions and first steps in battle plans... and thus likely kept those frightening possibilities in mind as he looked around at the Muroc/Edwards runway, pondering mankind's future.

Little wonder worried Mr. Eisenhower flatly rejected the opening extraterrestrial proposition.

The courageous space visitors persisted for a while, undeterred. Their leader proceeded to explain further. "They wanted to begin an educational program for the people of Earth," informant retiree Jerry told politician Lord Clancarty in the early 1980s. A global outreach, using the USA apparently as a platform, or first step. "Eisenhower told them he didn't think our world was ready for that," the ex-pilot recalled, adding "He was concerned this revelation would cause a panic."

Dwight Eisenhower surely realized our entire planet's business, religious, and social structures could go down the tubes in many ways and *fast*. This would wreck his once-sterling reputation, and cement his place in history as a thoughtless and irresponsible president. The fool who kicked off mayhem and economic ruin. Again, it all added up to a firm verbal rejection for the alien diplomats. A stunning official announcement of arrival? And an ET "educational program," huh? These initiatives just could *not* be allowed to take place, and Eisenhower told them so, right to their faces, as politely as possible, Clancarty's 1982 source remembered.

How did the visitors take "no" for an answer? Twenty-eight years after the encounter, Jerry Flier recalled the aliens seemed to understand and accept the president's negative decision - which makes one wonder how highly intelligent, earth-monitoring extraterrestrials could have proposed it all in the first place. *In 1954, aliens weren't really mainstream; the world's population just wasn't ready for this, psychologically.*

Allegedly, a new and different approach was then proposed by the landed extraterrestrials, eager to learn more about life on earth. The humanoids supposedly expressed their desire to quietly study conditions of plant, animal, and human life, as if the aliens were likened to ultimate foreign exchange students on college scholarships. They suggested to the chief executive that they could instead make contact with some isolated human beings, in quieter, more careful and discreet ways, looking to undertake their scientific research. Perhaps in remote locations, until the human race gradually came to fathom their reality. "Until Earth people got used to them," was how the retired aviator described the phrasing to Lord Clancarty, however long this gentler integration process took.

This secondary, or backup, plan did not thrill the president either, but he replied affirmatively yet cautiously. "Eisenhower thought this was all right," Flier recalled, as long as the human-like beings "didn't create panic and confusion." Keeping daily order was foremost on

Dwight's mind, as it should have been for any thoughtful, caring national leader.

A couple of contemporary sources have claimed they individually learned through document copies in military files that a written pact was formed from the Eisenhower encounter, supposedly entitled "The Greada Treaty," according to a source. {Was "Greada" their home planet? Or the name of their alien race?} This compact allowed aliens to tacitly study our life forms here and perhaps take off with a few samples for scientific research while the American military/government kept quiet, probably in exchange for some advanced ET hardware to study. This remarkable claim seems to have been backed up by retired Air Force serviceman Donald Phillips, who stated he at times worked with knowledgeable Central Intelligence Agency employees and personally reviewed once-secret records of Eisenhower's 1954 runway encounter and the subsequent formal written agreement it produced. "We were asked if we would allow them to be here, and to research, and the statement {from Eisenhower} I read said *"Well how can we stop you? You are so advanced."* Phillips asserted on camera in 2013 that the president's alien summit at Edwards "was on film" and well preserved, hopefully to this day.

Mr. Phillips said he once worked as a design engineer with Lockheed-Martin, long rumored to have been involved in reverse-engineering an alien craft. Don was given clearance to read the classified Ike-ET documents there, in the company offices as supposedly he was an employee on "clandestine aviation projects" after his military service years (in the mid-'60s). He further stated there were other covert high-level human-alien contacts after 2/19/54, with at least *twelve* different races of extraterrestrial beings over the ensuing decades. And also that American scientists learned from examining recovered crashed materials (and anything gifted to them) how to successfully apply the ET technology with man-made hardware, resulting in our latest high-tech jet planes. However, the more Don Phillips spoke, the more he seemed to repeat information originally relayed by another retired military source...

The late U.S. Army Colonel Phillip James Corso, Sr. (1915-1998) within his blockbuster 1997 memoirs, *"The Day After Roswell,"* and in TV and radio interviews, confirmed that extraterrestrials are indeed visiting earth, studying us. And that Eisenhower did indeed meet with them, he said in a media interview. The elderly author Corso once noted of visiting aliens: "We had negotiated a kind of surrender with them, as long as we couldn't fight them. They dictated the terms because they knew what we feared most was disclosure." Thus Colonel Corso edged close to describing the Eisenhower-ET treaty without details. What he did learn Phil eventually relayed to the RFK-JFK team in power in 1962 (see Chapter Eleven). Unfortunately for Mr. Corso, some of his colorful claims within *"The Day After Roswell"* were picked apart by military/government experts and historians. In his defense, the former Army officer (who knew Eisenhower personally) admitted privately he was upset about the technical errors in his book, apparently some coming from his memory, some the fault of others involved. But it's interesting to learn that an unearthed U.S. military record shows that communicative Colonel Corso was suddenly transferred to the National Security Administration's "operational coordination board" *on February 24th, 1954.* Coincidence?

The idea of a friendly treaty being drawn up, a mutually beneficial and peaceful agreement that was signed by friendly aliens and a somewhat nervous American chief executive, is not as entirely wild-sounding as perhaps one might think. It may have happened, felt a necessity, but most likely did *not* result in condoned coldblooded kidnappings, animal mutilations, and twisted scientific experiments, as some contemporary sources have claimed. Eisenhower and his military staff would never have agreed to that gruesomeness, not after having witnessed the cruel treatment of humans (and animals) in both WWI and II and the Korean War, all blood-soaked conflicts that were ended with formal written treaties. Signing accords to set the table for future relations was quite a par for this generation's course.

A noteworthy UFO researcher, lecturer, and radio/TV host in the '60s, '70s, and 1980s, Robert D. Barry (1922-1993) once developed quite a following on the American East Coast with his radio programs dedicated to understanding alien visitation. Mr. Barry — a WWII Army vet and retired radio station sales manager in Yoe, Pennsylvania - had informed his interested audiences over the decades that his various sources revealed to him that otherworldly beings had indeed visited Edwards Air Force Base - and left behind for officials a shiny circular spacecraft, kept in a well-guarded hangar. And that President Eisenhower did indeed secretly visit the site one night regarding such spine-tingling matters. However, Mr. Barry claimed that a military pilot at Edwards once reported seeing a circular alien spaceship sitting inside a hangar there in *1952*, during the *Truman* administration. {A check of Harry Truman's daily schedule as president shows no *official* trip to Palm Springs or Edwards AFB during his White House tenure, by the way.} Was this the crashed saucer that a base radar specialist from Chapter Five said he saw come down in '52? Or was it gifted by generous ETs? Or was the '52 dating off by two years? At any rate, the pilot who told others he saw this striking hangar sight supposedly undertook a routine flying mission the next day and was never seen again. During the ET airship's captivity at "the Muroc Dry Lake facility" the installation was placed on a special lock-down. "Nobody on the base was permitted to leave" and those from outside the site were not allowed in "for a period of three days." This matches up well with writer Desmond Leslie's information (see Chapter One).

"Colonel Jerry Flier" did not mention a base lock-down to the U.K. earl. Perhaps that information simply paled in comparison to the magnitude of the alien encounter itself and was forgotten, or purposely skipped over, by either man. But at this point, it might be a good idea to take an educated guess as to who the "retired test pilot" was, exactly...

Tall, thin, light-haired Richard James Harer (1924-2019) was a highly-educated, trusted, and courageous USAF test pilot stationed at Muroc/Edwards, one of America's very finest. He passed away at age 94 in November of 2019, apparently without saying anything, one way or another, about any alien event. His profile and background fit the bill perfectly here for "Jerry Flier," but there's still no hard proof since the ET encounter was an explosive state secret that a retired military officer on a fixed pension with benefits would not wish to publicize lest he loses his perks, position, or prestige.

While just 19 in mid-World War II, Richard Harer left his college training in Ohio to enter the Army Air Corps, and after training as a pilot he was shipped to England, where he served in the 392nd Bombardment Group, and then the 576th, *both located not far from Lord Clancarty*, supposedly so very fascinated by pilots and planes – and "Foo Fighters" in that era. During this time, Richard would have been under the overall command of General Eisenhower.

As his obituary reads, after the war young Harer "returned home to the United States and obtained his master's degree in Mechanical Engineering from California Institute of Technology and a Master's of Science degree in Systems Management from USC," proving himself an exceptionally intelligent young man, determined to learn all he could about flight technology and aerodynamics. He then returned to the USAF and was sent to Wright-Patterson AFB, in his home state of Ohio, the site of so many rumors of secretly recovered alien crafts over the years. Then Richard was transferred to Edwards AFB in the Mohave Desert, to helm experimental test flights. During the early '50s, knowledgeable Richard was briefly sent back to Europe as an adviser, to evaluate the latest French aircraft. When skilled, educated Richard spoke, people listened, despite his still relatively young age. Once back at Muroc/Edwards in '54 he resumed his test flights, including critical, high-profile ones in November and December. Then disaster struck. Richard's plane crash-landed on the dry lakebed and he was barely rescued by another pilot, suffering many painful burns and injuries. Tragically, both of Richard's badly damaged legs had to be amputated. Admirably, this still didn't slow Richard J. Harer down, not one bit. His bio explains: "He remained determined and committed to continuing a life involved in the field of aviation and testing of aircraft. He continued as a civil servant in many capacities including service in the Flight Research Division, Projects Administration Office, Project Control Office, Test Programs and Requirements Office, and was the Project Manager for the entire run of the X-15 program from beginning to end." Thus reliable Richard was involved with Eisenhower Pentagon connections *and* Edwards Airbase personnel for the next three decades until he finally retired in 1978. In his final four decades of life, aging Mr. Harer "enjoyed traveling," when not building and maintaining homes in his native northern Ohio and just outside the Muroc/Edwards area, in Tehachapi, California, surrounded by his growing family and friends. He had a rich, full, and exemplary life, perhaps more so than anyone ever imagined. He was, in short, an American hero and a role model.

Theory: R. J. Harer was a retired colonel and possibly in England for casual sightseeing and reminiscing sometime between late 1978 and mid-1982 when Lord Clancarty — still leading his headline-making government UFO inquiry - spilled the beans to the media of his recent encounter with just such a person. Harer would likely have been quite aware that USAF Commanding General Nathan Twining had passed away on 3/29/82, along with other Eisenhower administration figures in that more talkative era. As Clancarty made a name for himself with his media-covered UFO investigation in the British House of Lords, Harer would have been in his late 50s and free to speak at last, at least under conditions of anonymity. What's more, current online data shows that Richard was a longtime Republican and probably *very* keen on President Eisenhower back in his heyday. Therefore he would have been *the* most likely choice of any aware, Ike-hosting Edwards AFB commander, like General Stanley Holtoner. Stan even co-signed with Harer a photograph of his jet plane on the Edwards runway in '54! Most likely it was Rich Harer who was selected to stand next to the president and expertly assess the technical flight capabilities of the alien spaceships, relaying a younger generation's view of such momentous matters.

Again, R. J. Harer's presence on 2/19/54 remains an educated guess, but seemingly a very solid and reasonable one in hindsight. Still, it could be wrong, so the earl's helpful inside source will remain anonymous herein. But clearly, Harer was a great American worthy of praise today, whether he was selected for the historic close encounter or not.

In returning now to the '54 airbase narrative... standing about on the apron of the large airplane hangar, by the dusty runway... excited "Jerry Flier" and the five or six other men faithfully protected the alert American president... yet doubtlessly kept gazing longingly at the five fantastic spacecraft before them. They were as if hungry kids at a candy store window. All present had to wonder to themselves just exactly how the shiny alien ships worked and what exactly they could do in our skies.

They would soon find out.

CHAPTER EIGHT

Two Free Shows

"The UFO dematerialized before their eyes."

— author Frank Stranges

The time for small talk had ended - at least for a while - when it was decided by someone, probably within the alien contingent, to put on a free air show for the humans at Muroc/Edwards, this according to eyewitness Jerry Flier. "They demonstrated their spacecraft for the president," he remembered to Lord Clancarty, and the subsequent flying airship display suitably bedazzled all in attendance, even Jerry, who said he was specifically imported for this aspect of the meeting. "He had been called in as a technical adviser," the Dary Matera 1982 article highlighted, as Jerry possessed great "reputation and abilities as a test pilot."

How many of the five unique spaceships actually lifted off the ground and zipped about in the crisp California night air is not known, nor the number of extraordinary visitors who piloted those vehicles, but openly demonstrate the awesome aerial abilities they did. It proved to be yet another reason why the summit *had* to be set up in a rural, remote location. This could hardly have been accomplished unnoticed at a major airport in or near a large American city. It was one fantastic aerial circus, too, very much worth the undercover trip from Palm Springs for the president. While possibly some of the original ET landing party remained on the ground with the enraptured American audience, providing an informed narrative, the visitors exhibited their superior hardware in ways that likely made experienced pilots like Jerry drool.

We can effectively speculate at this point that the alien crafts soared at speeds our Air Force jets could not match, as has been alleged in countless other UFO sightings over the last half-century. One can conceive of the soaring extraterrestrial crafts likely turning on a dime in mid-air; stopping and restarting; banking, darting, and circling; accelerating and slowing; then zigzagging and rotating about, until finally making quiet, soft landings without the benefit of noticeable engines, wings, struts, flaps, or even exhaust pipes and vapor trails. Any cameraman trying to record the radiant, fast-paced display likely had difficulty keeping his lens on the flitting, speeding objects, at least until they resettled on the runway before them, and the celestial pilots stepped back outside.

To that end, an online UFO discussion site featured a forum message in 2009 that read: *"My friend said that Sam also told her about viewing a black and white movie of the meeting between President Eisenhower and human ETs which I assume was the alleged 1954 meeting. My friend says that it showed the three craft coming down over the runway doing some flight demonstrations and one craft landed and human-like ETs came out."*

Covering the Vatican beat, an Italian reporter and author whom we'll get to later has claimed this startling, supportive information: *"The meeting was filmed by the U.S. military with three 16mm cameras, placed at different points, loaded with color film and spring drive motors; that is because each camera operator had to change the film every 3 minutes and because in the presence of the aliens, electric motors did not work. In total, they shot 20 minutes of film in 7 rolls, each of them 30 meters in length."* Wow! What a detailed, knowledgeable-sounding piece of insight! Seemingly someone who was quite in the know spilled the beans in a tantalizing way, but *who*? And if this tale is true, it again indicates a well-prepared Muroc/Edwards operation, with multiple cameramen carefully spread out in advance, around the runway/hangar encounter site, recording it for posterity and security. But if so, where's the footage today? Why have only a few supposed eyewitnesses viewed it? Again, top military classifications appear to remain in effect for overall secrecy.

{We can also see that one allegation herein claims a "black-and-white film" was taken of the event, and the other mentions "color film," yet both sound reasonably believable. If there were three or more cameramen present, likely not all footage would be in one mode, and b/w film stock was cheaper and more widespread in '54.}

To learn more about the ET ships present, let's check with the April 1954 Army *"Special Operations Manual."* Under the heading "Description of Craft" there are some tasty samples of alien technology. For instance, *"Elliptical, or disc shape. This type of craft is of metallic construction and dull aluminum in color,"* and *"may have a raised dome on the top or bottom."* They are *"one-piece* construction," about *"50 to 300 feet in diameter,"* some with *"windows or ports, and lights on the top or bottom, which are not visible when the craft is at rest. Landing gear consists of three extendible legs ending in circular landing pads. A rectangular hatch is located along the equator or the lower surface of the disc."*

In other words, about what people of Earth already think would be your average alien flying saucer. *"Fuselage or cigar shape"* ships were also mentioned in the manual. One of them was described as a whopping *"approximately two thousand feet long and ninety-five feet thick, and apparently, do not operate in lower atmospheres."* If so, how did the U.S. Army find out such specific data? *"Radar reports"* suggest such an elongated craft soared along at *"7,000 miles per hour,"* far faster than any jet plane then, or now.

"Ovoid or circular shape" ET airships were also described in the 1954 instruction manual for intelligence officers. They are *"approximately thirty to forty feet long"* with *"an extremely bright light at the pointed end."*

And finally, the April 1954 Army *"S.O.M."* claimed that a fourth shape was possible: "Airfoil or triangular shape." Such unusual designs – reported more in UFO sightings of the early 1990s – were *"nearly three hundred feet in length, capable of high speeds and abrupt maneuvers."* The triangular craft mention brings to mind the Eisenhower White House stationary doodles, possibly showing a landed triangular ship and another one "flying" overhead on his notepaper.

The ETs permitted the men assembled with President Eisenhower to touch at least one of them, possibly to enter one or two grounded vehicles for a brief, up-close inspection. The metal ships proved to be amazingly lightweight, and one was supposedly dragged easily into a nearby hangar, one investigative UFO author – Dr. Frank E. Stranges, Ph.D. (1927-2008) - said he was told. At one point, as the president watched, "two individuals were able to tip it upside down." None of this appeared to concern the visiting alien ambassadors. "The craft was about thirty feet in diameter," Dr. Stranges recalled learning. {The highly-educated Stranges was the author of "*Stranger in the Pentagon*," about an alleged human-type "Venusian" named "Valiant Thor." The "alien" allegedly lived for three years in the Pentagon (1957-1960), supposedly offering President Eisenhower "a gift that would heal the world and end all disease and poverty" - but was turned down as, "It would ruin the economy." The "Valiant Thor" saga has since been debunked.}

Yes, the humanoids offered to help their earthly cousins with great gifts of knowledge and machinery, if not energy and medicine. The 2009 forum poster stated: "*They said that they were willing to cooperate and give mankind technology to cure disease, and cheap non-polluting energy technology if we would make concessions in regard to warfare and other things. But Eisenhower said the government was not ready for that, and that cheap energy technology would severely disrupt the economy.*" Once again, for a conservative president, fears of a damaged national economy were a very real, down-to-earth worry and might explain why business/financial experts like Edwin Nourse, George Allen, and Paul Hoffman might have been brought in for an assessment of the situation. Again, no one wanted another stock market disaster and global economic depression. But to turn down environmentally friendly "cheap energy technology" *gifted* on a virtual silver platter from advanced beings who just wanted to help? Eisenhower was tempted and soon conjured up a somewhat lesser deal, being a stout Cold Warrior who knew the value of finding ways of staying one step ahead of the Russians and Chinese.

"Claims of an agreement were made with the president exchanging technology" handed over by the visitors *"for a permanent base on earth."* This was boldly alleged in the 2014 *"MUFON Hangar 1"* television program, and the 1989 DIA document seemed to support that notion, referring to an airbase in very rural Nevada for possible ET use. But late that 2/19/54 night any sort of formal or informal treaty had to be carefully crafted with considerable thought and clear wording and then signed by the president at some point, and this would have taken some time. Perhaps days, or weeks, or months? Maybe even a full year? At least until that July.

Pacing a bit on the apron of the well-lit Edwards hangar, the great leader Eisenhower had to have scratched his bald head with a combination of amazement, delight, and utter dread. But the alien exhibition of very advanced ways was not yet over. The best was yet to come, as in any good show put on for an appreciative, mature audience. According to Lord Clancarty's "retired colonel," it was time for the big finish. A second free show to dazzle all...

Precisely how many extraterrestrial humanoids at this point were standing near their re-settled airships on the desert runway was not detailed by Jerry Flier, or at least not recalled by Lord Clancarty, but the retired test pilot related an amazing coup. Something that allegedly caused the patient president of the United States, Flier remembered, to worry greatly.

The aliens made themselves disappear! They became completely unseen... and then, came back into view again on the runway.

Yes, the otherworldly friends just seemed to vanish in front of their very eyes, Jerry Flier asserted. "They showed Ike their ability to make themselves invisible," the aviator told the earl.

Were the aliens able to make their entire molecular structure — and perhaps that of their airships — somehow physically move from the scene in an instant, into the ether? Or were they quite present, standing still, yet "cloaked" from view somehow? Either way, it was quite a shock to behold.

In a rare television interview in mid-1982 with popular BBC reporter Sir Michael Terrence Wogan (1938-2016), Lord Clancarty sat in his home's comfortable living room and recalled on camera learning from the confessing pilot-source that "These extraterrestrials demonstrated their paranormal powers — which are normal to them — and they went visible... invisible... *visible!*" The earl was serious, but the TV show's audience audibly chuckled, watching the video clip in a studio. Terry Wogan had little response to what seemed a little "bonkers," as he put it at the end of his televised report.

The aforementioned Frank Stranges - who was also a theologian - alleged he too gathered information mentioning "dematerialization" - for lack of a better term - going on at Muroc/Edwards and was even undertaken to the thirty-foot-long gifted spacecraft on the ground, the one that was allowed to be dragged about and tipped upside-down by the excited men. "The UFO dematerialized before their eyes," Frank recalled learning, then it came back, and as for proof, "there was motion picture footage of this event."

Film footage presumably classified. Again it seems obvious the military wanted to obtain proof of the historic presidential meeting just in case something went wrong and they needed to explain matters to the American people... *and...* they also would have needed evidence of the wild-sounding event for qualified military, aviation, and scientific leaders to study and learn from. Plus, the U.S. government would have the cold hard facts to air in public most indisputably someday when the time for full ET/UFO disclosure was at hand.

Alien people *and* their solid, metallic spaceships just *disappearing*. And then *re*appearing... over and over. It was beyond startling. It was unlike anything any human being had ever seen. This must have been even more shocking to witness than the sight of the humanoids and their five shapes of ships in the first place. *Where exactly did the vanished ETs go?* The humanoids had not actually "gone" anywhere, Colonel Flier recalled of the staggering event. To him they simply had given every man there the *appearance* of invisibility, possibly utilizing something like a "cloaking device" or method on the popular television/movie series "Star Trek." {American scientific minds are just now making inroads into such technology, in the news of late.} The airbase space brothers (or cousins) were present on the runway, and to prove it may have made a little noise on purpose while invisible, to show the befuddled homo sapiens the visitors were still there, just unseen.

The ET vanishing act brings to mind the strange case of UFO contactee/author George Washington Van Tassel (1910-1978), the subject of contemporary scrutiny five decades after his death. George wrote of his own otherworldly experiences that eerily mirror Ike's at Edwards. For instance, Mr. Van Tassel lived about forty miles north of Palm Springs (but still dozens of miles from Muroc/Edwards). He was apparently once an aviator affiliated with Howard Hughes' Aircraft, but in the 1950s was operating a crude desert airfield (that had no telephone) next to Giant Rock, near Landers, California. That's where Van Tassel said he was on the night of August 24, 1953, when awakened "around 2:00 a.m." He was sleeping just outside his cave-like home in the calm, moonlit desert when extraterrestrials showed up. George was soon led by a congenial human-like alien named "Solgonda" over to a "glittering, glowing spaceship" hovering about eight-to-ten feet over the nearby runway. It was disc-like, "about 36 feet in diameter and 19 feet high." Solgonda introduced himself and spoke to Van Tassel in English. Taken up inside the ship in a powerful light beam, George met three other smiling but speechless aliens, all about five-and-a-half-feet tall. They looked so much like tanned Caucasian males in their mid-twenties that the extraterrestrials could likely walk down any American street and draw no attention to them, Van Tassel recalled later. During his twenty-minute visit, Solgonda showed George his ship's vertical, hieroglyphic-symbol instrument panels (unlike any airplane's cockpit, he said), along with some retractable seats. George was then led into a power generating room, according to his esoteric 1958 book *"Council of Seven Lights."* In September of 1963, one of the aliens returned to Van Tassel, expressing impressive technical knowledge, and in front of nearly twenty eyewitnesses displayed his amazing ability to vanish from sight, and then reappear – *three times!* Sound familiar?

Were these the very same aliens that landed at Edwards AFB on 2/19/54 and met with President Eisenhower?

There are enough startling comparisons here to the Eisenhower-ET case at Edwards to create a Top Ten List again...

#1.) Van Tassel was a balding, devoutly Christian ex-serviceman from WWII whose family by the mid-1950s was grown and gone from home. Eisenhower the same.

#2.) Van Tassel saw a landed, circular alien ship in the Mohave Desert, in 1953, and supposedly other alien craft at other times. Eisenhower the same.

#3.) Van Tassel saw and spoke in English with friendly aliens in direct face-to-face verbal contact. Eisenhower the same.

#4.) Van Tassel's ETs were human-like, about five feet tall, and were peaceful and unarmed. Eisenhower the same.

#5.) Van Tassel witnessed the aliens demonstrate their ability to vanish from sight, yet still be there, cloaking. Eisenhower the same.

#6.) Van Tassel said the landed ETs discussed their worries about atomic bomb testing fallout (in automatic writing). For Eisenhower the same (verbally).

#7.) Van Tassel said the U.S. Air Force has suppressed UFO/ET information, keeping alien contact a huge secret. Eisenhower (and the USAF) did the same.

#8.) Van Tassel said in speeches the U.S. government could not allow open contact with citizens, it was too dangerous as it would cause a panic and social disorder. Eisenhower said the same.

#9.) Van Tassel said applied new ET technology would collapse the fragile U.S. and world economy, with automation jobs lost. Eisenhower apparently came to the same conclusion.

#10.) Van Tassel worried in speeches that U.S. and world citizens would drop their religious beliefs to worship the aliens. Eisenhower very likely worried the same.

Other eyebrow-raising details of Van Tassel's story are linked here. He said he received telepathic messages - "thought communication" - from aliens back in 1952, including technical data and an assurance from his celestial friends that Dwight D. Eisenhower was destined to become the next president of the United States, and that he needed to be informed as such. So George dutifully wrote to General Eisenhower, via his wife Mamie, with this claim early that critical election year. And in July of '52, Van Tassel wrote Eisenhower again, this time to warn him that "saucers were going to buzz the Pentagon" - and did five days later. "Everything in that letter came true, exactly as stated; the letter is now a matter of public record," housed in New York City, George asserted in a recorded 1958 public lecture. Two other similar letters were allegedly sent to Washington D.C., he said, presumably for and/or about Dwight Eisenhower.

Furthermore, in a recorded 1957 radio interview in New York City, Mr. Van Tassel let slip that he was "close enough to him {President Eisenhower} the time he came to Palm Springs to know what was going on."

In a recorded 1956 local Rotary Club lecture, Van Tassel spoke confidently that President Truman first spoke to friendly aliens (Setimus?), then-current President Eisenhower "flew out here to Palm Springs two years ago, specifically to be taken from Palm Springs over to March Air Force Base, {then} to Muroc Air Force Base, to converse with these people, at their request, when they landed there. Yet the public was never told of that. We know this happened as Ike was supposed to come up to our place to talk to *us*, and the night before his landing in Palm Springs, there was a GI six-wheeler truck with about forty M.P.s on it, ready to set up provide security for the president." Was Van Tassel referring with genuine inside knowledge to Eisenhower's Palm Springs arrival? If so, why did he need Military Police for protection there? Or did Van Tassel misspeak and meant in preparation at *Muroc/Edwards*? Or did George wildly imply that the president was originally supposed to arrive at *his* Giant Rock Airport, to be remarkably well-guarded, to be covertly transported out to Edwards AFB? Or was Van Tassel simply mistaken, exaggerating, or just plain lying?

Considered by some in his day as "eccentric," married Mr. Van Tassel was at the least a very bright and erudite high school dropout who hosted a yearly UFO convention at his Giant Rock airport, including one on April 4, 1954. He also wrote to the president that spring to inform him he would meet with Eisenhower at the White House on June 22, 1954, but George received no reply and apparently there is no particular evidence that he ever personally huddled with the nation's 34th president.

In returning to our 2/19/54 narrative... the landed alien beings completely vanished, to the naked human eye anyway. "This caused the president a lot of discomfort because none of us could see them, even though we knew they were there," pilot Jerry Flier recollected from the shocking Edwards AFB event, noting the landed alien beings then soon calmly reappeared before the assembled men, likely with impish smiles. Dwight's, however, was decidedly gone. Fretful President Eisenhower could picture in his mind what this cloaking achievement would do to various people and institutions if ETs displayed this technique with or without warning. Human-like aliens could move about undetected in our society, turning up in all sorts of places unannounced, giving citizens quite a surprise, an emotional jolt, or even heart attacks. To the faint of heart and poorly prepared, vanishing/reappearing space people and objects would be enough to make them "freak out." Mental meltdowns by already on-the-edge citizens seemed likely then, in reacting to such staggering displays.

"I have only one yardstick by which I test every major problem and that is: is it good for America?" Eisenhower was once quoted saying, and as he applied that standard here the imagined results came up short.

Within the 1989 summary leaked in 2017, we get confirmation of this worrisome point of view as far back as the 1948 Aztec UFO crash, feeling that a government policy of openness with the public would be *"causing a panic situation based upon fear of undetectable aliens among them. The thought of riots and murders was on everyone's mind."* Dwight likely knew this attitude, if not read such briefing papers during the Setimus situation back then but perhaps from witnessing it *in person* with Setimus '48-'49. He realized his handling of the humanoid landing party on 2/19/54 was most critical. Botching it, or not properly containing it, could lead to the sum of all fears.

Esteemed American author and former syndicated newspaper reporter/columnist Ruth Shick Montgomery (1912-2001) was friends with many a political bigwig in 1950s' Washington, including the Eisenhower's. Low-key but highly educated Ruth touched upon the presidential Edwards Airbase legend in her popular 1985 book *"Aliens Among Us."* As readers of metaphysics are quite aware, Mrs. Montgomery would produce some of the material for her series of classic, best-selling tomes in a most unusual manner: "automatic writing," which stemmed from her so-called "Spirit Guides." These high-minded deceased souls would allegedly type through conservative Christian Ruth at her desk for ten minutes every morning after meditation. They'd pass along uplifting spiritual messages that included predictions for the future and the reasons why aliens have been visiting our planet over the past thousands of years, stepped up in recent decades. On the topic of the Eisenhower-ET rumor, Mrs. Montgomery relayed: *"Ike saw and spoke to the space aliens. He saw the spaceships as well. He should have released that fact before he died."*

The socially-active, well-bred Mrs. Montgomery told this author a few years before her death in 2001 that, alas, she was not with Mr.

Eisenhower and the Washington press corps on that particular '54 California trip and thus completely unaware of what was going on in secret at the time. However, three decades later she researched the Edwards Airbase affair and came to believe in it, including the vanishing/reappearing alien angle, which her "Guides" say is done by mental processes currently beyond human abilities, in manipulating the molecular structure within all physical forms. {On top of that, Ruth passed along a spine-tingling nonfiction tale of a friendly extraterrestrial "highly developed master" from another star system, in human form, who visited a startled man in the wooded mountains of *Vermont*!}

Truly, the airbase-visiting aliens represented *tremendous* change, if not total social upheaval for sleepy 1954. Mr. Eisenhower was a cautious senior citizen, and they don't often embrace change swiftly, if at all. It had been a long day, now a long night. Dwight was determined he would *not* go down in the history books as the president who unleashed complete chaos across the land if some sort of open alien program went forward. Maybe, he figured, he could instead work out a secretive deal, to be set in print, to throw the ETs a bone while enriching America, but accomplished from the shadows, on government-guarded land in isolated Nevada.

Jerry Flier recalled that the anxious president informed the visitors that the human race "needed more time to get ready for this." His negative, fearful reaction had to have been a huge disappointment for all at this summit, especially if it had been quietly planned for over a year in advance. Nothing much was going to come of it all, seemingly.

Another specific topic was raised, one deeply important to the nature-loving visitors (see next chapter). The president listened but balked again. Afterward, things seemed to wind down. Perhaps more than an hour had passed. Evidently, Eisenhower felt that the ETs at Edwards AFB now needed to be gently persuaded to take their enticing airships and techniques elsewhere, and *not* attempt to "educate" our planet's people with it all again, at least not for a long, long time. Their technology was over our heads (literally). Their unexpected invisibility cloaking was downright *dangerous* and scary to contemplate.

Perhaps taking a deep breath, President Eisenhower screwed up his courage and verbally rejected the humanoids once more that night, firmly but fairly, according to Jerry Flier. Dwight took the time to courteously explain some of his reasoning behind why the open ET presence was ultimately unsatisfactory and had to be erased. The visitors listened attentively. The ex-pilot recalled they surprisingly accepted Dwight's decision, remaining calm, to everyone's great relief. The visiting ETs seemed to understand all of the overriding reasons spelled out for them by the sage commander-in-chief.

This was a key moment in "UFO history," as it were. If not human history. The highest-ranking, most respected government official on earth told the friendly aliens they could not show themselves openly, that at best they could visit here only fleetingly and keep their business undercover. The humanoids signed off on this official policy (see the 1989 DIA report). And a further decision was later made – perhaps by Eisenhower himself – to deny, undermine, and dismiss UFO reports, and perhaps even harass American eyewitnesses – in order to keep the overall peace and tranquility of the nation, if not the world. Thus the monumental Muroc/Edwards summit conference and its presidential decision reverberate to this day.

In the cool, still desert night air, President Eisenhower realized that folks back at the Smoke Tree Ranch – including the potentially restless press – might begin to wonder aloud where he was. And that perhaps George E. Allen was waiting for him with his car back at the intermediate airfield, outside Palm Springs/Indio/La Quinta, or at least back at his upscale home. Thus the clock was ticking to get back there and keep a lid on all of the stupefying events of that Friday night/Saturday morning, by the time weary, worried Eisenhower got back to his ranch quarters – hopefully undetected - and went to bed.

Yes, the time for farewells had come. "The aliens then boarded their ships and departed," Clancarty quoted Colonel Flier summing up. All eyes at the Edwards hangar entrance were on the physical reality of liftoff and exit from airbase airspace. Just as they had come in, apparently, the five amazing crafts soared out of sight, silently and sleekly into the night sky. The sagging humans probably breathed a sigh of relief, yet were also sorry to see their amazing new friends leave. The assembled men encircling President Eisenhower, the "Secret Six," stared at the sky... then looked back down and at each other... back and forth, still overcome with emotion and unsure what to think, emotionally spent.

It was just after this aerial departure, Jerry Flier allegedly told the Irish-British Earl of Clancarty, that the men at the base were gathered around for the president to solemnly swear them all to complete secrecy. Even the nearby protective six, so trusted, were asked to raise their hands for a rather quick, informal but military-style loyalty oath to repeat. *None of what they just witnessed and learned could be allowed out of the dusty Edwards hangar that night for reasons of national security.* The same went for any welcoming committee; soldiers or M.P.s on guard along the outer perimeter; or cameramen. The event had to stay bottled up inside, at least until some point in time where the president felt it reasonable and acceptable to admit it publicly in some manner. No one ever seemed to break this sworn allegiance, apparently, until the aging (or even *dying?*) pilot spoke up to the UFO-curious parliamentary lord sometime in perhaps mid-1982.

It's possible the president at this point agreed to pose for a commemorative but private photograph at this time with his special protection squad, quite possibly troopers from Georgia (see Chapter Ten), not USAF or Secret Service officials at all. The distant alien ships had disappeared into the dark upper atmosphere, lost in a jumble of memories and emotions now. A sad emptiness must have settled in for all concerned. The event of a lifetime was all over. "They" were really gone.

Or were they?

CHAPTER NINE

The Light Letter and The Omega Secret

"Eisenhower was spirited over to Muroc one night during his visit to Palm Springs recently..."

— author Gerald Light

Jerry Flier's amazing story, as told to Lord Clancarty, has effectively ended. From this point on we have to fill in the Eisenhower-ET encounter blanks with tidbits of indisputable truths, plus some informed and reasonable conjecture. And then later in this chapter, we'll utilize a stunning near-"smoking gun" letter, typed up nice and neat for posterity. First, let's cover some sensible supposition mixed with firm facts...

The helicopter or airplane that imported Dwight and his entourage to Edwards was undoubtedly fueled and prepped for a return flight while resting on a nearby runway, perhaps General

Harold Bartron standing by. The president meanwhile undoubtedly met with the base commander, Brigadier General Stan Holtoner, and perhaps some well-decorated Edwards AFB officers who were quite curious as to how the private outdoor meeting went. Dwight needed their help in clamping the lid down and keeping it there. General orders were issued to maintain great silence and security at the base, and to be prepared for any sort of further otherworldly developments. All soldiers out on leave were ordered kept out, with gates locked, until "the dust cleared," so to speak, for what if these or other adventurous humanoids came back? Possibly classified reports were hastily typed, sealed, and locked away by a trusted base secretary or stenographer (who then had to be sworn to secrecy also). Any possible photographs or film footage taken at the encounter had to be confiscated, sealed, and classified "above top secret." The hangar – if it had a gifted ET ship within - had to be guarded with MPs and kept isolated until further notice. *Everyone* on the base had to be lectured on not spreading rumors. Nothing could be left to chance, to leak out someday and conceivably start a public panic. The heart of the matter was kept on a strict "need-to-know" basis.

Probably after nearly an hour or so of hammering out these details and instructions, Dwight hopped his flight back to the intermediate airfield near Palm Springs, taking along whomever it was he brought with him, including Secret Service agents. It might have been getting close to midnight. All of the excited men involved would have experienced great difficulty calming and sleeping, wondering how they could just go back to dull, day-to-day duties - but that was reality. Life went on.

At the Palm Springs-area airfield in the valley, Eisenhower was driven back home, perhaps stopping at George E. Allen's home first. *If* ex-President Truman was at Allen's place, he'd get a quick briefing on how it all went, and how he apparently would not be needed further. Mr. Allen probably learned little. Then it was time for the drive back to the Smoke Tree Ranch, the streets nearly empty and quite dark. Dwight couldn't help but ponder all that had just taken place while idle in the passenger seat, still numb.

Upon his later arrival back at the Smoke Tree Ranch home of Paul Helms, likely now after midnight, uninformed Mamie Eisenhower and any aides (some feeling a bit loose from drinks at the hotel party) may have quizzed him innocently on the latest lowdown: "Where have you been? Is everything all right?" Dwight in all likelihood said little in response. Loose lips sink (space)ships. His cover story was probably that he and chatty George Allen had a few drinks, played some bridge (Dwight's favorite), watched TV, and let the hours slip away without notice that night.

Saturday, Sunday, Monday, Tuesday... the days slipped by at the Smoke Tree Ranch and the local country club golf courses without a word or deed out of place, no one the wiser. No reports of any return of alien entities, at Muroc/Edwards, or anywhere else in America. By Tuesday night the 23rd, after sundown, it was time for the president and his traveling party to climb back on Columbine II at the Palm Springs airport and fly home to Washington D.C. The international skies were quiet, few UFO incidents were reported in the past few days. It was felt safe, without perceived repercussions for telling ETs to "please leave and stay aloof."

At 7:45 a.m. Eastern Time, the president's plane landed at Washington's National Airport on Wednesday, February 24th. The somewhat tanned and rested commander-in-chief was back in his executive mansion by 8:00 a.m. Congressional Republican leadership hustled over to the White House early, to huddle in private in the West Wing with the president at 8:30, something was so important.

What was discussed likely had to do with legislation, domestic issues, and McCarthyism, a growing problem in the press and halls of congress. It seems very unlikely that the president talked to mere congressmen or low-to-mid-level aides even a mere sliver about his riveting top-secret encounter in California.

All the press knew was that the golf-obsessed president was seen on the lawn of the White House a bit later that Wednesday morning, hitting a few chip shots with an iron. Subsequent biographers learned that Dwight Eisenhower purposely smacked golf balls on the grass of the executive mansion to project a clear public image of serenity and normalcy for the American public, its allies, and its enemies (in particular the Soviets). Was that the same public facade he purposely projected by golfing in Palm Springs on Saturday, 2/20/54, after the ET summit the night before?

Minus the press-obsessed issue of the congressional Army-McCarthy hearings, the rest of February passed quietly, and March of '54 seemed uneventful as well. We do know that President Eisenhower dictated a letter sent on March 9th to his Palm Springs host Paul Helms (the bakery executive), complaining of the "plateful of problems and headaches" he was struggling with once he got back from southern California. The president mentioned "the many grave problems" the country was facing later in the same missive, nothing specific.

Was there nothing of substance taking place at the carefully-selected ET landing site? One source claimed that by either late March or early April, *plenty* was up at Edwards Airbase - because he was *there*, soaking it all in, possibly interacting with the very same humanoids the president had supposedly dismissed and watched depart some fifty days earlier!

And that's where we dig into a most extraordinary letter...

Gerald Light was an aging metaphysical researcher, writer, and lecturer of some renown in Southern California in 1954. He was also artistic and crafted paintings reflecting his spiritualist beliefs. Gerald once lived in England but in '54 resided in Los Angeles (10545 Scenario Lane), sporting a reputation as something of a mystic or psychic in his own right, keenly interested in any rumored tales with a supernatural bent. To this end, he did some work for "Borderland Sciences Research Associates," a metaphysical laboratory located in San Diego (3524 Adams Avenue) since 1945. The unique lab was created for studying various aspects of the occult, a very rare bird in the button-down 1950s. Gerald also at times wrote paranormal essays for a Borderland publication under the name "Dr. Kappa," and claimed to have had his own, personal encounter with "Etherians," alien visitors who allegedly arrived in his presence in 1950.

The educated but esoteric Mr. Light carefully composed and typed up his neat one-page letter just after the second weekend of April 1954; *it was all about his first-hand knowledge of Edwards Airbase goings-on with aliens.* The information relayed was for "Mr. Meade Layne," his Borderland contact and the director of that laboratory, and likely took two days for the postal service to get it down the coast, from L.A. to S.D., ASAP.

Newton Meade Layne (1882-1961) was the founder and director of this paranormal research institute, back in 1945, and acted as the editor of their bi-monthly magazine in the 1950s. He was a graduate of USC and later the University of Oregon in 1926, then became an educator at various schools around the nation. He penned a great deal of philosophy, poetry, and paranormal papers in his day, and described his friend Gerald Light as "a man of rare gifts and unquestionable integrity." Mr. Layne also stated in a Borderlands publication that Mr. Light's 1950 alien contact was, intriguingly, "a singular and unhappy adventure." Meade – who retired on June 1, 1959, at age 77, was a regular correspondent with Gerald, sharing his proclivity for typing up his experiences in letter form. {Director Layne was also pen-pals, evidence shows, with UFO writer Desmond Leslie, mentioned in Chapter One, and once typed a detailed description of alien craft to the FBI in 1947, now viewable on the internet.} Why Meade and Gerald didn't telephone each other with their thoughts seems odd, but not everyone owned a phone in those days.

In one riveting letter passage, erudite Mr. Light pecked out the following statement on his manual typewriter: *"President Eisenhower, as you may already know, was spirited over to Muroc one night during his visit to Palm Springs recently."*

Wow! This statement certainly indicates that Gerald had recently learned the stupefying alien secret and that he also suspected his paranormal investigative colleague Meade had too. Gerald excitedly affirmed it as true for us all. But his marvelous missive revealed much more, some of it confirming precisely what "Jerry Flier" and "Sergeant X" claimed in later years, as we'll see, giving the overall tale more credence.

When precisely the startling document surfaced decades after its construction is not entirely clear, but it first made its way into the public record by its inclusion within the pages of the Berlitz and Moore 1980 Roswell book. It has become rather legendary in alien-government conspiracy circles ever since, and popular on the internet. The document turned up in the estate of the late Mr. Layne's family, following Meade's death at age 78 in a San Diego rest home, in May of 1961. It certainly seems to be quite authentic; included also are the apparent handwritten notes of Meade Layne in the open upper area of the paper, partially to record when he received the mailing on an April Friday (*"4/16/54"*). Meade also curiously scribbled the name of two San Diego area airbases: *"Huramon Airfield / Gillespie Airfield."* A simple *"5"* rests atop this printed remark, and a line across the page connects the inexplicable airfield statement to a rather chaotic doodled design on the left side of the upper part of the paper, with a circle around it. Strange! Was this to represent the five alien ships that had arrived and landed?

Gerald Light's birth and death dates are unknown; he remains largely a mysterious, highly intelligent but eccentric figure. He was described by one researcher as "elderly" in '54 and died long before the contents of his typed revelations became public knowledge, and the same can be said of Meade Layne. The specific people Mr. Light mentioned within the letter were also all deceased by the time it surfaced. {Was this why someone waited so long to release the letter?} Frustratingly, Gerald's other writings for Borderland Sciences are hopelessly muddled, rife with strange terms and mystical claims that make almost no sense, and are not worth repeating here, frankly. They're still found today online, at borderlandsciences.org.

What private paranormal researcher Layne found in the body of Light's letter likely caused the hair on the back of his neck to stand up. Gerald's exciting account of *"those forty-eight hours at Muroc"* later in the neatly typed paragraphs seem to indicate he was likely physically *there,* probably over the weekend of April 10th-11th, '54. Then we can reasonably assume he arrived home to quickly put together his thoughts down on paper, at his desk, before eagerly mailing it to his pal in San Diego by the 12th or 13th. Gerald was a *writer*, by golly, quite used to pecking away on a typewriter to express his thoughts. We can be deeply grateful today he did. Light's opening remarks to Director Layne certainly help make a case for the Eisenhower encounter allegations. To wit {italicizing added}:

"My dear friend: I have just returned from Muroc. The report is true - - devastatingly true!"

Here again, we logically assume that both Gerald Light *and* Meade Layne had recently heard the ET landing gossip in the southern California area - *"the report"* - sometime *before* Light's trip to Muroc/Edwards, likely via Frank Edwards' popular Mutual Radio show, mentioned in Chapter One. Based upon first-hand experience Gerald learned it was all quite thrillingly genuine. He was chosen by someone within the federal government and/or the military, perhaps selecting Gerald due to his public claim of possessing previous experience in fathoming both dematerialization and extraterrestrials. Oh, and that he also lived in L.A., for the group car ride to the isolated airbase:

"I made the journey in company with Franklin Allen of the Hearst papers and Edwin Nourse of the Brookings Institute (Truman's erstwhile financial advisor) and Bishop McIntyre of L.A. (confidential names, for the present, please.)"

Here we have a brief description of an apparent sociological "study group," one likely appointed in a careful, deliberate way. The unusual foursome was allowed to not just enter Muroc/Edwards for the intention of looking over gifted alien hardware, but to survey the ongoing actions and reactions of both humans and aliens in a hangar there. And once again, right off, the name "Edwin Nourse" flares up, much as in August of '49, during the Truman Oval Office meetings while handling the Vermont "Setimus" episode (see Chapter Three).

Gerald Light, the "student of occultism" (his words) who had written essays and even a previous copyrighted book (well, a 28-page mimeographed pamphlet) on the subject of visiting inter-dimensional space beings and their ships, was therefore quite naturally selected to participate. It may well be that someone in charge of handling the Edwards alien visitors contacted the rare parapsychological "Borderland Science Research Associates" and asked specifically for this man.

In 1953, Light boldly wrote for Borderland Sciences' publication: *"The flying saucers are real, truth-in-action. The skies are literally teeming with beings from other worlds; swarming with instruments and machines carrying living beings as real and vital as ourselves (and in some cases a thousand times more vital). We must be prepared to meet them at once!"* Remember, this was a year *before* the Edwards Airbase landing, typewritten by an old man who felt he was in occasional telepathic contact with entities from "Etheria," the astral dimension beyond the physical world where he felt beings existed and/or possibly traveled through, to arrive in our planet's atmosphere.

Let's now take a closer look at the three named men allegedly traveling with Gerald Light to Muroc/Edwards...

First, there was Winthrop Franklin Allen (1874-19??). In early 1954 he was age 80, a retired Hearst newspaper reporter (and book author) who had covered the sometimes-secretive actions of the U.S. government in Washington D.C. for many years. Mr. Allen's reputation was solid, serious, and studious; he could have given President Eisenhower and his top aides his view of the sustained alien contact situation in regards to its potential impact on congress and the national media, and governments around the world when dropping such a huge bombshell. {One wonders if Winthrop F. Allen was related to lawyer/businessman George E. Allen. Answer unknown.}

The aforementioned Dr. Edwin Griswold Nourse, Ph.D. (1883-1974) was age 71 at the time, retired from the fields of economics, agriculture, and commerce. He served President Truman as the first Chairman of the Council of Economic Advisers. A 1972 taped interview with Dr. Nourse explored his past actions in government but also revealed *he was good friends with Eisenhower's Smoke Tree Ranch co-host, Paul Hoffman.* Dr. Nourse was a Cornell-educated, worldly gentleman and a consultant for the Brookings Institute, the famous and reputable private think-tank in Washington D.C. Ed Nourse could have given President Eisenhower advice on how the news of the alien contact would potentially have influenced global financial markets and more specifically Wall Street, and thus the American economy overall.

Important note: Nourse's Brookings Institute produced a special study for NASA in 1960, carefully constructed during the Eisenhower era. *It discussed the potential impact of extraterrestrial visitation upon the largely unprepared public.* Such a coincidence! The report stated that contact between ETs and humanity "could happen at any time," and that some scholars felt that "the earth may *already* be under closed scrutiny by advanced space races." The $96,000 study's author concluded it was better for *the American government to keep the lid on all evidence for alien visitation*, that any "*discovery of extraterrestrial artifacts should be covered up for fear of paralyzing research and development enterprises*" already underway.

Cardinal James Francis Aloysius McIntyre (1886-1979) was age 68 in early 1954, the rabidly anti-communist Archbishop of the Roman Catholic Church of the Los Angeles diocese from 1948 to 1970. The future Bishop McIntyre was the highly-influential spiritual leader of a particular organized worldwide religion that would have been knocked for quite a loop if the ET revelations had gone forward en masse. In fact, McIntyre was based out of New York City in much of

1948, just like Dwight Eisenhower at Columbia University that year; did the cardinal and the general become friends during this time-frame?

Interestingly – and quite suspiciously – J. F. McIntyre's various saved written correspondences over the years "just happened" to have been abruptly closed to UFO researchers in the 1980s and beyond. McIntyre might have been casually selected for the Edwards study group simply because he was already available in the Los Angeles area... or... he was very carefully selected to give his own trusted secret report to the Vatican in Rome. He also could have given President Eisenhower and his top advisers some Catholic-based Christian counsel on what the news of sustained alien contact would have had on American (and the world's) citizens' religious faiths, beliefs, and passions.

{Side notes: in Chapter One, we learned of some insight by prominent Los Angeles journalist Frank Scully, whose real name was Francis Joseph Xavier Scully, a devoted Catholic who was once knighted by the "Order of the St. Gregory" in 1956. Was he in tight with His Eminence, Cardinal McIntyre of L.A.? According to data online, it was Archbishop McIntyre who created the "St. Gregory The Great Parish" in 1951, and the award wasn't just for anyone. Plus... President Eisenhower was never a Catholic but was baptized a Presbyterian Christian in D.C. just weeks after being sworn into office. Nonetheless, on December 6, 1959, he became nearly the only American president by that point in history to have met with a sitting pope when he conferred in Vatican City with Pope John XXIII; only Woodrow Wilson (in 1919) had ever previously done so as a seated U.S. president. Every American chief executive since Eisenhower has met with a pope, who also nowadays oversees Catholic astronomical observatories and the search for alien life!}

Let's recall that William Brophy (mentioned in Chapter One) expressed that his father, a B-29 Bomber pilot, told him that it was his understanding President Eisenhower met with peaceful aliens at Edwards Airbase in February of 1954... *and that James F. McIntyre was there then too.* Did Brophy refer to the Gerald Light claim, of McIntyre being imported in the summit's *aftermath*, in early April of '54, to learn more information from the visiting ETs? Either way, Cardinal McIntyre was *already* informed on the subject of ETs on earth, Brophy claimed, as the Italian government had once recovered a crashed alien craft in June of 1933 and subsequently contacted the Vatican about the matter. The pope told this shocking story to his American representative, McIntyre; how Eisenhower or one of his aides discovered that McIntyre knew all of this remains a mystery. Did Dwight contact the pope *before*, or *after* his airbase encounter? If Edwards AFB contact was prearranged well before Friday, February 19th, a notified pope might have recommended that his man McIntyre be included, as his emissary. But... if such an airbase visit by the cardinal was undertaken only in April, then McIntyre presumably had not yet seen any ETs previously.

Now we come to another fascinating facet of this scintillating saga, straight from Vatican City...

A dedicated UFO/ET buff and magazine writer named Cristoforo Barbato (1972-) has claimed that from 2001 to 2005 he received sensitive insider information from a Jesuit priest working inside the Vatican. Much of the resulting shocking data accumulated led to Barbato's controversial 2006 article (available online) *"The Omega Secret,"* highlighting the lowdown from high up in the Vatican. The unnamed secret source supposedly told Chris that it was his understanding that *Cardinal James F. McIntyre from California did indeed go to Edwards Airbase and witness extraterrestrial beings for himself, right alongside President Eisenhower on 2/19/54.* And further that McIntyre was so moved by the dramatic experience he quickly flew to Rome, Italy, to speak directly to Pope Pius XII (Eugenio Pacelli, 1876-1958), briefing him about the shocking ET situation, despite being sworn to secrecy. In fact, along the way, McIntyre was stopped and warned by nervous U.S. government officials to keep his mouth shut but refused the order. According to Barbato's information, the cardinal was part of a 2/19/54 "delegation with the president." This again indicates a prearranged landing event with a "welcoming committee" on hand, waiting patiently perhaps for *days* at the base, hoping that aliens would land as promised and that also the president would arrive to help greet them. {Recall the MUFON allegation that air traffic at Edwards was restricted in advance, for the 19th, 20th, and 21st.}

Supposedly Cardinal McIntyre quickly arranged for a private tell-all with the pope, just days after 2/19/54. The trusted Jesuit found this out from existing records within the Vatican and further informed Barbato that the intrigued Pius XII in '54 decided in response to form his own high-level intelligence committee called "Vatican Information Services." This unit would inform the papal see of future major secrets, whatever they may be, somewhat like the Vatican creating its own CIA. Two major American information coordinators for this intel group, Mr. Barbato alleged, would have been James Francis McIntyre and also the Archbishop of Detroit, Edward Aloysius Mooney (1882-1958).

{Interestingly, Archbishop Mooney was chosen to deliver the benediction at President Eisenhower's second inauguration in January of 1957. In October of '58, he was attending a papal conclave in Vatican City when he suddenly collapsed and died of a heart attack. Cardinal McIntyre was present and granted Edward Mooney absolution before James left the secretive conclave, which was held to select a replacement for the late Pope Pius XII, who had just died of heart failure, in bed, after serving as pope since 1939.}

The risk-taking Jesuit source for Barbato wasn't finished with his Eisenhower–ET inside scoops. He told the Italian UFO magazine writer/editor in communique and secret meetings that three different 16-millimeter cameras were utilized at Edwards Airbase by military operators during the big runway ET event (see the previous chapter). The mechanical power systems of the alien spaceships were said to have overwhelmed at least one large film camera and inadvertently disabled it. But other resulting footage taken showed the famous American leader with a few other people around him for protection greeting the human-like entities stepping from their landed high-tech ships.

Is there any precedent or history of Dwight David Eisenhower getting involved in a UFO matter with a Catholic inspection/opinion afterward? Oddly enough, there is.

As shown in a later-leaked 6/30/47 memorandum revealed within www.majesticdocuments.com, President Truman's Army Chief of Staff, General Eisenhower, ordered a colonel to look after U.S. East Coast Archbishop Francis Joseph Spellman (1889-1967) on a tour of New Mexico military installations around the time of the Roswell UFO crash recovery. Cardinal Spellman was referred to in this paperwork as "Military Vicar of the Armed Forces," set to enjoy "complete security at all times and that his presence at any airfield will not be disclosed." Was McIntyre *with* Spellman? It's unknown, but wouldn't be surprising. The delicate, secret alien retrieval/cover-up was to be undertaken "at the personal direction the President of the United States," Dwight's memo stated. So it was Truman's call in '47, not Eisenhower's, but it was something "Ike" obviously took note of.

Catholic or not, all three selected "wise men" with Gerald Light that spring of 1954 were very respected and successful in their chosen fields, evidently issued passes and given a brief thumbnail sketch of what they were to study at the airbase upon arrival. Perhaps they took turns driving the few hours necessary to reach their destination until they finally passed through the guarded checkpoint gates of Edwards AFB. It was probably a little taxing for the old men, but that was nothing compared to the endurance test that came next:

"When we were allowed to enter the restricted section (after about six hours in which we were checked on every possible item, event, incident, and aspect of our personal and public lives), I had the distinct feeling that the world had come to an end with fantastic realism."

Certainly, the security precautions at Muroc/Edwards would have been substantial, but it seems the military operatives in charge of "protecting" the secret alien visitors were a little over the top (if writer Light described events accurately). *Nearly six long hours* for highly-regarded professional men - all of them senior citizens – *invited* to the base, to endure constant questioning and background checks? And not just about their jobs and their home lives, but their own deeply-held personal beliefs? The grilling the foursome received by security agents must have seemed interminable and perhaps a bit outrageous. But once inside the base hangars that day, what they eventually experienced after the intense security check was a total, mind-blowing surprise, well worth the trip. They were allowed inside the so-called "restricted section" to absorb what had to have been the most impressive sight and exciting highlight of metaphysical Gerald Light's long and colorful life. The friendly humanoids who had landed in February were back!

Thus there had to have been a "second landing event" at Edwards, perhaps in late March of 1954, it is clear from Gerald's letter. Apparently, he took it fairly calmly, but others did not:

"For I have never seen so many human beings in a state of complete collapse and confusion as they realized that their world had indeed ended with such finality as to beggar description."

The fearful, stunned responses had to have been both amusing and unsettling to observe.

"The reality of "otherplane" aeroforms is now and forever removed from the realms of speculation and made a rather painful part of the consciousness of every responsible scientific and political group."

Seven months later, a riveting statement at a press conference held by Dr. Hermann Julius Oberth (1894-1989), one of the fathers of rocket science, caught the attention of some alert Americans. Esteemed physics Professor Oberth stunned the attending media with some seemingly-knowledgeable statements about advanced extraterrestrial visitation to Earth. He declared that he knew quite well that aliens had not only come to our planet but that *they were working with scientists* in various fields to advance various technologies. The German scientist also claimed to know how ET crafts worked, via "distorting the gravitational field and converting gravity into usable energy." {See more of his eyebrow-raising quotes in the October 24, 1954 edition of *The American Weekly*, the article entitled, "Flying Saucers Come from a Distant World."} Where in the world did Dr. Oberth get such staggering claims? Could he have been among those great brains allegedly called into Edwards Airbase after the late March second landing?

"During my two days visit, I saw five separate and distinct types of spaceships being studied and handled by our air force officials - with the assistance and permission of the Etherians!"

None of these pilots or USAF "officials" - minus "Jerry Flier" - evidently ever came forward with such surprising first-hand tales. But at least we have further confirmation one more time of Flier's and Sergeant X's allegation of *five* alien ships landing at Muroc/Edwards. Even Mr. Light said he saw this specific number, lending even more credence to his letter's genuineness and believability.

1980 UFO book co-authors Berlitz and Moore, mentioned earlier, once interviewed Mr. Reilly Hansard Crabb (1912-1994), a paranormal researcher/lecturer/writer and one-time head (from 1959 to 1985) of the same Borderland Sciences Research Foundation that Light and Layne labored at. Crabb alleged that an unnamed Air Force sergeant blabbed to him in 1971 that he was stationed at Edwards AFB back in 1967 when he saw something quite out of this world. The sergeant claimed he had struck up a conversation with a trusted test pilot at the base, and the subject of UFOs and life beyond earth came up. The helpful, knowledgeable pilot then allegedly took the curious sergeant into his confidence by leading him to one of the well-guarded airplane hangars. The pilot - who remained unidentified - supposedly had full access inside the vast structure, and allowed his guest, the sergeant, a long look behind a parted curtain. Together they peered at a saucer-shaped craft "sitting on high landing gear" of some sort on the pavement. This highly unusual flying machine was said by the sergeant to have been "completely circular" and featured "sharp edges sloping up to a domed cockpit area" at the disc's center. The apparent alien spaceship was in very good shape but seemed to be capable of only holding two or three human-sized persons. The vehicle was estimated to be "twenty-five to thirty-five feet in diameter." {Sound familiar?} Edwards AFB personnel in coveralls were allegedly moving about the parked ship quite nonchalantly, working on something, the anonymous sergeant told R. H. Crabb. After seeing all of this, the pilot was shipped out to Vietnam, where he subsequently died in combat. The sergeant revealed the friendly pilot warned him that day in 1967 upon leaving the hangar that complete secrecy on what he had just witnessed was required. The sergeant also disclosed to Crabb that Edwards Airbase guards he later became acquainted with stated unequivocally that *there had been extraterrestrial contact made at the airbase in years past.* The odd saucer was left over from that cosmic exchange era.

In 1980, Reilly Crabb went on to pen a 44-page pamphlet, stapled together, on the 1954 aliens at Muroc/Edwards, entitled *"Flying Saucers at Edwards AFB"* (not read by this author). In this obscure booklet, Mr. Crabb apparently raised an intriguing notion: "It is quite likely that similar landings, and warnings, were made at secret military bases in China and Russia at the same time." Was this inside information, or just speculation? Did Eisenhower's ETs give equal time to leaders of the communist nations, after he essentially turned them away?

On October 28th, 2016, a caller named "Robert from Ohio" (then 65 years old) contacted "The Mary Joyce Show" podcast, to tell of his life as a USAF machinist with top-secret security clearance, in service for four years total. {The program was placed on *YouTube* on November 7th, 2016.} Robert said he worked at Edwards AFB in 1971, and it was the site of many "black ops" projects. One day, he saw a large, empty hangar in the distance "at the main base," with people walking into it, but strangely not out of it. This was a special test base hangar for new technology, he said, so he went over to it and boldly entered too. Robert looked around, then headed down a stairwell, to an elevator. He got in, went down fast, and soon discovered underground roads and tunnels, working spaces and offices... and a saucer-shaped metal spacecraft with windows and thin tripod legs. Security guards quickly jumped Robert with M16 rifles and escorted him out, with an electronic device held to head. He eventually passed out. Upon awakening later, intimidated Robert was threatened with recriminations if he talked – which he did, now and then, he said. For instance, an Air Force doctor he once spoke with told him that he had discovered that *President Eisenhower once met with aliens at Edwards AFB and even signed a treaty with them, in 1954.* "Eisenhower was one of the first ones that were allowed on the alien crafts," the physician asserted, and that he personally saw photographs of ETs "shaking hands with Eisenhower." Robert also learned that *the Brookings Institute was involved with the alien direct communication project*, but members in the know are instructed to deny everything.

Keeping all of that in mind, let's now return to Gerald Light's remarkable letter from mid-April of '54...

"I have no words to express my reactions. It has finally happened. It is now a matter of history."

Yet, official history does not record or acknowledge this amazing incident, only scattered hints and allegations remain. But let's ask ourselves now an important question: what was so urgently critical on Earth that could have caused advanced extraterrestrials to send repeated messages; doggedly negotiate for a landing site and date, and then set down as prearranged at Muroc/Edwards on February 19th for a meeting with the most powerful and influential person on earth... *and then come back to that very site just a month and a half later?*

In short, here is the likely answer, described within a modern website on the "explosive" subject:

"A hydrogen bomb is, by far, the most destructive weapon that mankind has ever invented. It is the most powerful type of nuclear bomb, in some cases reaching more than 2,000 times the yield of the nuclear bombs dropped on Hiroshima and Nagasaki, Japan."

Let's chew on that two-word phrase for a sec: *"two thousand times"* - than the worst devastation ever seen (in 1945). It's a mind-boggling figure, and it was being tried out, experimentally, as dangerous, recklessly destructive, and insane as that sounds today.

Since just after he took office in January of 1953, President Dwight D. Eisenhower ordered a whole series of these hydrogen bombs to be test-detonated, between late February and mid-May of 1954. The biggest of them all was due to be touched off March 1st of '54. It proved to be an enormous mistake, a gigantic atmospheric explosion, and a subsequent environmental calamity for much of the Pacific Ocean and its inhabitants - human, plant, and animal - spreading radiation across the sea, land, and atmosphere, far and wide. And it was only one of *several* controversial nuclear bomb tests that were rocking and rolling the planet that spring.

Guess who warned against detonating this monumental 3/1/54 calamity days in advance while at Muroc/Edwards on 2/19/54? And were pretty unhappy about it when they were ignored... so they came back to complain again in late March/early April before the environmentally disastrous program was to be concluded? American military scientists were meddling with high-yield atomic forces that they didn't fully understand, it is clear in hindsight, dangerous matters that affected our so-called "outer space," not just our planet's *lower*, breathable atmosphere. Human beings in positions of power weren't just acting like foolish little boys playing with matches, they were playing with *dynamite*. *Lots* of it. And some sources have alleged that the humanoids who landed and spoke on the runway to Eisenhower expressed their serious misgivings on the subject. It might have been the whole point of setting up the conference in the first place.

Should President Eisenhower go ahead and discuss the alien warning - or even the hushed landing event - in a public speech to the world? If Gerald Light's eye-popping letter was an accurate overview of the situation, the startling notion of a public declaration *was* being bandied about – and opposed in some powerful quarters:

"And it is my conviction that he will ignore the terrific conflict between the various "authorities" and go directly to the people via radio and television if the impasse continues much longer."

Such an astonishing statement, apparently based on the scuttlebutt Gerald heard in early April at Edwards AFB, perhaps even from the very military officers who represented at least some of the *"authorities"* he mentioned in seemingly sarcastic quotes. Such a televised delivery would undoubtedly shock the entire planet. Perhaps held at the United Nations? Or from the Oval Office? Or even at Edwards Airbase, possibly alongside some of the peaceful alien beings? At least it was *pondered* if Gerald is to be believed.

Air Force chief Nathan F. Twining might have been *there*, at Edwards, perhaps in February and but more likely in either late March or early April of '54, for the apparent second landing. Which side did he lean on regarding going public? In mid-May of 1954, General Twining gave a speech in Texas, after which he was asked about the validity of UFOs, as reported in *"European Stars and Stripes,"* among other publications. "The best brains in the Air Force are working on the problem of Unidentified Flying Objects, trying to solve this mystery," Twining was quoted by a reporter as telling his audience. Was this a direct reference to Gerald Light's claim of a covert Edwards examination of ETs by military officials? Trying to make sense of their high-tech spaceships and mysterious vanishings? Twining then tried to backtrack by adding, "No facts have been uncovered to show that there is anything to flying saucers," but there are "very reliable people" who have reported seeing them. So the general was all over the map in his response for the public, but at least he was talking to the press. Perhaps he realized he had said too much on a top-secret, classified subject.

Another prestigious figure at Edwards was likely President Eisenhower's Secretary of the Air Force, Harold Elstner Talbott, Jr. (1888-1957). He served Dwight from February of '53 to August of '55. He showed up with his family in Palm Springs *in late March*, as recorded in the *Desert Sun* 3/29/54 edition, and they stayed *at the Smoke Tree Ranch*. The Talbotts hobnobbed with Dwight's pal Paul Helms, according to a gossip columnist, making one wonder if they stayed in the very same Helms guest facilities that the First Couple occupied a month earlier. The esteemed Talbott family settled in for a week, but Secretary Talbott didn't stay too long, leaving to supposedly "tour southern California airbases." Like Edwards AFB, no doubt. Recall that Gerald Light said he saw "Air Force officials" working with the aliens, and you can't get any more "official" than Secretary Talbott.

Incredibly, *Harold Talbott had his own UFO sighting* while flying as a passenger over the Fresno, California, area on March 24, 1954! The "metallic ship" allegedly followed his plane "about 1,000 yards below and behind," easily keeping up. Others on board also witnessed the startling, extended sight. At one point, the flummoxed pilot was ordered – by Secretary Talbott himself? - to turn the plane around, "but the UFO outmaneuvered them and raced off." {Source: Loren Gross, *UFOs: A History, Jan.-May 1954*.} Officially, Talbott later denied the story - what else would he say? - but the incident was tellingly scratched from official flight records, which showed his aerial journey that day as having ended with a landing in Palm Springs.

The U.S. Army Intelligence *"Special Operations Manual 1-01"* (readied in March, for an April '54 release) repeatedly emphasized the need for secrecy on all UFO/ET matters and even the steps to be undertaken to discredit or destroy the reputations of those who came forward with credible stories for the American media. It read at one point: *"Any encounter with entities known to be of extraterrestrial origin is to be considered a matter of national security and therefore classified TOP SECRET. Under no circumstances is the general public or the public press to learn of the existence of these entities. The official government policy is that such creatures do not exist, and that no agency of the federal government is now engaged in any study of ETs or their artifacts. Any deviation from this stated policy is forbidden."*

If that wasn't harsh enough, let's not forget that uncovered government documents reveal that on March 1st, 1954, the U.S. Department of Defense issued a stern directive demanding silence on alien beings. *"Under no circumstances are the general public or public press to learn more about the evidence for these entities,"* the report declared of alien entities. This was considered "new classified policy (MANDATE 0463) in regard to extraterrestrial encounters." The staggering memo was sent out "to all departments and military service branches." It is nearly a smoking gun for revealing Eisenhower's reaction to his memories of the 2/19/54 summit, and how he originally wanted their extraordinary presence and abilities kept completely rejected and covered up, lest it trigger a national (or global) panic. The DoD directive relayed "the official government policy that such creatures do not exist." {Source: MUFON *"Hangar 1"* season premiere in 2014.}

So now President Eisenhower, the ex-Army strategist, was rather boxed in, perhaps partly by his own doing. A speech revealing even some of the blockbuster event would likely open the proverbial floodgates, especially in the eager, probing press. He had just ordered everyone to zip their lips, likely with threats of very negative repercussions, but... Mr. Eisenhower probably felt *someone* was going to inevitably leak the bombshell saga. Overall, he knew that as commander-in-chief, he could make his own rules. So he at least seriously pondered the possibilities of going public first, in theory to get ahead of the story.

Gerald Light informed us precisely when he heard it would all come spilling out:

"From what I could gather, an official statement to the country is being prepared for delivery about the middle of May."

If he had made this big broadcast speech, Dwight could potentially spin it to make it sound like friendly, advanced ETs were waiting for only *his* competent administration to make contact as they trusted only *his* sparkling wisdom and leadership. He'd come across as the hero, to aid his future re-election, if not his place in the history books. And thereby rather stick it to ex-President Truman. It was likely *very* tempting for Dwight's ego and future planning to contemplate.

Yet onward did the atomic testing program march, and no ET announcement ever surfaced. According to the story of retired Marine sergeant Charles L. Suggs II, recalling his naval commander father's first-hand tale of the Edwards secret summit, the human-like aliens stepped down from their crafts and "posed questions about our nuclear testing." This seems to be a recurring theme in *other* UFO/ET cases over the ensuing decades; aliens are terribly worried about what humanity is doing to the planet. And remember that early 1952 UFO-buzzing of the U.S.S. Franklin Roosevelt, with pajama-clad Eisenhower aboard... and how that aircraft carrier was rumored to be carrying *nuclear* weaponry? Was that Dwight's first clue to this anxious alien theme? Or did Setimus warn of reckless bomb testing first, back in 1948-'49, to Ike and/or President Truman in Vermont? Remember, Harry dubbed the Soviet bomb program, "Vermont."

Unfortunately for the fretful humanoids, as the spring of '54 went along they were unsuccessful in convincing Commander-in-Chief Eisenhower to halt the hideous "Castle" program. A unique "dry fuel hydrogen" device was set off as planned on March 1st and "Castle Bravo" turned out to be the largest and most destructive blast in human history. To reemphasize: Bravo expended *far* more energy than originally figured and did much greater damage to the Bikini Atoll detonation site near the Marshall Islands in the South Pacific than U.S. scientists had initially predicted. It was approximated to be *1,200 times more devastating* than either of the two atomic bombs that were dropped by American forces in the late stages of World War II, in August of 1945. An estimated *250%* more destructive than first postulated by poorly calculating U.S. scientists! Bravo was a devastating, shocking blunder; did ETs see this coming and try to warn head honcho Eisenhower?

To make matters worse, the startling '54 devastation spread wind-blown atmospheric nuclear fallout. The poisonous pollution wafted a reputed *six thousand square miles* within the earth's atmosphere, expanding across the Pacific Ocean, headed downward, making some people and animals sick for several years to come. Members of the American detonation team had to be rescued from an island twenty miles away, wisely covering themselves with bed-sheets to keep the fallout from touching their bodies. Twenty-three crew members of a Japanese fishing boat were not so informed or lucky. They felt atomic ash falling from the sky and sticking to their ship – and their bare skin. The group quickly fell ill with various symptoms, and one of the men eventually died. The Japanese press reported the tale and national outrage ensued. It grew internationally, naturally as March and April passed.

Needless to say, angry criticism of the American soldier-statesman Eisenhower and his heedless atomic policies eventually reverberated around the globe as the news of the sickening contamination spread – but it took a while. The nightmarish testing scenario slowly grew into a political morass for the president and his staff, scrambling to apologize and fix the fiasco as best they could. Two entire islands were evacuated – permanently - and quarantines for unlucky others took effect in the area downwind of the blast site. It took about $250 million in American government funds to clean up the disaster (as best they could) and pay off sickly victims.

So when was Eisenhower's controversial Castle program in the South Pacific specifically planned to come to a halt? *The middle of May!* Perhaps we can see now why the president would reverse course and consider going public with the news of the alien landing and communication at Edwards: *it would change the subject*. And turn around his suddenly-sagging poll numbers. By April 11th or so, Dwight knew he was in trouble, but stubbornly wanted the plotted Castle program completed first, perhaps to show who was boss. Castle program test detonations went off March 22nd and 29th, did they lead directly to a "second landing" and renewed pleading by the concerned ETs at Edwards Airbase?

{The mighty atomic blasts concluded on May 14th-15th, 1954, with serious study of the effects went on for weeks after. Other plotted tests, on other types of bombs, continued as well.}

As the nuclear controversy sizzled, it is possible the gentle extraterrestrials asked a favor of the military, perhaps realizing Eisenhower was vulnerable now. The aliens required and thus requested a more permanent place in America to safely land in privacy in order to conduct their own scientific studies on a more regular basis. This would call for a site more remote and peaceful locale than the sometimes-bustling Edwards AFB. They needed their own laboratory, it seems clear. The 1989 "MJ-12" documents mention how the ETs were accommodated. A special site at an American airbase in rural, obscure Nevada, far out in the burning desert, surrounded by imposing mountains, was allegedly turned into a special base for friendly humanoid ETs. Whether this accounts for the many UFO sightings in Nevada over the past decades is subject to debate, but the site mentioned in the DIA document was likely *not* the legendary "Area 51" but apparently, located not too far away.

Speaking to journalist Linda Moulton Howe exclusively in 1998, an anonymous source from the U.S. Army Signal Corps (loaned to the CIA at times), nicknamed "Kewper Stein," alleged that he briefed President Eisenhower in the late 1950s. Dwight was most curious during his tenure in office about the covert Nevada aerial facilities and their alien connection (as reported in Howe's marvelous www.Earthfiles.com). Alien hardware and relations were allegedly handled within a facility entitled "S-4," not far away from Area 51, said Stein. At the time of his interview, Kewper was 77 years old and in ill health, wanting to spill secrets to Howe before he left this world. The top-secret S-4 site, he alleged, was built into the side of a Nevada mountain and contained gifted or recovered alien craft, plus comfortable quarters for the visiting members of "Majestic Twelve," and on another guarded level, for live space aliens as our guests! Stein recalled he was once summoned to the Oval Office by President Eisenhower (with Vice President Nixon present), to discuss the captured and gifted alien hardware and creatures at "S-4," which an irritated Dwight eventually threatened to invade with an entire Army division if the site's CIA-heavy leadership didn't start producing intelligence reports on their progress, as they had originally promised him. The secret bases known as "Area 51" and "S-4" were actually specifically initiated *by* President Eisenhower (within a year of his '54 California meeting with extraterrestrials), Kewper noted, adding that "MJ-12" eventually made it their "main base of operations" during Dwight's tenure. This was to Eisenhower's eventual chagrin as key Central Intelligence figures involved pretty much took charge there and remained aloof from their own commander-in-chief, Stein explained. Eisenhower had his day-to-day duties in D.C. to perform and couldn't go rushing off to S-4 to try to poke his nose into delicate, guarded matters; he had to rely on good intel. But it is possible these Nevada sites were touched upon in the 1989 DIA briefing... while S-4 remains off-limits but of great interest to UFO researchers to this very day.

In returning to Gerald Light and his wondrous April '54 letter... we're up to his opening sentence in the final paragraph, which reveals that perhaps he was a little optimistic on how many people were going to be contacted and informed within the scientific community on what was happening inside the guarded Edwards Airbase hangar that spring:

"I will leave it to your excellent powers of deduction to construct a fitting picture of the mental and emotional pandemonium that is now shattering the consciousness of hundreds of our scientific

"authorities" and all the pundits of the various specialized knowledge that make up our current physics."

The initial eye-catching claim within this statement is of course the word *"hundreds."* Had Gerald gone over the top in his recall? Were the number of scientists Gerald saw during his two days at the airbase *truly* that many, or was he projecting a future scenario? He went on, regarding his typed-up sympathy for the human frailties he had absorbed:

"In some instances, I could not stifle a wave of pity that arose in my being as I watched the pathetic bewilderment of rather brilliant brains struggling to make some sort of rational explanation which would enable them to retain their familiar theories and concepts."

Some of the great scientific thinkers of his day Gerald witnessed at the Air Force installation were reduced to sad, irrational states, a noteworthy percentage of them scrambling to somehow slam their stubborn, preconceived (or misconceived) scientific notions into ill-fitting slots that did not jibe with the new reality the humanoids were presenting to them.

Herein lies the rub with the entire ET saga: *it was over our heads.* Most of the "Etherian" abilities and technology were simply unfathomable to human comprehension in 1954.

Within the final sentences in the marvelous missive, more is revealed about the background and experiences of Gerald Light than anything else. It is obvious he was quite fascinated by the field of metaphysical mysteries from a fairly early age:

"And I thanked my destiny for having long ago pushed me into the metaphysical woods and compelled me to find my way out."

Bear in mind that Borderlands institute's director, Meade Layne, once wrote of Light: "He is a gifted and highly-educated" person who, according to authors Berlitz and Moore, "liked to dabble in clairvoyance and the occult." Gerald found the answers to the great enigmas and powers he probed, if he truly did *"find my way out."* At any rate, Gerald continued to type at his L.A. home:

"To watch strong minds cringe before totally irreconcilable aspects of "science" is not a pleasant thing. I had forgotten how commonplace such things as the dematerialization of "solid" objects had become to my mind."

So now it would seem for certain that the visiting humanoids were not just able to make themselves appear invisible (while still being there), but they also "vanished" or "cloaked" most any object they wished, perhaps even human beings! To accustomed Gerald and his supernatural talents (and years of personal research), the process seemed like no great feat, but he was reminded how "mere mortals" like the straight-laced scientists at the airbase were simply not well-prepared for the remarkable experience.

"The coming and going of an etheric, or spirit, body has been so familiar to me these many years I had just forgotten that such a manifestation could snap the mental balance of a man not as conditioned."

Here we may have hit upon the ultimate "secret" to moving material objects, or at least the body of a visiting humanoid: his thinking soul or *"spirit"* was responsible. The "overall intelligence" or *"etheric"* mental makeup of a being is responsible for maneuvering the physical shell that encases one's self, or what makes up an object. In other words, *it was mind over matter*. It all came down to thought commands to conceal or expose its mass of molecules.

{Note: this is something that was also asserted by Ruth Montgomery's "Spirit Guides" in her popular books, culminating in *"Aliens Among Us,"* that mental molecular commands are used by some advanced extraterrestrials, now coming to earth in larger numbers to worriedly observe and examine our environmental decay.}

Finally Mr. Light wrapped up his letter to Mr. Layne, almost abruptly, likely because he was running out of words to explain his unique experience, and also because he was simply running out of room at the bottom of the page...

"I shall never forget those forty-eight hours at Muroc!"

An understatement if there ever was one. Who *could* forget such a life-altering event?

After this succinct summation, the author simply scribbled his initials: *"G.L."* in cursive, and that was it. Gerald's letter was finished and folded, enveloped, and stamped. It was then mailed and later received by his pal Meade, but the memories in typeface were to last forever, giving us plenty of exciting insight today.

Perhaps the very first author to touch upon Gerald Light's claims was UFO researcher Gray Barker (1925-1984), via his fascinating 1956 tome, *"They Knew Too Much About Flying Saucers."* It seems to be the very first book to mention the notion of scary, intrusive "Men in Black." Within one chapter, Mr. Barker wrote that Meade Layne had recently informed him of the ET spaceships landing at Muroc/Edwards, being "closely studied by our technicians and inspected by President Eisenhower himself during his stay in Palm Springs." Meade said his anonymous source for the tale - Gerald Light - was "a highly responsible person who himself spent two days at the base," with "three fairly well-known names who accompanied him." The alien ships were "five different types, and they are said to have completely baffled scientists and 'experts.'" Barker wrote that he had *another* West Coast source that assured him the Eisenhower-ET airbase story was quite valid, but "the technicians studying the saucers were going quite nuts" as "the strange craft were unlike anything on Earth and represented technology far beyond our present knowledge." Layne added that "a nationally known news commentator of a large radio network" - undoubtedly Frank Edwards - assured him that he was "determined to break this matter wide open," but was "subsequently silenced." Gray Barker also recalled in his book chapter "a news item" that mentioned reporters in February of '54 "had been trying to find the President during his stay in Palm Springs, but he had completely eluded them. He wasn't really in Palm Springs at all!" Sadly, in the years beyond this groundbreaking book, Gray Barker strangely engaged in some foolish but minor UFO hoaxing, wrecking his good name, and he subsequently faded from the scene. Yet his enticing 1956 book still stands out for tapping into more data than the author initially seemed to realize.

Intrigued Mr. Barker wanted to know more, and perhaps so did an old friend of Mr. Eisenhower's...

According to biographers, sometime in late February of 1954, British Prime Minister Winston Churchill contacted President Eisenhower and passed along a request to meet with him in person. The old WWII partners who had squelched a UFO report back in the day (see Chapter One) had just seen each other in December of '53, at a conference in Bermuda. On March 9th, "Winnie" contacted the White House again on this proposed new summit. He didn't seem to get anywhere. By late that month, the news of Eisenhower's nearly out-of-control Pacific Ocean hydrogen bomb test and its troubling contamination had reached the British peoples' ears, and they grew understandably upset. Now more than ever, the prime minister felt he just *had* to meet the prez, face to face. On April 5th, Churchill spoke at the British House of Commons and officially called publicly for a summit conference. The pressure worked. President Eisenhower acquiesced. The two great leaders finally nailed down in mid-May of '54 the firm details of an intimate conference for late June, to be held at the White House.

As we have seen, "the middle of May" has turned up twice before in this saga. Was a bewildered "Winnie" Churchill eager to get the inside scoop on extraterrestrials? Did Winston even want to travel to Edwards Airbase for himself when he reached the United States? If so, this notion was quashed as he didn't travel beyond the American eastern seaboard and eastern Canada in June of that amazing year.

In addition to all of this, in early 1954, a "Foreign Ministers Conference" was undertaken in Berlin, Germany, from January 25th to February 19th, the very day of the extraterrestrial landing at Muroc/Edwards. A Geneva Conference was also going on that spring of '54, with Secretary of State J. F. Dulles in attendance. Plus, the Bilderberg Society held their first-ever meeting in late May, with representatives of America and England present, interacting with other Europeans present. {Rumors over the years that have claimed that this closed-door confab was about handling visiting aliens are likely inaccurate.}

Churchill felt passionate that he and Eisenhower had something quite critical to discuss that just could not wait; could not be done by aides, and could not be accomplished by mail, or by telegram, or by long-distance telephone calls. It was something so critical and high-level it *had* to be in person, behind closed doors, with no aides allowed in the room, as it turned out. Hmmm...now what could that be?

A once-secret memo from Winston Churchill to his "Secretary for Air, Lord Cherwell," from July of 1952 (that "D.C. UFO flap" period when President Truman popped off to cameras), quotes the legendary leader asking plainly: *"What does all this stuff about flying saucers amount to? What can it mean? What is the truth?"* What Cherwell's private response for Churchill was no one knows, but the British Air Ministry let loose some misinformation two weeks later, not helping matters. Distracting false data was officially released to the public. "This {cover-up} is evident," one experienced UFO researcher has mentioned, "in a secret memo Cherwell sent two months later to Walter Bedell Smith." General Smith (1895-1961) was Eisenhower's close military aide, intimate adviser, and one-time CIA director. To keep the lid on things, those in power in the USA and UK were saying one thing to the people and doing quite another, complicit partners behind the scenes, it is obvious.

At any rate, Winston Churchill proceeded to fly from London on June 24, 1954, to meet with Eisenhower at the White House on the 25th (escorted inside by Vice President Richard Nixon). The conservative, conventional old wartime friends huddled in private, behind shut Oval Office doors, discussing secret subject matters that were strangely not explained to the press or the public. *Historians and biographers are unsure to the present day what exactly was so critically important that it just couldn't wait or be explained later.* What just *had* to be explored, person to person, within the West Wing, with no one else within earshot? And why is it kept under wraps to this day?

Certainly, the two great men talked for a little while in the White House of sensitive Russian and Chinese issues, the Cold War, the

Korean conflict, etc., but once again, they could have easily done *that* by written messages or assistants, and via their state department officials. And the same might have been said regarding talks regarding the dreadful "Castle" atomic bomb testing program.

Remember that UFO researchers have learned that the United States government considered alien activity to be "a bigger secret than the atom bomb." It was incredibly hush-hush in those more button-down times. And it might *still* be today.

Did titillated Churchill wish to see some photo-filled Muroc/Edwards contact files? Or even some film footage? Or even the ET hardware? Again, a perfectly natural reaction, curiosity. When the executive mansion meeting was completed, Churchill and Eisenhower stepped out onto the White House lawn, settled into chairs, and posed for photographers. They sat alongside seated Secretary of State John Foster Dulles and Britain's Foreign Secretary, saying nothing of substance. The four days of high-level talks remain mysterious in some ways. It is difficult to believe the amazing alien landing and spaceship inspection saga did not reach Churchill's ears and create a need for the private D.C. summit.

Also in late June of 1954 – the 26th, to be exact – a special "Housewarming Party" was set up at Edwards Airbase. According to a recently-discovered party invitation, among the guests to see a newly-completed "High-Speed Flight Station" at the base included General Twining, Jerome Hunsaker, and Detlev Bronk, all members of the covert "Majestic Twelve" UFO committee. Remarks to the assembled group were to be given by base commander J. S. Holtoner, the USAF general who may have been coordinating "Air Force officials" and scientists regarding inspections of the aliens and/or their craft at his base back in April (if Gerald Light is to be believed). Or was that was still quietly taking place in late June?

Mentioned also in the uncovered "Housewarming" list were some members of academia associated with the "National Advisory Committee for Aeronautics," seemingly the very type of brainy scientists Mr. Light mentioned in his letter.

And all during this time, perhaps much of 1954, an apparent delicately-worded agreement for the aliens and Eisenhower to sign was supposedly being worked on, perhaps by one or two U.S. military aides or diplomats, under the president's secretive direction. Then this polished, highly classified "homework" needed to be turned in... possibly in July of '54 (when the 1989 DIA report said it was "ratified"), and perhaps in more polished, agreed form in February of 1955. The only questions are "how" and "where"?

Paul Blake Smith

CHAPTER TEN

Mr. C on 1955: More Ike & ETs

"The ETs will refrain where and when possible from an open display of their presence."

— a 1989 DIA briefing document

Coincidence or not, the dating of mid-February for Eisenhower-ET affairs pops up again as we take a look at the smashing research of a late, great American UFO investigator who pinned down further otherworldly presidential exploits in 1955...

As far back as the mid-1950s, ex-serviceman Arthur Campbell (1930?-2017) of the Pacific Northwest (and Kansas City, Missouri) had been an enthusiastic ET/UFO researcher and writer. Having completed his stint in the United States Navy during the Korean War, Art went on to work with the likes of NICAP (National Investigative Committee on Aerial Phenomenon) and even the Boy Scouts of

America, since he was once an Eagle Scout. By profession, Art was a schoolteacher and gym coach but always held a deep-seated need to more thoroughly explore under-reported Unidentified Flying Objects cases. Sightings and sites, even digging in the dirt for crash clues, that's what intrigued doggedly determined Art Campbell the most.

While looking into a 1947 UFO crash-landing near San Agustin, New Mexico, Mr. Campbell began to accumulate startling data on another Eisenhower-alien affair in the so-called "Land of Enchantment." In a nutshell: it seems the president undertook a covert trip to Holloman Air Force Base (in southern New Mexico) in 1955. Art created enough material regarding this stunner to put it into a well-constructed website (one actually dedicated more to his archaeological digging for alien artifacts). The following will be a summary of what Arthur wrote about; gave public speeches about; and reported over the airwaves about since the year 2006 until his death eleven years later...

President Dwight Eisenhower spoke to the gathered press at the White House on Wednesday, February 9, 1955, and informed them he planned to take a quick trip south, via Columbine III – his newest Air Force One plane - to modest Thomasville, Georgia. Once there he hoped to do some quail hunting for a few days with his friends. This we have seen he did the year before, at the very same Georgia farm called "Milestone," owned by Treasury Secretary George Magoffin Humphrey (1890-1970), before returning to the White House, then jetting off to Palm Springs. Now a year later Dwight announced the coming trip himself and allowed members of the press to follow him to Georgia in their chartered airplane, creating a very above-board atmosphere in '55, seemingly. But there appears to have been another Eisenhower ruse afoot, a diversion for the press.

That Thursday morning, February the 10th, the president met early (8:30) with his seventeen-man National Security Team at the White House, including both Dulles brothers. The First Couple left for the airport at 12:45 p.m. and were airborne by 1:05. There were fourteen crew members and various aides on board the president's flight, and no side trips were announced, nor rumored. Columbine III and the press plane went straight to Georgia without incident. The two planes arrived around 4:30 p.m. at Spence Air Force Base, near Moultrie, Georgia, about 35 miles north of the rural Humphrey estate, located about a dozen miles north of the state's border with Florida.

Dwight and Mamie, plus her mother and the accommodating Treasury Secretary (and his wife) were driven to the 2,000-acre plantation accompanied by a Wall Street banker and financial adviser. Oh, and presidential press spokesman James Hagerty, of course. Plus Mamie's aide and Dwight's valet. And an unusually large contingent of Secret Service agents, at least twelve instead of the usual five or six, an Air Force One security guard recalled later to Mr. Campbell. In particular, a rather unique Secret Service *linguist* who spoke at least six different languages was memorably along for the alleged bird-hunting trip. He was a "Communications specialist." Did he do bird-calls? All this for a quick outdoorsy *hunting* vacation?

Many local citizens gathered on a motorcade route between the Georgia airbase and the enormous farm to watch the presidential party roll by, guarded as usual by the Secret Service, the Treasury Department's most dedicated and hardworking employees. By nearly 5:30 p.m. on Thursday, 2/10/55, the sun was setting and it grew quite damp outside, but travel-weary Eisenhower was seen heading out to the duck blinds anyway, along with his shotgun and two similarly-armed friends. The press corps — said to have been representing a whopping 120 different news outlets - was not allowed many, if any, further glimpses into the carefully crafted presidential visit. In what must certainly sound like a familiar modus operandi, reporters were kept at bay, eight miles away at a hotel in the nearest town. They were kept informed at times by spokesman Hagerty, generally bored.

A *Time* magazine writer stated that he learned the president and his cabinet member "bagged two birds apiece" that Thursday evening, despite the light rain. Eisenhower was said to be in good spirits, dining later with friends, then playing cards while Mamie and her mother Elivera played Scrabble with Mrs. Humphrey. The next day - Friday, February 11th - the press gathered for a conference headed by imposing Hagerty. He told them that due to the area's precipitation the morning Milestone quail hunt, starting at 9:20 a.m., was not successful. No one seemed to have witnessed this, however. The alleged hunt was wrapped up a little early, Hagerty explained, and the president would not be around for a while since he had come down with "the sniffles." He now needed quiet bed rest and privacy on the farm. "The president remained indoors the rest of the day," his logs read. Was Dwight *really* now a bit ill with a slight cold? Or was this the thin cover story he needed to sneak away?

{Author Larry Holcombe checked Eisenhower's diary at his Presidential Library in Kansas and found notations for the Georgia quail hunts but mentioned that clever strategist Dwight's diary "could have been deliberately adjusted" and that he likely wasn't at the chilly estate much that Friday, 2/11/55.}

It continued to drizzle on and off during the cold, gray, dull day in Georgia. To appease the restless White House press corps, Hagerty told all that Secretary Humphrey was going to host a big cocktail party for them at a local country club that Friday night. Sound familiar? *The same distraction method of operation as in Palm*

Springs, hosted by Paul Hoffman and Paul Helms on a Friday night at the El Mirador Hotel. The '55 party invitation caused some reporters to hit the Thomasville, Georgia, shopping district, to prepare for the shindig. Thus the press and the public were effectively distracted, not realizing that behind the scenes, a healthy Eisenhower had quietly taken off, with meeting aliens in private once more on his mind.

{Two trivia notes: Art Campbell found that newspapers that day ran the syndicated one-panel cartoon *"Blondie"* which featured the character "Dagwood Bumstead" dreaming of riding in an alien's flying saucer! Plus, during this time a future U.S. president was busy toiling 100 miles away on his farm in Georgia, growing his agribusiness while serving in the U.S. Naval Reserve: James Earl "Jimmy" Carter, then age 30, the son of a late State Representative and fourteen years later himself a UFO eyewitness in Leary, Georgia.}

Strangely, at this point, February 19, 1954, suddenly rears its remarkable head again. It was the specific date found noted in the president's daily appointment logs for Saturday, February 12, 1955! Supposedly at 4:10 p.m. that day, the chief executive's records state that *"The president autographed a group picture taken February 19, 1954, showing members of the Georgia state police who assisted the Secret Service in setting up the security on that occasion."*

Wow! What's this now? *Could we have here a tremendous clue on exactly who it was that surrounded President Eisenhower at Muroc/Edwards for the well-planned alien encounter of 2/19/54?* The "Secret Six?" What other reason would there be to fly some state cops a couple of thousand miles out to a simple "California golf vacation?"

Perhaps these were trusted Georgia men, off-duty and in civilian attire in '54, briefed and ready to protect their leader at all costs, just like they had done for him in the past decade when Dwight came to Georgia to golf and fish at Augusta.

The Secret Service was of course around, too, on 2/19/54, along with local police in Palm Springs and likely California state troopers here and there, not to mention the regular U.S. Air Force troops on guard duty all around Edwards Airbase. Plus MPs. *So why would anyone import such Georgia lawmen?* For "that occasion" they were "setting up security," which means the Dixie cops weren't in Palm Springs for a mere convention, or to play golf. At some point that day or night they posed for a group picture with Dwight; why do so if nothing noteworthy was afoot? And why then have the commander-in-chief autograph it in February of 1955... unless it was on the day of a *second* alien encounter out west, where perhaps the same special Georgia unit was again utilized? It's speculative, but fits.

Let's remember that President Eisenhower was a member since 1948 of the exclusive Augusta golf club, an all-white-male organization that played on the finest course in the country, where "The Masters" tournament is held annually. Dwight visited there a whopping 45 times! It would seem quite likely that in the past, President Eisenhower utilized this very Georgia state police unit – consisting no doubt of WWII vets - to help guard him when visiting that southern state in the past. And let's recall that even more importantly, just a couple of days before the 1954 Palm Springs trip, the president visited Secretary Humphrey's farm for alleged "bird hunting." That was on Friday, February 12th through Sunday the 14th of '54. The special Georgia police unit was almost assuredly utilized during that brief stay in the Peach State... and then ordered to help out in southern California days later too? {The president's party departed Washington D.C. on Wednesday afternoon, the 17th - *with* the "Secret Six"?}

"There would be huge crowds" to greet and sometimes shadow popular Mr. Eisenhower when he arrived in Georgia in various past visits, according to a professional photographer who captured images in those more law-abiding times. State police officers - likely from Troop E, Post 25, that patrolled Augusta and Richmond County (and some neighboring counties) - were deemed necessary to help keep the enthusiastic onlookers at arm's length. So there could have been quite a previous strong connection with Eisenhower, and genuine trust established, well *before* the idea of any historic 1954 ET runway summit at Edwards AFB.

What's more, official 1955 White House records say President Eisenhower signed the 2/19/54 cop photo with this inscription: "*For Sgt. L. H. Bass, with greetings and best wishes, Dwight D. Eisenhower.*" Hmmmm, L. H. Bass, eh? A sergeant in the Georgia State police force – Troop E? - was a long away from home, some 250 miles away from his regular post, on 2/12/55. Sgt. Bass and the Georgia unit's other members were welcomed in the Thomasville area but had no particular legal authority in the state of California, it should be noted.

In his research for the 1955 ET drama, Art Campbell interviewed a former Secret Service agent who acknowledged some of the strange extra protection for Chief Executive Eisenhower during the Georgia trip that mid-February. Campbell quoted this retired agent as recalling he was notified one night at 3:00 a.m. that they'd all take off within the hour, with Dwight in his presidential airplane, but a half-hour before that 4:00 a.m. departure, he saw two cars rolled up to the aircraft at the dark airfield. With a dozen T-men *already on the plane*, out of a pair of the parked sedans "six agents came on board," apparently having been holed up in a local motel "for a day or so." *Who were these six special men?* The two vehicles had USAF markings on the sides as if someone in authority within the United

States Air Force was handling this part of security (like Stan Holtoner, perhaps?).

Six men in suits, apparently, specially ordered to go to the New Mexico alien landing with the president, much like California in '54. Let's recall the retired pilot "Jerry Flier" who said around 1982 that he was "one of six people guarding the president" at Edwards Airbase. And now this special photograph's troopers likely hailing from central to South Georgia, but willing to travel quite a ways to help out their president.

The February 1955 "hunting vacation" in Georgia, Art Campbell's Secret Service source recalled, *did* include a covert middle-of-the-night trip "somewhere out west," confirming the remarkable Holloman ET "runway summit" notion. Something quite unusual was up, it seems.

Theory: the "Secret Six" were a tight-knit group of serious-minded Georgia men who kept in touch with each other over the years – and with the ex-pilot, "Jerry" at Edwards AFB – well beyond their retirement, bonded by the incredible alien landing memories and Eisenhower's somber, sworn oath to keep it all from the public. It was like a special, exclusive club. Thus by mid-1982, the pilot knew it was finally time to spill some secrets when he learned that the last one of these Peach State troopers had passed away. It was finally time then to get the story out (still anonymously). More on this intriguing situation later in the chapter.

In returning to dedicated Mr. Campbell's original research on 1955 subterfuge... President Eisenhower was taken by his Secret Service chauffeur in a car at close to 3:00 a.m. on early Friday the 11th, back up the road to Spence AFB near Moultrie. From there he flew without fanfare on Columbine III (Air Force One) across the country, leaving around 4:00 a.m., headed for Holloman AFB, New Mexico, near the town of Alamagordo. The isolated desert locale was the same general area of practice military bombing runs, missile testing, and special secret experimental aircraft flights – and many reported UFO sightings. {It was also not too far from where Setimus once was housed at Los Alamos and later picked up by his landed ET brethren in August of 1949, at Kirtland AFB near Albuquerque.}

The president's plane approached Holloman Airbase in broad daylight but was being observed in more ways than one. Art Campbell estimated that "probably three hundred" Holloman base employees and military personnel were potentially able to have seen the famous plane land that sunny day. It was said to have come down on the runway around 8:45 to 9:00 a.m. Mountain Time. It rested at the farthest point possible, away from base hangars, offices, and workshops. At one point a worker or two supposedly brought out a metal stairwell to the famous plane's door, then likely exited. All airbase radar technicians were supposedly given orders to shut off their equipment, although smaller radar mechanisms were allowed to operate. Soon some personnel on duty found out why...

Two unidentified "bogies" or unusual flying objects had been sighted in the area, Campbell says he learned. {A third alien airship was said to have been spotted a few minutes after the initial pair, but this vehicle does not seem to figure in the story.} Swiftly the pair of UFOs hovered directly over inert Columbine III, perhaps 300 feet up in the air, Campbell said eyewitnesses told him. They were silvery discs with no tails, propellers, wings, exhausts, or visible motors, just as in 1954's runway encounter. The first vehicle was supposedly set down gently on the ground about 200 feet from the president's plane. The second came down lower, but only somewhat, slowly sweeping the sky across the grounds, near some hangars, as if keeping a silent watch in mid-air.

According to those at the base observing, at times with binoculars, the landed alien airship opened up a hatchway, then a metallic ramp pushed out quietly and set down on the pavement. The craft waited quietly; no figures seen around it.

As the tension and drama built, the door to Columbine III opened. A grown man stepped out and then down its rolled-into-place steps. Arthur Campbell stated the mysterious person was none other than President Eisenhower. Dwight moved from the stairs, across the runway, and walked right up to the landed alien ship. He stepped up its ramp, extended his hand, and a humanoid creature leaned out to shake it, supposedly. Soon brave Mr. Eisenhower trooped inside, just after his peaceful ET host, both now out of view from any observers at the base. {Where were the imported "Secret Six?"}

Holloman AFB personnel who were able to see from a distance what was going on felt that the Friday meeting between the chief executive and those within the non-terrestrial craft lasted for "about 45 minutes." If this shocking account is accurate, it shows the president was comfortable and trusting of his ET hosts, and had something very important to discuss with them, unafraid, perhaps realizing if they wanted to harm him, or the nation, they'd have done so long ago.

How long the shipboard communications lasted no one is sure, but when this phenomenal direct contact was over, it was claimed that President Eisenhower stepped back out of the craft's hatchway and walked calmly down its ramp, across the runway, and back over to his parked airplane. It seemed pretty clear to those with binoculars that bald Dwight was hatless, walking with a certain military bearing, and appeared quite unharmed. He made his way back up the portable stairs to his airplane and slipped inside

Columbine III (again, also known as "Air Force One"). Anxious observers and staffers had to have breathed a tremendous sigh of relief.

On the surface, the Arthur Campbell story sounds a bit outlandish and hard to swallow, but we do know that a dozen or so Secret Service agents were on board the first flight, from D.C. to Georgia, including the language specialist; it was an unusually high number. Some of them could have been imported specially for this second and secretive trip, from Georgia to New Mexico.

On his website, researcher Campbell alleged that he gathered most of his data from two main eyewitnesses, evidently respected military men that he assigned fictional names to protect their identities. "Wilbur" and "Dorsey" related they were told *days before* that Friday, February 11, 1955, that the president was going to be visiting their airbase fairly soon. At first, a military parade was assumed by base commanders to be necessary and prepared for, to officially greet the arriving commander-in-chief, but the idea was suddenly quashed. In fact, the two were told that the whole mention of Dwight's impending arrival was to be "forgotten," and not discussed with anyone.

Dorsey saw the strange silver disc on the runway, telling Wilbur it looked to be of highly polished steel or aluminum construction, about "20 to 30 feet in diameter." Dorsey said he witnessed this circular ET craft *twice* that day, separated by about thirty minutes when he was moving about the airbase commissary. The two men also overheard a pilot on the base who speculated that the tower radar was turned off as it might have interfered with not the president's plane, but with a visiting alien "saucer's guidance system." At this point, a question from the talkative pilot overheard may be most revealing to us now. Wilbur heard the flier ask another man about the UFO: *"Do you think the ones today are the same from Palmdale last year?"* In this remark, we might well have confirmation of the original '54 Eisenhower encounter. That is, "Palmdale" is located not far from Muroc/Edwards Airbase (37 miles driving distance). There *is* no "Palmdale," New Mexico.

Another supportive eyewitness tale came to Arthur Campbell by way of a woman who said her father, an electrician, was working on the base that specific, memorable day. He climbed up an electrical utility pole on the Holloman base to get a glimpse of the presidential plane on the runway and got a good look at it. Then he said he saw the spaceships come down near the parked Columbine III. He anxiously scampered down his pole, moving fast, fearing for his safety, perhaps even a possible conflict or "alien invasion" to come.

From what Art learned, however, Mr. Eisenhower did not just quickly take off that day, right after returning from the alien craft. Instead, he eventually left Columbine III and headed for a base building, likely surrounded by security agents and an aide or two. Supposedly, in the early afternoon hours at Holloman, Dwight hunkered down with base officials, then gathered about 225 other personnel and addressed them in a kind of pep talk, telling them to "keep up the good work" but that what everyone saw that morning was to remain a top-secret matter, not to be discussed. This speech was allegedly repeated later within the "base theater" to again about 225 or so people, with Eisenhower mentioning that his visit was quite private and was to remain that way, not to be related to the American public or the press for reasons of "national security."

Interestingly, one source of information for the Holloman presidential-alien summit, relaying his data to a different UFO investigator/lecturer decades later, was *allegedly a crew member from the president's plane.*

The entire Hollomon AFB visit allegedly took several hours, dragging on, for some reason. When base business was completed, the president then finally returned to Columbine III, which was likely refueled and safety-inspected during his time indoors. It took off late in the afternoon "over the residential area of the base," and even this was memorable as it was normally restricted, empty airspace.

Coincidence or not, a series of atomic test detonations were set to begin in Nevada, just days later. From February 18th through May 15th, 1955, fourteen atomic warheads were set off, incredibly, within just 65 miles of Las Vegas. Eisenhower learned no lessons from the troubling '54 "Castle" program. Dubbed in '55 "Operation Teapot," it was more of the same ol' nuclear experimenting, just with smaller scale detonations, but emitting plenty of radiation in the desert. Still more reckless testing in the land underground, under the sea, in the atmosphere, and on the earth's surface went on, unabated by any extraterrestrial concerns in the years to come.

Eventually, Columbine III uneventfully flew President Eisenhower and his entourage back to Spence AFB in Georgia where they landed safely, presumably well after dark Friday night with no fuss or fanfare. The press at that time would have been neatly out of the way, gathered at the Thomasville area's country club for the big dinner party hosted by Secretary Humphrey. The distraction worked perfectly, and thus the Eisenhower-to-Holloman trip didn't leak out via the media at all, but only after determined Art Campbell's insightful spadework in New Mexico decades later. Whether Secretary George M. Humphrey was ever fully informed of the true, otherworldly nature of the New Mexico journey remains unknown. No one was the wiser when the president was driven without fanfare the 35 miles from the airport to the Milestone Plantation to secretly return to his guest cottage, the distant media naively believing the "sniffles" story. According to Campbell's research, the president's plane did not arrive at Moultrie/Spence AFB until around midnight, and Eisenhower did not make it "home" to Milestone until about 1:00 a.m., on Saturday, February 12, 1955. He likely tried to sleep in his guest quarters, and by the late morning was finally back up and around; he signed the telltale Georgia trooper photograph from 2/19/54 just after 4:00 in the afternoon, perhaps while entertaining the "Secret Six" in his guest cottage or the main house. Had that special unit been utilized in the past twenty-four hours as well, on the ground at Holloman, and this was part of their president's quiet gratitude?

Whatever the case, Mr. Eisenhower had been out of sight from the press a total of 36 hours, giving him plenty of time to have made safe ET contact and follow-up business at Holloman. Dwight's dance card was filled on Sunday the 13th, with some public appearances in and around the Thomasville, Georgia, area, before departing Spencer AFB for D.C. at about 3:00 p.m. He had to have been pretty jet-lagged when he reached the White House by 6:00 that evening. Some sharp-eyed reporters noted the next day that Eisenhower looked a little tired for a casual "hunting trip" or quiet presidential vacation.

Interestingly, it was Art Campbell's opinion that the '55 Holloman Airbase affair was *not* Eisenhower's first meeting with friendly extraterrestrials. That the president *had* to have been assured in advance that the ETs were peaceful and openly communicative to have made such brazen contact on the New Mexican runway. That previous safe encounter had given him experience and confidence to undertake more, Art reasoned. Thus, negotiations had to have been going on well before this carefully arranged, secured Holloman Airbase runway summit, from 9:00 in the morning to around 4:45 in that warm afternoon. Campbell's informants did not speak out about the benumbing occurrence until the mid-1990s.

Author Larry Holcombe pointed out that his sources informed him that previous "saucer sightings" in the area of the New Mexico military installations were so common in that era of weapons testing in the desert "they were expected and virtually ignored."

It's worth noting that something unknown seemed to hold up the completion of the human-alien exchange at Holloman AFB. Soooo many hours on the ground there, for the president. What was the source of the "dead time" of waiting around? Was it finalizing the Ike-ET agreement and its need for firm commitments and signatures? Was it waiting for trade-worthy data and materials to arrive?

Let's go back to those 2017-leaked "Majestic-12 Documents," containing information about U.S. contacts with visiting extraterrestrials. Again, mention was made within its DIA-written pages that on July 18th, 1954, President Eisenhower *first* ventured to New Mexico. Thus in '55, he flew to Kirtland AFB "to ratify and sign" a treaty with aliens, after having first hammered out the contractual details with his secret "MJ-12" control group, over which he had the final say as its most powerful member. The 1989 DIA document claimed the president on this July '54 date – a Sunday - personally handed over this "statement of intent" to "an individual on behalf of the EBEs." Was that "individual" an alien, or a human? Were there arriving alien saucers at Kirtland AFB on July 18th, like there supposedly would be in February of '55 at Hollomon? Many questions arise, but none can be answered for sure at this point.

President Eisenhower's official daily appointment logs show us that on Saturday, July 17, 1954, he had lunch at the White House *with none other than ubiquitous businessman George Edward Allen,* the name so familiar in these affairs. The meal was suspiciously labeled *"Off the record."* Dwight and George also golfed together at a course in the D.C. area (Burning Tree Country Club) that Saturday afternoon. The president supposedly returned home at 5:30 p.m.; was that time fudged? Sunday the 18th is shown as nearly a blank, with a brief notation of Mr. Eisenhower meeting with a wealthy businessman at 4:00, and then-Secretary of State John Foster Dulles from 5:10 to 5:48 p.m., valid entries or not. In other words, on Saturday morning, Dwight could have flown to New Mexico on a hush-hush, sun-drenched July '54 trip to an airbase, and then gotten back by late Sunday afternoon. Or even have left early Sunday morning and taken much of the day there, keeping it all off the books.

Within the official White House records, it states that first thing Monday morning, 7/19/54, President Eisenhower met in the Oval Office with Secretary Dulles and Joint Chiefs honcho Arthur Radford again, along with two others, and this was again considered *"Off the record,"* meaning it was top tier stuff with no notes taken. Radford stayed for more meetings, most suspiciously with Dwight and USAF General Nathan Twining at 10:30 a.m. Again, *the very type of people a president would meet with after he had just transacted some secret, classified extraterrestrial matters.*

Thus the DIA "MJ-12" document might well be telling the truth once more. A July 18, 1954, meeting in New Mexico with landed ETs *could* conceivably have happened as described in the DIA summary that was leaked in 2017. But what was agreed to in writing, as relayed in the '89 government briefing paper?

"The extraterrestrials will refrain where and when possible from an open display of their presence to the public at large. The extraterrestrials will submit substantiating proof and listings of all persons contacted from among the public at large, or that have been

---

removed from Earth for purposes of contact or cultural exchanges. In no case shall anyone abducted by the EBEs be subjected to knowing harm, or kept against their will for longer than 48 hours."

These are words that Dwight D. Eisenhower himself may have uttered that first night in southern California on 2/19/54, so protective as he was to the fate of the American people, those he was sworn in to protect and preserve as president... thus this paragraph looks and sounds pretty believable. Alien beings were most curious about human beings and wanted to look them over within their flying laboratories, in a sense, so to keep this otherworldly desire undercover, it appears our commander-in-chief issued more stipulations that were agreed to by the visiting entities:

"The extraterrestrials will avoid any willful contact with representatives of the public news media or any private investigators of the UFO phenomena, groups of writers dedicated to the same intentions."

In other words, "Keep your visiting alien mouths shut to inquisitive folks, and the press, and make us an accurate list of people you pick up to examine and release, and we'll be cool, atomic testing agreement or not." Keeping ET visitation out of the papers and TV/radio airwaves, and also published books if possible was once again a key factor to the Eisenhower administration. Once more, we see keeping the American public in the dark at all costs was imperative to avoid cultivating a fearful mass panic and to maintain secret communications with the friendly ETs.

Now we come to the DIA document's statement on what the American government secretly agreed to in the top-secret alien-human treaty:

"The U.S. government will provide, through the Defense Logistic Agency's "Reutilization and Marketing Service," such items as needed for the personal comfort of those visiting EBEs who may be sequestered in its care. The U.S. government will provide a section of the MAJESTIC headquarters base in Nevada as an embassy compound for the EBE visitors and equip it to their needs."

Not only does this sound again like what "Kewper Stein" alleged in 1998, but the Eisenhower administration was going to covertly and cleverly "help" aliens get settled in America by providing part of a sprawling military base in remote Nevada. In that way, they could keep their eyes on their "special guests" and make sure they weren't getting carried away, all while protecting them from the public. But what possible "personal comfort" could we humans possibly give advanced aliens? *"In its care"* sounds like babysitting children, nearly. This was – and still is - pretty mind-boggling stuff, and one wonders if it all continues today.

Oh, and one more thing Mr. Eisenhower supposedly wanted in writing:

"Any exchange of technical, scientific, or social information will be conducted item-for-item and in such a manner as to assure that both parties have equal gain from the process."

So if we gave the aliens some inside scientific data on the human race or planetary ecosystem – DNA samples, for example - they had to give us something similar, of equal value we longed for, or no deal. Perhaps their DNA, blood, or tissue samples for scientific study. Fair enough, but this stipulation sounds very tough to assess and enforce.

Was all of this agreement detail signed, sealed, and delivered on a sunbaked runway in steamy New Mexico? In July of '54 at Kirtland

AFB as the DIA "Majestic-12" alien document claimed, or in February of '55 at Holloman AFB as Art Campbell discovered? Or perhaps at both?

One source for Art Campbell summed up the odd length of time for the February 1955 airbase visit after Eisenhower returned to Columbine III from the landed alien spaceship on the Holloman AFB runway: "It was almost as if they were waiting for something," or killing time until something else took place. Possibly a new or follow-up alien message, stipulation, snafu, or item to be received, either at Holloman or elsewhere? Another Campbell airbase source, a pilot, told Art he flew a load of cargo into Holloman AFB that day as scheduled, but wasn't allowed to leave until President Eisenhower and his party did. This flier personally attended one of the two airbase personnel confabs that the president addressed, where Dwight stressed the need for base personnel to keep quiet and maintain security on his covert presence there. *Could his cargo load have been something either side desired at the runway summit*, agreed to be provided for aliens by humans in the signed treaty, and patiently waited for? Conjecture, yes, but not unreasonably so.

A check of President Eisenhower's White House daily appointment log shows that after his return to D.C. from New Mexico in February of '55, he quickly held high-level meetings on Monday morning the 14th in the Oval Office with three top advisers: Admiral Radford (at 10:30); Charles I. Wilson, his Secretary of Defense (at 11:30); and John Foster Dulles, his Secretary of State (at 1:00 p.m.). Once again precisely the sort of military/government officials you'd need to confer with regarding very classified recent contact with visiting aliens. After the Dulles lunch confab wrapped, dutiful Dwight was down for the day, with no further official appointments, which was pretty unusual. Likely he needed a substantial nap, thanks to jet-lag.

Backing up his overall research, Arthur Campbell alleged, was an unexpected letter that arrived from a mysterious source within British military intelligence, specifically someone who had access to the juicy archives within "MI5" ("Military Intelligence, section five). The letter-writing Brit stated that it was his understanding that friendly human-like aliens "had landed in several places" in the years 1953 to 1955 and specifically "asked for a meeting" with President Eisenhower. If this is true, Dwight undoubtedly felt like he *had* to go meet them, *somewhere* in private, or this potentially explosive landing and exposure situation would continue until the lid was blown off nationally in some unsecured manner.

Also, the February 1955 Holloman Air Force Base summit was quite real, the British source told Art, and that it was "one of the first" meetings that this particular race of visiting alien species had undertaken. The humanoid ETs liked and/or trusted Eisenhower more than his predecessor Truman, who some say – like Linda Moulton Howe, after much research - once ordered the U.S. Air Force to *shoot down* UFOs, back in 1947. Arthur Campbell once spoke with aging Harry Truman in his retirement in western Missouri, according to author Larry Holcombe. The Truman's were old friends to Cambell's family, both based out of Independence. When Mr. Campbell brought up the subject of UFOs to Truman, Harry's face and friendliness frosted fast. Arthur also noticed that a Secret Service agent showed up that night to his hotel lecture on alien visitation, undoubtedly sent by the ex-president, but nothing seemed to have come from the hawkish federal monitoring.

In his lectures and within his website, researcher Campbell passed along still more information he uncovered on the Holloman secret summit, including some of the names of the passengers who went along from Washington D.C. to Moultrie, Georgia, to begin the trip. It was here however that Art made a substantial mistake that harmed his overall credibility somewhat. He stated that he learned that a name on the passenger list for the president's plane was "Arthur Godfrey", so he naturally assumed this was the popular radio and television entertainer of the same name. Campbell was not aware that one of the toughest, most respected Secret Service agents working the White House detail in the 1950s and '60s, traveling often with the president, was none other than "Arthur Lincoln Godfrey" (1921-2002). Campbell thus went a little overboard in the wrong direction; Art Godfrey the famous emcee/singer had nothing to do with the ET contact (although a decade later he reported a UFO while flying his plane, on the East Coast). But we can forgive that small error in the otherwise compelling and convincing circumstantial case that Campbell put together overall.

{On a minor note, it is worth mentioning that on the day of the first anniversary of the Muroc/Edwards summit with aliens, President Eisenhower (according to his records) held a 2/19/55 Saturday Oval Office meeting with Admiral Radford and USAF General Twining; then had lunch about an hour later; and soon called it a day, leaving a substantial, mysterious gap again in his schedule. Was there an alien-human agreement to attend to in private during that slow weekend?}

Overall, what Art Campbell's exciting research shows us is that President Eisenhower wisely utilized a "vacation" approach a second time, a la Palm Springs, to covertly meet with aliens in 1955, but via a shorter plane trip to an equally remote desert airbase (in New Mexico), saving many hundreds of miles further west in travel, to southern California. And it was pulled off again by distracting the media with a hotel party, and all effectively kept under wraps, even long after Dwight Eisenhower's death in 1969. And perhaps also after the passing of his special six-man entourage/eyewitnesses years later. No one expressed a public peep or a monument concerning the covert, historic landing events, and any data learned from the summits.

Or... *did* they?

Let's say you were part of the "Secret Six" cautiously flanking President Eisenhower at Edwards Airbase in '54, and possibly also at Holloman Airbase in '55. *Probably* five or six guards – Georgia state troopers? - and maybe one high-ranking Air Force pilot who knew the president well and was trusted by him. You remembered the mid-1950s extraterrestrial contact and discussed it privately, only among yourselves. Over the passing years, wouldn't you, as a member of this exclusive club – probably based in rural Georgia - long to create a memorial to these mighty events? And perhaps also get a special message out from the ETs out to the public, in *some* anonymous fashion? All without giving away your identity and that of the off-world messengers?

A generation after the '54 and '55 encounters, something quite monumental appeared in a central Georgia pasture that has since boggled the minds of people across the planet, and has remained a puzzling, unsolved enigma ever since. Specifically, we're talking about a strange rock monument nicknamed "The Georgia Guidestones." This unusual public design consists of five tall granite slabs featuring ten messages - simple suggestions, really - for humanity, expressed in eight different languages. The slabs stand in the middle of a hilly cow pasture near Highway 77 in the Georgia countryside. It's located about 84 driving miles from Augusta, or about a two-hour car trip north, resting atop a pastoral slope in Elbert County, 90 miles east of Atlanta. Some folks call the structure "America's Stonehenge." It turns out the available land was purchased in mid-1979 and a local "granite finishing company" was contacted that summer to create the mysterious edifice, with a large, deep, steel-reinforced foundation. A hair-raising "Top Ten List," of sorts, is chiseled into the rock, simple, straightforward words of guidance in how mankind should govern planet earth. It is very much like the "Ten Commandments" brought forth by Moses, from all-powerful but caring God.

The project got underway a full decade after Dwight D. Eisenhower, who so loved rural Georgia, passed away in a D.C. army hospital. The person who funded the unusual 1979 construction is alleged to have called himself "Robert," or "R. C. Christian," but his true identity has never been revealed. Did "R.C" stand for "Roman Catholic" perhaps? Was surviving Stan Holtoner or "Jerry Flier" such a source? Unknown. The sculptor who created the monument upon instructions recalled that the well-dressed, gray-haired Mr. Christian was "a middle-aged gentleman" who initially said he wanted the pricey monument built on land "stretching west of Augusta" (which had its own remarkable UFO sighting in 1952). Was the wealthy stranger a former Georgia state trooper/Ike bodyguard from the Augusta area that the famous president so often visited? Rumors have it that R. C. Christian had a great grandmother who hailed from Georgia and that he had once served in World War II (under Ike?).

{Note: someone calling himself "Robert Christian" wrote an odd book – supposedly in 1986, but not published until 1990 - that tried to explain the Georgia Guidestones' messages, called *"Common Sense Renewed,"* which asserted that "Atomic arsenals should be dismantled and their warheads converted to peaceful uses," sounding very much like the '54 aliens, but... who knows if the book is authentic and genuinely related?}

The mysterious R. C. Christian said in 1979 that he represented *a small group* that anonymously wanted the monument built on Georgia rural property formerly utilized for peacefully grazing cows.

Christian said his group had been planning the monument for over twenty years, which means it was originally inspired in the 1950s. Money was no object, so construction was quietly undertaken despite the very curious unexplained nature of the enterprise. On March 22, 1980, the finished monument was unveiled to many a baffled and confused citizen. What did it all mean? Who or what did R. C. Christian and his "small group" represent? Who was the source of the unexplained information imprinted in the Guidestones' granite?

To be more specific, the simple sentences put into the solid stone slabs were in English, Spanish, Swahili, Hindi, Hebrew, Arabic, Chinese, and Russian. It translated into this Top Ten List:

#1.) Maintain humanity under 500,000,000 in perpetual balance with nature.

#2.) Guide reproduction wisely — improving fitness and diversity.

#3.) Unite humanity with a living new language.

#4.) Rule passion — faith — tradition — and all things with tempered reason.

#5.) Protect people and nations with fair laws and just courts.

#6.) Let all nations rule internally resolving external disputes in a world court.

#7.) Avoid petty laws and useless officials.

#8.) Balance personal rights with social duties.

#9.) Prize truth — beauty — love — seeking harmony with the infinite.

#10.) Be not a cancer on the earth — Leave room for nature — Leave room for nature.

Now then, under our scenario... who do we know in Georgia that were a small unit of concerned citizens, likely wanting to anonymously get a message for humanity out to the world, for advanced ETs, but were dying out by 1979 to 1982?

Well obviously, the answer would be the "Secret Six" from the Eisenhower-ET encounters, trying to leave an insightful extraterrestrial's statement for the planet before they too passed away. Can we draw an alien-themed conclusion here? Seems logical, does it not?

Was there in any way an otherworldly feel to the monument besides the odd "Top Ten List" printed on it? Consider now a helpful small guide marker, left in the base of the unusual structure. It mentions the "Astronomic Features" of the edifice. Which are: "#1. Channel through stone indicates celestial pole. #2. A horizontal slot indicates the annual travel of the sun. #3. Sunbeam through capstone marks noontime throughout the year."

As *Wikipedia* explains it: "The four outer stones are oriented to mark the limits of the 18.6-year lunar declination cycle. The center column features a hole drilled at an angle from one side to the other, through which can be seen the North Star, a star whose position changes only very gradually over time. The same pillar has a slot carved through it which is aligned with the Sun's solstices and equinoxes. A 7/8-inch (22 mm) aperture in the capstone allows a ray of sun to pass through at noon each day, shining a beam on the center stone indicating the day of the year." Pretty complex and impressively precise, accurate stuff.

Additionally, enigmatic R. C. Christian stated that the monument stones "would function as a compass, a calendar, and a clock." Oh, and that the structure should be able to withstand catastrophic events – a rather chilling description to contemplate.

How in the world did some Georgia citizens come up with all of *that* complicated, far-out data (from the '50s)?

The special info marker also mentions that the monument was created by "a small group of Americans who seek the Age of Reason." But was this *really* who passed along the strange, ET-sounding guidance for all humanity in the multilingual messages? As of now, we can also ask: did the five tall slabs represent the five alien spaceships that came down at Edwards AFB? Or perhaps the five special security men – plus one person more, the test pilot, represented by the top capstone piece? - who surrounded President Eisenhower as he met with landed, off-world ambassadors in '54?

The ground-level marker also asserts that a special "time capsule" was placed six feet under the structure and then allowed an open space for the date that it should be opened... which was inexplicably left blank. Could there still be something that commemorates the Eisenhower encounters buried below the imposing monument?

We just might have an explanation for the whole odd structure at last.

Let's face it, the "Secret Six" *from 1950s Georgia* certainly could not have erected a large, special, explainable monument to honor aliens on government land at Edwards Airbase, nor at Holloman AFB, in their heyday. They would have waited decades, and wanted it done anonymously in their home state, to keep their identity and that of the ETs secrets but relay what the human-like aliens passed along to President Eisenhower. They would likely have wanted the messagey Guidestones built reasonably close to their homes, within driving distance, and may have found that the nearest available land for sale was up near Highway 77. Perhaps nearly everyone else involved from the 1954/55 secret airbase contacts were now deceased, so the six men felt free to act at last. Even former First Lady Mamie Eisenhower died one day after Halloween in 1979, when she eerily assured a relative visiting her - in the same Washington D.C. hospital that her beloved husband died in - that she would be passing away on the following day – and *did*, in her sleep.

While none of this is concrete, indisputable evidence for a water-tight verdict on the enigmatic monument, it sure makes a solid circumstantial case that seems to add up here, every aspect of it.

Let's put it this way: does anyone have a *better* explanation for the puzzling "Georgia Guidestones" than this?

CHAPTER ELEVEN

The Presidents After Ike

"For the purpose of inspecting things from outer space."

— a 1962 CIA summary

You become president. You receive highly sensitive, classified intelligence briefings on military, defense, and space matters. You meet with your most trusted advisers. Even before you move into 1600 Pennsylvania Avenue, you come up with a pretext for traveling to Palm Springs. You arrange a suitable place to stay while in the Mojave Desert, at a wealthy friend's house, to be able to duck out quietly. You distract the media with a hotel party. You attend to alien issues at a nearby military airbase, with no reporters or civilians around. Then you go home and pretend like nothing ever happened.

That was the workable method of operation for Dwight D. Eisenhower, as we've seen, and this template was copied by some *other* United States presidents, as we're about to understand. So let's take a closer look at Palm Springs and presidential sightings...

In February of '54, vacationing President Eisenhower told the Palm Springs press pool he wanted to come back to Coachella Valley the following year, but records show he did not return to the region until early October of 1959. He and Mamie also spoke in '54 of enjoying their Smoke Tree Ranch stay yet when they arrived in town five years later the First Couple bunked down at George Edward Allen's pad in La Quinta, and records show that Dwight didn't even visit Smoke Tree, nor hobnob with wealthy exec Paul Hoffman. {Paul Helms had since died.}

As was his custom, the president played plenty of golf during that early October '59 lull, although there were substantial openings in his printed schedule which *could* have allowed for sneaky shenanigans, left unrecorded of course. In theory, the president could also have even brought with him "Jerry Flier," or General J. Stanley Holtoner, since Eisenhower had recently returned him to the Pentagon in D.C. in 1959, where Stan was assigned to the newly created "Office of the Director of Defense Research and Engineering." Perhaps the kind of work that reverse-engineering captured or *gifted* ET technology with defense industries would have required coordinating very discreetly by a knowledgeable old hand.

Starting in early 1961, newly retired *ex*-President Eisenhower settled into a quiet, somewhat-secluded life, partly on his cattle farm in Gettysburg, Pennsylvania. Dwight and Mamie often stayed long stretches in the wintertime at their rented golf course home at their Eldorado Country Club in Palm Springs, where he penned much of his autobiography. {Even *supporters* referred to Dwight's memoirs as dry and dull; he barely commented on the period of February through

April 1954 and never mentioned Palm Springs, nor Edwards, Kirtland, or Hollomon airbases, understandably.}

In his retirement – from January of 1961 to his death of congestive heart failure at age 78 in March of 1969 - Dwight Eisenhower met with two sitting United States presidents that we know of in Palm Springs, and at least two future ones, possibly more. Leaders seemed to make a beeline for his 11th fairway door. Was this done partly to discuss in secluded privacy the ongoing covert alien visitation situation?

According to the Thunderbird Country Club website: *"President Eisenhower on two occasions brought his Vice President Richard Nixon to play golf at Thunderbird. He was also responsible for President Lyndon Johnson visiting Thunderbird and playing the course on several occasions."* As a "Veep," Richard Milhous Nixon (1913-1994) was *not* with Eisenhower in Palm Springs in February of 1954, nor in October of 1959. What the contemporary website was undoubtedly mentioning was during Dwight's *retirement*, when he hosted travelin' "Tricky Dick." It was pretty rare for "Ike and Dick" to golf together, for both security and personality reasons. {Nixon privately complained Eisenhower often treated him like a lowly subordinate, almost as if he was an army private reporting to a general.} Nixon mostly golfed at "Sunnylands" in Palm Springs – 14 times between 1969 and 1992 - especially as president, staying at the upscale, 220-acre estate of the mega-wealthy publisher and diplomat Walter Hubert Annenberg (1908-2002). Naturally, it was situated near well-watered fairways.

V.P. Nixon flew to Edwards Airbase for an inspection of the latest high-tech U.S. aircraft on October 15, 1958; what else he saw in private while touring the installation before making a speech to a crowd there is unknown. And if Mr. Nixon made any other open or covert visits at Muroc/Edwards in the 1950s, well, that remains a mystery too. Obviously, as a native southern Californian, for Richard Nixon to have flown to Edwards AFB directly would not have been very unusual or suspicious. {On that particular 10/15/58 afternoon in Washington, President Eisenhower shot a round of golf at a country club with George E. Allen, and five days later Dwight flew to Los Angeles himself, but there were no side trips to Palm Springs or Edwards Airbase.}

In 2019, an excellent story hit the internet from writer Marcus Lowth of www.ufoinsight.com. It detailed a strange aerial crash near Edwards in the summer of 1971, during Nixon's White House tenure. A woman living near the installation said she heard a roar and a crash outside her property at that time; she and some other neighbors rushed outside and to the accident site, expecting an errant airplane in ruins and injured people in pain. What they found instead was a bizarre mushroom-shaped alien craft on the ground, broken open with "three gray humanoids" on board... along with a grown woman in a pink outfit, a dazed human scrambling out of the wreckage. She had been abducted from her Los Angeles area home! Decades later this "Woman in Pink" came forward to say she was removed from the downed alien craft by base military personnel and taken to a facility on the north side of Edwards AFB, where memories were hazy but... there might have been military and humanoid ET personnel standing over her as she was examined by medicos. If President Nixon was notified of the strange incident, it remains unknown, but seems likely.

As a hands-on president, Mr. Nixon was ultimately in charge of the Apollo space program, which was shaped partly at the Edwards Flight Research Center. His friend, conservative comic Jackie Gleason (1916-1987), was glued to the Apollo project and had its Edwards-trained pilot-astronauts as special guests on his Miami-based TV variety show. In the 1950s, Jackie undoubtedly supported fellow Republican Eisenhower while living in a special "Mother-ship" round home outside New York City, from the mid-1950s to the early 1960s. Mr. Gleason was also an *enormous* UFO/ET buff (weight pun not intended). Jackie told a few people he was privately informed – and *shown* – actual crash-recovered dead alien bodies and ET hardware at a south Florida USAF base, by way of his Miami-area golfing buddy Nixon, a subject explored in many online articles since it broke in the tabloids in the mid-1970s. It is not a tale to be taken lightly, but did Jackie ever golf with Dwight Eisenhower, and found out more? It is possible, yet whether Ike took a showbiz comic into his confidence is unknown. It was tough enough for *Nixon* to get Eisenhower to reveal important government matters to him.

When precisely Nixon learned of President Eisenhower's February 1954 encounter with aliens is anyone's guess, but it now seems a solid bet that Richard *was* briefed at some point and later patterned his own mid-February 1973 trip to Florida's Homestead Air Force Base, just south of Miami, for personally reviewing ET evidence (with Gleason) based upon Dwight's action plan. To examine this claim in some small detail, let's stop and compare notes on the two presidents and their methods of operation, via another Top Ten List. It simply cannot be considered coincidental that...

#1.) Ike arranged in advance a "relaxing vacation" pretext, involving golf in order to make his secret ET connection – and so did Dick.

#2.) Ike chose February 19th to handle his otherworldly business – and so did Dick.

#3.) Ike sneaked out at night – and so did Dick.

#4.) Ike made sure the distant press was distracted with a party at their hotel - and so did Dick. (Well, *probably*.)

#5.) Ike traveled many miles that late night to an Air Force Base and back under the cover of darkness – and so did Dick.

#6.) Ike saw aliens and their spaceships – and so did Dick (only *his* were autopsied remains of both).

#7.) Ike had bodyguards and witnesses with him – and so did Dick (well, *one or two* witnesses, plus guards around nearby).

#8.) Ike ducked back home safely around midnight, with no one the wiser – and so did Dick.

#9.) Ike got up the next morning, February 20th, and kept his set public schedule like nothing unusual happened – and so did Dick.

And finally... #10.) Ike remained completely mum on the topic for decades, even to his death – and so did Dick.

An important question arises: did President Nixon stick around Homestead AFB after Jackie Gleason was taken home that 2/19/73 Monday night? The president could always order a car, or a helicopter to take him back later to his "Winter White House" in Key Biscayne. But did he stay to secretly meet with some landed ETs on a base runway as the night wore on? Or was he planning to, but chickened out? Was there a formal treaty that needed renewal?

"The Council of Five" is a contemporary website that purports to give inside ET data; its writer Dante Santori describes a visiting alien race called "Emerther" beings by noting: *"They met with President Eisenhower on three different occasions, and they also met with two high-ranking USSR leaders on three occasions, and they tried (they do not "force" anything upon Humans) to meet with President Nixon but he refused, claiming that it would be too dangerous as they could maybe read his mind and find out about delicate national security secrets concerning the relations with USSR."* It seems beyond belief that Nixon "just happened" to show up at an airbase *on the very night of the exact 19ᵗʰ anniversary of the Eisenhower-ET airbase summit,* so to have signed or officially renewed an alien-American treaty seems at least logical, whether any "live ones" showed up or not to co-sign it.

Richard Nixon made eight total trips to Palm Springs as commander-in-chief from January 1969 to August of 1974. Just as one example, Richard made a sudden and unannounced motorcade drive from his home in San Clemente, California, to the Palm Springs mansion of wealthy ambassador to the United Kingdom in mid-January of '74. What the controversial president was doing, precisely, at this upscale estate, behind closed doors, for two full days remains unknown. Did Richard make any side trips to a nearby airbase for an ET inspection? It is at least possible as the press was kept at bay. It was a month shy of the twentieth anniversary of Eisenhower's historic visit/summit. When his sudden and enigmatic Palm Springs idyll was complete, Nixon flew out of the local municipal airport on Air Force One to D.C., yet his daily diary is a bit incomplete for this day, January 12ᵗʰ, as *"a restricted document was removed from this file folder."*

{Digitized records show President Nixon spent the actual twentieth-anniversary date, 2/19/74, at the White House, with nothing of any consequence going on, at least not officially and reported.}

As the Watergate scandal closed in and impeachment loomed, Nixon resigned in disgrace, on August 9th, 1974. That's when he flew directly from Washington D.C. to El Toro Marine Airbase in Orange County, California. But then, oddly, Nixon nearly went straight to Palm Springs, where he was frequently seen over the next days, weeks, and even years (despite living elsewhere). In fact, retired Richard Nixon was golfing (at "Sunnylands" and the Annenbergs' home again) when his historic official legal pardon from the new president was announced one month later.

Back in the 1950s, when both Eisenhower and Nixon separately enjoyed hitting the links in the D.C. area — mostly at the "Burning Tree Country Club" course - they might well have run into a handsome young United States congressman nearly as obsessed with golf as they were: John Fitzgerald Kennedy (1917-1963).

Youthful JFK directly succeeded aging Eisenhower as president in January of 1961 and during his relatively brief administration, Kennedy visited Palm Springs at least three times: late March of '62; December of '62; and late September of '63. Remarkably, records do not show President Kennedy playing any golf on these three desert community trips! If he did not hit the links, *then what was the official excuse for going to Coachella Valley? Why bother?*

As soon as he got elected Kennedy's relationship to Palm Springs mirrored Dwight Eisenhower's, almost eerily so. For instance, instead of Paul Hoffman hosting the First Couple, the nearby Paul Helms home at Smoke Tree Ranch was selected instead, for "security reasons." Some years later, President-elect Kennedy contacted his own wealthy friend about making a very similar Palm Springs trip: world-famous singer/actor Francis Albert "Frank" Sinatra (1915-1998). Just a week after the November 1960 election win, excited Sinatra quickly drew up plans to add a special wing to his remote desert house to accommodate the new president, plus a helipad and guest cottages for the Secret Service. Ground was broken for these new additions in early December, *even though Frank already had an upscale mansion in Beverly Hills*. And JFK had plenty of *other* friends and well-heeled donors in southern California, and almost always stayed with his sister and "brother-in-Lawford" when in the L.A. area (beachfront in Santa Monica), for example. Why not stay there, or at the Beverly Hills Hilton, as the Kennedys had done at times also?

Thus we can speculate reasonably that perhaps the only need for Sinatra's sudden "home improvement" project in Palm Springs was for *Kennedy to copy Eisenhower* and set the excuse of a "relaxing desert vacation" in order to be in the vicinity of a well-guarded desert airbase for more private alien matters. {Sinatra was undoubtedly *not* told the real reason for the president's Palm Springs visit, however.}

Throughout 1961 expansion work on the classy Sinatra desert house proceeded, and like Paul Helms before him, Frank paid for the pricey additions and installed many special telephone lines. Again it should be noted, John F. Kennedy could golf anywhere in the country (and did), and could party with women any place (and did), and could stay at any ol' place in southern California. And as it turned out, when March 23rd-25th of 1962 rolled around, JFK did just that. He went elsewhere. President Kennedy flew into Palm Springs on Air Force One (without his wife) and stayed with another singer/actor, Harry Lillis "Bing" Crosby (1903-1977). Then after settling in... *JFK quickly visited ex-President Eisenhower.* {Sinatra meanwhile flew into a rage; his place had been scrubbed from the Kennedy schedule just two days before the president's arrival, supposedly thanks to his past associations with gangsters. Frank was told it was for reasons of "security" instead. He thus took a sledgehammer to some of his own home's improvements, by all accounts furious at being snubbed.}

Yes, at 11:00 a.m. Saturday, JFK left the Crosby residence and motored over to the Eldorado Country Club, to meet Ike at the Eisenhower home. When they were done about an hour later, the famous duo stepped outside, strolling around the pool deck to pose for photographers and a gathered crowd that loitered on the nearby golf course. The rest of the youthful president's schedule that day is officially left blank. He undoubtedly went back to Crosby's place at some point. Der Bingle's modern, private Palm Desert home within the then-sparse "Silver Spur Ranch" development near Shadow Mountain, on 49400 Della Robbia Lane, was utilized for all three of Kennedy's area visits. The president was able to do whatever he wanted in much-guarded secrecy.

Just a few hours before the president's party arrived in town in March of '62, President Kennedy toured California's Vandenberg Air Force Base, where inside one hangar he was shown "missile equipment during a tour of spacecraft displays," according to his presidential library website. JFK hovered over what appears eerily like a small, stereotypical "flying saucer," in some of the resulting hangar photographs. Was this still on his mind when he got settled in at the Crosby estate? Or was it something more down-to-earth...

On Saturday, 3/24/62, it seems pretty clear that the president had a romantic rendezvous with superstar actress Marilyn Monroe (1926-1962), witnessed by others and even described decades later by a visiting Los Angeles government employee. Supposedly in the late afternoon, Kennedy entertained guests in Crosby's large living room, then would duck out to a guest cottage where a smaller gathering was held, including Monroe "in a kind of robe thing." A bit later that evening, Monroe called her masseuse and let Kennedy speak to him. But perhaps from 8:00 p.m. onward, nothing is known of the president's whereabouts (along with noon to possibly 4:00 p.m. before that). That same Saturday night the naughty president's famous press secretary, Pierre Salinger (1925-2004), *held a "lavish party" for the distracted media on Saturday night at a Palm Springs hotel.* Sound familiar? The town's Riviera Hotel was in fact host to celebrity soiree entertainers that entire "gala weekend," imported to keep the press happy. Was it more accurately designed to keep intrepid reporters away from the steamy Kennedy-Monroe tryst, or perhaps something more otherworldly, a la Ike at Muroc/Edwards in '54? Or perhaps for *both* top-secret reasons?

After church services Sunday morning the 25th, nothing appears concrete about JFK's schedule that day, and the local papers reported he left for the airport "after 11:00 p.m." for a takeoff to D.C. That leaves quite a wide-open second window of unobserved Sunday presidential goings-on; the entire three-day desert visit was the talk of the town, of course, but for so much of it, President Kennedy was far more discussed than seen in public.

Overall it seems strange as to why Kennedy was in "Eisenhower's ballpark" so many times in such a short span. After all, Dwight had previously traveled to Camp David to quietly summit with JFK, and they of course had occasional phone conversations. So something pretty substantial had to have been afoot when Kennedy was in Palm Springs.

Shortly before her mysterious death in August of 1962, Marilyn Monroe told a close friend – producer/author Robert Slatzer (1927-2005), interviewed about it on the mid-1990s TV show "Encounters" - that the handsome president had admitted to her that while on "a trip out west" to "some Air Force base" he covertly undertook for viewing some dead, gray, black-eyed, alien bodies and crashed ET hardware! This covert airbase inspection was also mentioned within a controversial 1995-leaked document that some feel is an authentic CIA office memo, summarizing on 8/3/62 various topics gleaned from wiretapped Monroe's recent phone conversations, while others suspect the one-page report is somehow a fake.

Did JFK secretly inspect UFO crash corpses and debris? Consider the case of former LAPD intelligence officer Mike Rothmiller, who said he read secret Los Angeles police documents regarding Monroe's early August 1962 death, and of her ties to the loose-lipped Kennedy brothers. To this day, Rothmiller refuses to give details of something quite explosive he learned, but he spoke tantalizingly on camera once, for a 1999 documentary, and spilled just a few beans. Rothmiller claimed that from the sizzling LAPD intel reports of Monroe's bugged telephones and Brentwood home, he discovered that "President Kennedy had told her the truth about this event," which he declined to describe but added, "It was a phenomenal event that would literally change the world," far beyond Miss Monroe's normal topic of discussion. Certainly, the shushed '47 Roswell alien fiasco fits that bill, and would also cause Rothmiller to keep his lips sealed out of fear of government recriminations five decades later.

In 2013, an anonymous online book reviewer stated the following on the JFK and RFK assassinations, Marilyn Monroe's death, and UFO crash recoveries: *"There was indeed a connection in these horrific murders, and the three were silenced for knowing too much about "The Big Secret." I work for the U.S. Government and know and can prove this. The UFOs/ETs are indeed real, and every U.S. President since Franklin Roosevelt has known it. I cannot disclose my real name, but rest assured JFK was ambushed in a military-style killing. There was no way "THEY" were going to let him live and be President again in 1964. He was considered a real national security risk. So was Marilyn Monroe."* Of course, *anyone* can make up a story online without giving their name and pass it off as valid, so this comment should be approached warily. But it just might be support for the presidential '47 Roswell ET recovery inspection by John F. Kennedy during his brief presidency (1961-1963).

The alleged 8/3/62 Central Intelligence memorandum — leaked in 1995 - also mentioned wiretaps on aforementioned gossip reporter Dorothy Kilgallen, who knew both Monroe and Kennedy and had previously expressed in print data on governmental knowledge of ET visitation, as we've seen in Chapter One. A paragraph within the disputed '62 memo stated that Miss Kilgallen had recently told a phoned friend that she first learned "in the mid-fifties" of a "secret effort by U.S. and U.K. governments to identify the origins of crashed spacecrafts and dead bodies." It added this now-famous nugget regarding Miss Monroe's mid-summer telephone chit-chat: *"One such "secret" mentions the visit by the president at a secret airbase for the purpose of inspecting things from outer space."* Was this during the March '62 idyll in southern California?

UFO researcher, lecturer, and author Timothy Good (1942-) included a thumbnail sketch of the '54 Ike-ET allegation in his 1991 book *"Alien Contact,"* claiming Eisenhower "disappeared for four hours, causing considerable confusion" among those left behind in Palm Springs while at Edwards Airbase. British Mr. Good described interviewing Lord Clancarty over the prior decade but being unable to pry the true identity of the mysterious "retired colonel" who confessed his presence at Eisenhower's ET runway summit. Timothy, a classically trained orchestral violinist, was interviewed in 2012 on BBC2's talk show *"Opinionated"* about the '54 alien saga and was featured in a 2012 London *Daily Mail* newspaper article on it.

Did JFK find out Eisenhower's top-secret summit information and want in on the fun? In 2007 Timothy claimed he had "an impeccable source" that told him *President Kennedy did indeed inspect an American military airbase regarding extraterrestrial evidence* after having been briefed on the subject by intelligence bigwigs. "Special access" was granted in 1961 or '62, and JFK arranged for Air Force One to fly him directly to the military site. In guarded privacy, Kennedy personally reviewed seemingly indestructible silvery-gray metal spaceship materials and also small, dead alien bodies. {Mr. Good then claimed he learned that this inspection took place at Tyndall Air Force Base near Panama City, Florida, oddly enough.} Tim's source stated the event was not allowed to be recorded in a White House log, and no member of the press was taken along to observe the trip, either, so the explosive allegation remains difficult to confirm or deny to this day.

Author Tim Good further explained he was told by another source that *President Kennedy once privately met and spoke with peaceful extraterrestrials who had landed at a military airbase near Desert Hot Springs!* That town was of course situated just a few miles from Palm Springs/Palm Desert, but precisely what military airfield this could have been remains clouded by time (many have closed in the past sixty years). Was it the very same airfield that handled Eisenhower's brief, intermediate military transport flight to Muroc/Edwards on 2/19/54, as mentioned in Chapter One? Was alien material moved closer to Palm Springs in the interim, for either Kennedy or retired Mr. Eisenhower to more easily monitor? Much greater detail is needed to fully believe in this amazing allegation. However, a fairly well-known UFO "contactee" of the day - George Adamski (1891-1965) - *also* once stated that it was his acquired information that President Kennedy traveled to Desert Hot Springs to meet friendly humanoid aliens in private. {Desert Hot Springs online today boasts that JFK's lover, movie queen Monroe, journeyed to their town to enjoy their spas on occasion, and did so for a full week not too long before her abrupt and extremely suspicious early August 1962 demise.}

All we know for certain is that, like Eisenhower, official records show that on 3/25/62, President Kennedy attended Sunday morning services at a (Catholic) church in the area (Palm Desert), then he returned to the Crosby house. But that lazy Sunday from noon onward, with another party for the press going on in Palm Springs... all we know for sure is that the Kennedy presidential party left town that night at 11:30 p.m. Pacific Time. They made it back to the White House in the early morning hours of the 26th, and then... Kennedy's first appointment Monday morning in the Oval Office was with an Air Force general with UFO ties!

USAF General Lauris Norstad (1907-1988) huddled alone with the handsome young president in the West Wing on March 26th, but the content of their chat is still unknown. Lauris retired a month after President Kennedy's murder and joined the RAND Corporation, which has been rumored for years to have been quietly working on recovered UFO technology. General Norstad was noted in official White House logs as being summoned to Harry Truman's Oval Office during the height of the mid-summer 1947 Roswell response, along with some other Air Force honchos. {And by the way... young Congressman Jack Kennedy was said in a later-leaked summer of '47 military brief to have been informed about the true otherworldly nature of the Roswell incident (see www.MajesticDocuments.com.}

Hours after the Norstad 2/26/62 huddle, JFK met in an *"off the record"* confab in his office with another worldly-wise major-general, mostly regarding atomic testing. Coincidence? That was the subject humanoid aliens were most concerned about, supposedly, in the Eisenhower years. They had every reason to fret during the Kennedy tenure.

In December of '62, after stops at key military/science sites in *New Mexico* on Saturday the 8th, President Kennedy and his small entourage again flew to Palm Springs, where they once more settled in Crosby's upscale home, by 12:45 p.m. Again, the official records of appointments that day stops cold. Whatever the president undertook that day and the rest of the night was left off the books. Sunday morning, Kennedy went to a church mass, then returned to Crosby's place by noon. The rest of that day is left unrecorded also, in fact completely until 24 hours later, when the presidential group packed and motored to the airport to leave town.

Adding to all of this, low-key California UFO investigator Timothy Cooper stated that a "reliable source" had told him that President Kennedy "did fly out to an air force base to personally watch an "unidentified bogie" track an aircraft under tight security, which got no press coverage in 1962." Mr. Cooper – the 1995 source of the controversial 1962 CIA summary on Monroe and Kilgallen - further stated he learned that as chief executive Mr. Kennedy also once flew to Holloman Airbase for a tour and while there received a classified military briefing on the UFO situation. Cooper's source was likely his father, then a USAF investigator based out of Holloman AFB, at times digging into serious UFO allegations as part of his duties. Much of this story is absolutely, provably true: the press recorded JFK and his vice president, flying in separate airplanes, arriving at Holloman in early June of 1963 – with rare color footage of it found in 2011 and placed on *YouTube*. Kennedy gave a speech to a crowd gathered there, then both men reviewed something pretty important behind closed doors on the base, the press not allowed in to follow. However, the timing for this was ten months *after* the death of Marilyn Monroe, so obviously this wasn't the western airbase alien inspection she mentioned over her tapped telephone.

Existing photos and video footage show that on another occasion, President John Kennedy – along with his "Veep" and also Harry Truman's pal during the August 1949 "Setimus" affair, New Mexico

Senator Clinton Anderson — openly visited (on December 7, 1962) Albuquerque's Kirtland AFB. Then they hit nearby Sandia National Laboratory, located near the Manzano Storage Facility, all three long rumored to have been involved in secret UFO hardware examination and reverse engineering. Their later additional visit to Los Alamos laboratories was said to have been concerning aspects of the burgeoning space program. A closed-door, classified confab was held there, too, no press allowed.

Dashing naval Lieutenant "Jack" Kennedy was a free man in early 1945, discharged by the military but still eager to do his part. When in Frankfurt, Germany, he first met "Ike" Eisenhower, on August 1st of that eventful year. The odd couple met again fifteen years later at the White House to discuss, historians note, top-secret, "off the record" government matters — probably including ET visitation — on December 6, 1960. The duo did so again within the Oval Office on January 19, 1961. The new president's younger brother, Robert Francis Kennedy (1925-1968), was so curious about UFOs he called in aforementioned Army officer Phil Corso for such discussions "on several occasions" in 1962, the retired colonel recalled three decades later in his popular book. Corso said he knew that by briefing Bobby he was also informing Jack, fully realizing RFK - the U.S. Attorney General and virtual co-president - would swiftly take the data back to his big brother, who was so famously enthused by NASA and the growing space program and its noble moon landing goal.

JFK-era ET tales inevitably lead us to this aging but important claim: retired Air Force One "load-master and flight steward" William "Bill" Holden revealed in later years that he once brought up the subject of UFOs to a seated President Kennedy as the young man served him on board the famous plane (in June of 1963, on a flight to Germany). Kennedy gave the ET matter some quiet thought before replying that he'd love to reveal all to the public on UFOs "but my hands are tied." Was this a quick reference to the same military/governmental barriers that the previous president found himself up against when contemplating a public speech in the mid-1950s?

Bill Holden worked on Air Force One for Presidents Kennedy, Johnson, and Nixon (but only one trip.) Holden said in an interview he had heard talk about the amazing Eisenhower '54 encounter. "I believe he was in Palm Springs and he was getting ready to play golf and all of a sudden he said, 'I've got a toothache,'" Holden told questioner Kerry Cassidy on camera in 2007. "So he goes all the way to Edwards Air Force Base," where "a mother-ship was seen coming in. There were several UFOs coming in," Holden recalled learning. The airbase was shut down, and this lock-down lasted for three days. "An agreement was signed between the U.S." and the visiting ETs, retired Mr. Holden noted. "I have been able to find in civilian records, newspaper accounts, and everything else" confirming evidence the Edwards ET event did happen, William stated firmly (despite missing the mark on the "dental emergency" saga, as we've seen).

Although its authenticity is in dispute, there exists a CIA memorandum from Director Allen Dulles to President Kennedy from June of 1961 that mentions "MJ-12 activities" - or the study of recovered spaceships and data from and about friendly aliens - and how they were once "classified under the *Atomic Energy Act of 1954*." So once again we see the subject of atomic power linking the American scientific community; the federal government; and extraterrestrial issues... and there's that special year again: 1954.

So now we come to another tantalizing tale of JFK and UFOs/ETs with a possible atomic bomb twist to it...

An American gentleman who runs a paranormal website claims that in the autumn of 2000 he communicated with a USAF vet who was once stationed, in 1963, at an airbase in Corvallis, Oregon. We'll call him "Perry." His specialty was as an Air Force photographer. It seems Perry made a most startling claim 37 years beyond his heyday: that he was asked in September of '63 to fly in a small private plane for about three hours "with two men in suits" to an unnamed "secret airfield." There he met President Kennedy and snapped his picture - posing with a real live alien!

To inject an important point here first: JFK seems to have been quite fond of having his photo taken. He posed a great deal during his presidency with family, friends, administration members, Oval Office visitors, and foreign heads of state. For most of this, he employed his own official White House photographer, Cecil William Stoughton (1920-2008), formerly of the Army Signal Corps. Respected reporter/author Seymour Hersh (1937-) stated that to his astonishment in his JFK research, he learned the promiscuous president also loved to pose in a White House bedroom with his private mistresses, sometimes wearing masks but little else. The resulting adult snapshot would be taken by a Secret Service agent to a D.C. art gallery, where the owner would fit it with a nice frame. The agent in a dark suit would then monitor the framing process and make sure no copies of the astonishing sex photo were made. When done he'd take the item back to JFK at the executive mansion. Allegedly, Kennedy loved somewhat reckless, brazen fun, *and* recording it for his own sake. So therefore, was staging an alien greeting photo at a "secret airfield" the same general modus operandi?

Perry said the peaceful extraterrestrial being with President Kennedy that memorable day was "a head taller" than the chief executive, sporting "a gray jumpsuit," with long limbs and "big black eyes." Not far away was the alien's round spacecraft, "with a ladder" leading out of an opening, down to the flat runway. Curious lettering was visible on the side of the airship; Perry alleged it read "A-TIPACIL," which might have meant, "Atomic Testing In Pacific Islands."

While all of this sounds far-fetched and unproven, it is a fact that in September of 1963 President Kennedy went on a substantial "conservation tour" of U.S. western states, stopping at Air Force bases and airports, speaking to large crowds to gin up support for preserving the earth and establishing peace through reduction of atomic weaponry and its testing (including in the Pacific Islands). The last stop on this noble, lengthy tour was Palm Springs. Yes, it was back to the Crosby estate at 3:10 p.m. on Saturday, September 28th, but *why?* There was no big speech, no golf, no public appearance, and no activity listed at all, in fact, *nothing* is listed on Kennedy's official diary of appointments from 3:10 until the following morning. That Saturday evening a special cocktail party was set up for "the presidential press corps, entertained by the Desert Press Club," according to the Palm Springs newspaper. *Obviously, this was the key opening JFK needed for a covert trip to a nearby airfield, to meet 'n' greet ETs in secrecy,* at least in theory. After Sunday morning church services on the 29th the president and his party zipped to the Palm Springs airport by 11:20 a.m. and quickly took off for our nation's capital. He was back at his desk early Monday morning, the 30th.

Could President John Kennedy during that Saturday late afternoon/evening have been quietly flown out to Edwards Airbase, and then back without being recorded? Well, yes, of course. And that desert installation was about three hours in flight time for a twin-engine craft, from Corvallis, Oregon, the webmaster reported discovering after carefully measuring Perry's claim. But Edwards AFB was hardly "secret airfield" with just one tower and a small ground crew, as Perry remembered seeing while picture-taking unless it was a far-flung part of the huge Muroc lake-bed facility. But about those lingering rumors regarding a smaller airfield in Desert Hot Springs or Palm Desert... one that Kennedy may have visited before, regarding ETs and UFOs... *that* matches Perry's wild story well.

{To conclude Perry's fascinating but unsubstantiated story, he said he was flown with the federal agents from the mystery airfield back to his Oregon base, where he developed the photos in his office and handed them (and the negatives) over to the feds. They left after warning him to keep silent or else. Perry said he *did* take one fully developed and secretly stashed photograph of JFK and the ET back to his own home to allow his wife to view it, as a witness, then he destroyed it. After relaying these statements in 2000, Perry stopped responding to further communications, so that seems to be the end of the mysterious Kennedy-ET claim. The UFO website's owner/researcher felt that the Air Force photographer's service record was solid, and his story was at least possible.}

Throughout his time in office, John Fitzgerald Kennedy pushed hard for a global nuclear test ban, precisely what aliens wanted. He managed to negotiate successfully with the Soviet Union and the United Kingdom and the resulting "Limited Test Ban" agreement was signed in August of 1963. The new accord banned detonations in the air, sea, and or up in space, what Dwight's "Castle" testing program exploited. It was to take effect in full in the coming year – 1964, a decade from the Muroc/Edwards encounter and its possible ten-year treaty with atomic-bomb-concerned aliens. {Unfortunately, such huge atomic detonations continued within American *and* Russian soil, exploded underground – in fact more than ever, sadly. This area was not covered in the historic new agreement.}

Tragically, JFK was murdered in Texas on November 22, 1963, under still-murky circumstances, but he should be remembered and lauded to this day for at least scaling back what President Eisenhower escalated – the U.S. arsenal of nuclear bombs went from just over 1,000 when Dwight took office to over *22,000* when he left the White House! Little wonder visiting, observing aliens were aghast and landed to express their concerns.

Texas-based Lyndon Baines Johnson (1908-1973) took over that dark day in Dallas as the new president, eager to keep the country on an even keel and its standing in the world community reliable. He was seemingly *very* busy... yet naturally, within a month in office, *President Johnson surprised the press by suddenly announcing his plans to visit arid Palm Springs.* Less than two months later he too traveled to the far-flung desert, just like his predecessors.

It seems that in late December of 1963, Johnson decided to meet with the president of Mexico, mostly over resolving a minor but nagging land dispute on the two nations' border, near Texas. The conference between the two leaders and their top aides would not take too long since, in LBJ's own words, "Relations between the United States and Mexico have never been better." It is customary for a U.S. president to receive a foreign head of state at the White House, perhaps with an official South Lawn greeting ceremony and even a state dinner. And to confer in the privacy of the Oval Office with the door shut, after press photos. Or maybe at the LBJ ranch outside Austin, Texas, much closer to Mexico for its president, Adolfo Lopez Mateos (1909-1969), and also to the problem area in question. But that is strangely not what was planned or took place over two months later.

The lanky liberal Lyndon decided to fly with his wife; his press secretary; and his loyal Secretary of State (plus a State Department contingent) across the country to Palm Springs. Of all the times and dates for this act, Johnson chose the evening of Thursday, February

20, 1964... missing by *one* day the exact tenth anniversary of Ike's excellent adventure!

Private meetings between LBJ and Mexico's Mateos were also held in Coachella Valley on Friday the 21st. According to White House records, the two famous leaders then took limousines to the Eldorado Country Club in Palm Desert, where they met private citizen Dwight D. Eisenhower, and then posed for news photographers. After dinner, the trio reconvened for drinks at the Eisenhower home on the 11th fairway, from 6:20 to 6:45 p.m. Then the two current leaders left Dwight and Mamie at Eldorado and headed elsewhere that night. What was discussed behind closed doors that night remains a mystery, but it was likely mostly small talk mixed with governmental affairs.

Records reveal that President Johnson and ex-President Eisenhower met again on Saturday, February 22, 1964, at a private home in the Las Palmas suburb of Palm Springs where the Johnsons were staying, existing news photos and articles reveal. "Johnson Changes Plans, To Remain at Resort Extra Night," read an Associated Press headlined news article for the afternoon editions on the 21st, indicating an unscheduled extension in his Palm Springs visit, just like Eisenhower a decade earlier. LBJ and Mateos "had breakfast today" in the early morning, then for some reason, the American president was too busy to participate when the Mexican president held a press conference, keeping the media occupied. Press shutterbugs at one later point snapped images of Johnson and Eisenhower conversing outside the sunlit upscale house, then heading inside, deep in thought that was never detailed to the public. What happened after that is unknown.

Oddly enough, meanwhile, at the Palm Springs airport, *two* "Air Force Ones" were parked, the press noted. One was for the president, and one was an identical backup airplane, landing about fifteen minutes ahead of LBJ's aircraft, the night of 2/20/64. "Air Force Two" is normally assigned to the vice president, but Johnson had none in 1964. Both big planes came to a halt in front of the bright lights of the press and eager public, wanting a good view of the relatively new American First Couple as they initially arrived.

It has to be asked, speculatively: did Johnson and Eisenhower somehow find a way to sneak over to Edwards Airbase that Saturday 2/22/64 for any alien-related matters? As we'll see, there certainly was an open window for "jumping out" and attending to such spine-tingling issues. {This is not to be confused with LBJ officially inspecting the Edwards base on 6/19/64, for that was for just one hour, surrounded by staffers, news people, congressmen, records show.}

Later on that Saturday the 22nd, Johnson and Mateos reconvened to dine at the private estate of "a Texas oil and real estate developer" on West Stevens Road. The twosome – with a secretary present - talked out a host of issues, nothing very critical, as White House notes (found digitized online today) explain. The Palm Springs summit conference between the two nations' presidents was deemed a success, coming on the heels of their initial LAX meeting and UCLA ceremony the previous day. An agreement was drawn up that February of '64 about the Texas-Mexico land dispute and signed by Mr. Johnson and Mr. Mateos. But was that the only written treaty that was of importance during the special presidential visit to Palm Springs?

The fact is, when first talking to reporters back in late December of 1963, in what was dubbed "a surprise announcement," President Johnson mentioned openly that he would likely visit retiree Eisenhower, who was going to be briefed ahead of time by none other than the Director of the Central Intelligence Agency – Dwight's former Atomic Energy Commission chairman - John Alexander McCone (1902-1991) to prep for Johnson's visit. *Atomic energy?* It was for some reason *very* important for Eisenhower to have the lowdown on sensitive intelligence matters in that field before he had a chance to sit down with Lyndon in his Eldorado home almost two months later. News articles even mentioned how unusual this was, and that such impending presidential visits are not normally declared to the press and the public until a few weeks beforehand. The mid-February Eisenhower-Johnson encounter was quite calculated and prepped for. But like Ike in '54 and '59, and visiting JFK two years earlier, why didn't LBJ simply stay at a hotel? Why did it *have* to be at a private estate? It belonged in this case Louis J. Taubman (1923-1994), a wealthy Texas/Oklahoma oil executive. Back in December, the Taubmans were contacted about utilizing their estate at 925 Coronado Avenue for hosting the Johnsons. Did Mr. Taubman – like Helms and Sinatra before him - also add some extra phone lines and Secret Service accommodations in time for the president's visit in late February? Their mansion already boasted five bedrooms and a whopping *ten* bathrooms, so adding an entirely new guest wing was likely felt unnecessary. And of course, news reporters were not allowed anywhere near the Taubman estate for the high-level meetings; only later did the State Department reveal some of the nature of the summit chat, seemingly rather mundane.

Adolfo Mateos left Palm Springs for first Los Angeles on Saturday evening, then Mexico City. Johnson oddly remained, and what he did that night, and on Sunday morning and afternoon, remains an intriguing mystery. He did not leave until Sunday night, 2/23/64, headed back aboard Air Force One for D.C. with the First Lady and a full entourage. This late Saturday/most of Sunday time gap certainly left Lyndon Johnson – with Dwight Eisenhower? - plenty of time to duck out of view of the press and public to attend to secret, classified extraterrestrial matters.

The 1989 DIA briefing document about "Majestic-12" stated: *"During a contact debriefing in 1964, an EBE explained that this was a hardship for them."* This was a reference about ETs having to "rotate at twenty-two-year intervals" their "stationed mother-ships" where they cannot be detected by mankind, just beyond our ever-moving solar system. But take note of two keywords: *"contact"* and *"1964."* Could this alleged alien-human interaction have taken place at Edwards AFB (or another, smaller airfield nearby) during Johnson's February '64 visit? Speculative, yes, but it would make sense, considering the expense, time, and trouble it took to arrange the tall Texan's special, out-of-the-way trip. It might also explain a second Air Force One being present. {We can't ask Dwight's personal pilot, who commanded the three different Columbine "AF1" planes, USAF Colonel William G. Draper (1920-1964); he allegedly committed suicide by hanging himself in November of '64.}

Things gets more "coincidental," five years later. Appointment logs show that *on February 19, 1968 – the ET summit's precise 15th anniversary - President Johnson received at 12:17 p.m. an Oval Office long distance phone call of about ten minutes long from "President Dwight Eisenhower, Indio, California."*

The Palm Springs *Desert Sun* newspaper noted that President Lyndon Johnson came back to the valley "to golf and soak up the sun" - with Eisenhower. Naturally, this next co-presidential event took place on February 21, 1968. The press noted that on the day before, war-weary Johnson "made an impromptu tour of military installations in this area." Was Edwards Airbase included? With aging Ike? All we know for sure is that LBJ made a surprise visit to the Navy carrier U.S.S. Constellation in San Diego harbor and even stayed there overnight, supposedly, before flying to Palm Springs and huddling with elderly Eisenhower in private, and out on the links.

Additionally, Truman administration member Charles S. Murphy recalled in an interview meeting with President Johnson on April 18, 1968, on LBJ's way back from a trip to Hawaii. Johnson made sure to stop *at Edwards Air Force Base, "and President Eisenhower came up* and had breakfast with him." Murphy vividly remembered being impressed at how coherent and insightful Eisenhower was, despite his increasing health woes, at a wider meeting besides the two chief executives conferring alone within an Air Force One private cabin, from 7:15 to 7:40 a.m., and then again from 9:05 to 9:30. a.m., records show. {However, LBJ's logs claim this all took place during a stop at *March* Airbase, 100 miles from Edwards AFB.}

Mr. Eisenhower died in March of 1969 and Mr. Johnson died in January of 1973, so both men did not live long enough to see the *next* tenth anniversary of any alleged alien agreement's update in 1964. However, LBJ's Oval Office audiotapes reveal the two men spoke fairly often over the telephone, so any face-to-face meeting about *any* matter that was not revealed to the public becomes increasingly intriguing.

"Ufologists" have not found a great deal to dig into regarding the rest of the Johnson administration (1963-1969) when it came to possible alien visitation - minus the puzzling Kecksburg, Pennsylvania, incident. That's when something round and metallic came crashing down in some woods near that small town on December 9, 1965. The impact site was about 140 miles from Dwight and Mamie Eisenhower's rural Gettysburg home, but more contemporary research shows that this "UFO" crash *might* have been in reality merely a downed Russian satellite.

The Kecksburg affair originally began way up in the North American sky with "a large, brilliant fireball seen in six states, dripping hot metal," most notably in the state of Michigan. That was the home state of the U.S. House Minority Leader, Gerald Rudolph Ford (1913-2006). A Freemason; a Republican Party leader; and a U.S. congressman since the late 1940s, Ford was pretty familiar with fellow conservative Eisenhower as well as liberal Johnson, who appointed Jerry to the controversial Warren Commission in 1963. Future President Ford certainly showed genuine interest in UFOs when in 1966 the representative from Grand Rapids tried to get a federal investigation started into a controversial wave of UFO sightings in his home state, one that eventually the Air Force looked into and famously (and ridiculously) dismissed as "swamp gas." In a spring 1966 letter by Congressman Ford to the Chairman of the Armed Services Committee, Jerry wrote: "I strongly recommend that there be a committee investigation of the UFO phenomenon... It is important that we learn where UFOs come from and what is their purpose."

Jerry Ford's later presidential administration was so brief (1974-1977) it produced nothing of substance on UFOs, but when it was over retired Mr. Ford sent a letter to an American citizen interested in the subject stating he received *zero* help from his government on the matter during his time in office. The Fords had retired to the Palm Springs area following his presidency, buying up *two* homes fronting Dwight's beloved Thunderbird Country Club golf course. Jerry golfed the many desert courses there quite often after Eisenhower's death and perhaps a few times before it, possibly even meeting him there. {Ford was an early 1952 political supporter of Ike's.} But what Gerald R. Ford knew about any presidential alien airbase encounters at Edwards or in New Mexico is not known.

President James Earl Carter (1924-) took office just after Ford, and as previously mentioned once filed an official UFO report years after having witnessed a rather large flying craft of changing colors move slowly about in the Leary, Georgia, sky. Although Carter originally recollected this event happened in October that year, records show that it had to have been at 7:15 p.m. on January 6, 1969. Several other startled people watched the craft alongside Mr. Carter outside a Lions Club meeting hall that evening. "It seemed to move towards us from a distance. It stopped, moved partially away, returned, and then departed." It was a luminous object "about the size of the moon." But the moon had not yet risen, and there was no breeze. "It was bluish at first, then reddish." The closest it came was at about 300 yards away, then it disappeared in the distance.

During his presidential campaign of 1976 Jimmy — an amateur astronomer - told reporters: "It was the darnedest thing I've ever seen. It was big, it was very bright, it changed colors and it was about the size of the moon. We watched it for ten minutes, but none of us could figure out what it was." Jimmy Carter filed a report with the National Investigations Committee on Aerial Phenomena (NICAP) on September 18, 1973, a year before he decided to run for president, it should be noted. Carter promised to bring transparency to the U.S. government's dealings with UFO reports if elected president: "If I become president, I'll make every piece of information this country has about UFO sightings available to the public. I am convinced that UFOs exist because I have seen one." He walked that promise back when he took office, saying he had concerns relating to "defense implications." Shirley MacLaine in 2007 wrote: "I discussed the UFO phenomenon with President Jimmy Carter. He told me once that he tried to shed some sunshine laws" on the topic because he had seen one himself, "but he said elected officials are told such things only on a "need to know" basis."

In 2007 elderly Mr. Carter strangely, abruptly backtracked on his UFO incident, claiming to the media he simply saw something skyward he didn't recognize back in '69 and that he now doubted it was truly extraterrestrial in nature. His filed report description and various other statements certainly sound otherwise. Mr. Carter very rarely golfed as president (from 1977-1981) but may well have visited Palm Springs on another pretext, however, no one seems to have a record of it. The same could be said for his possibly stopping by Edwards Airbase as president. His rural home/farm in Plains was/is 220 miles from the Georgia Guidestones, notably created during his presidency. Jimmy probably never met Dwight Eisenhower, so we'll move on to a commander-in-chief who knew Ike pretty well...

President Ronald Wilson Reagan (1911-2004) was a visitor to Palm Springs so many times no one can count them all. First as a Hollywood actor and occasional golfer, then as a political figure. Reagan spent many a stint campaigning in the desert community. He was in town for various official functions as a two-term governor of California, such as when Reagan set up a Republican Governors Association meeting in 1968 in Palm Springs, with then-House Minority Leader Gerald Ford addressing the esteemed group. Dwight Eisenhower attended too, still residing at nearby Eldorado. Aspiring to the presidency even then, Governor Reagan huddled with Dwight and posed for pictures with him, and again when visiting the area at other times.

One person who claims to have learned that Ronald Reagan personally reviewed photos and documents on otherworldly humanoids who once landed at Edwards was a rather esteemed physicist/engineer who supposedly once worked there: Dr. Edward Leverne Moragne, Ph.D. (1915-2000). Nearly eighty when he spoke up, Dr. Moragne publicly declared that he worked at the legendary airbase while researching acquired alien hardware for the U.S. Department of Defense in the late 1960s and early 1970s when Reagan was governor of California. This was a special, top-secret DoD project back then, Ed said, under the aegis of the Defense

Intelligence Agency (which, again, produced the January 1989 briefing report on aliens, while Reagan was still in office). But here's the upshot: Dr. Moragne told Linda Moulton Howe that *there was indeed a landing by humanoid extraterrestrials at Muroc/Edwards, perhaps more than one, "sometime in 1964," and that alien technology was gifted upon Air Force officials during that time.* Which could well mean that President Lyndon Johnson *did* go to Edwards about ETs during his mysterious Palm Springs summit that mid-February! And maybe Dwight Eisenhower (again) too?

All of this became the subject of a classified report that Governor Reagan supposedly absorbed in the mid-'60s, highly intrigued, understandably. Dr. Moragne alleged that nearly four rows of military guards and even more rows of electrified fencing secured where he worked, within the special Edwards Airbase "Hangar 8," where a gifted alien spaceship supposedly was being kept for scientific testing. {For more details on Dr. Moragne's singular claims, see Howe's mighty www.earthfiles.com.}

During World War II, liberal actor Ronald Reagan served as a captain with an Army Air Force Public Relations Unit. Conservative politico Ronald Reagan in later decades was said by his pilot, Bill Paynter (a former Air Force colonel), to have witnessed with others an otherworldly flying "bright object" in the night skies of September 19th, 1974. He saw it at length while peering out of a window of his campaign airplane as it zipped along near Bakersfield, California, some 200 miles north of Palm Springs and just 80 miles from Edwards Airbase. Paynter remembered decades later: "It appeared to be several hundred yards away," initially approaching from the rear. It was "a fairly steady light until it began to accelerate. Then it appeared to elongate. Then the light took off. It went up a 45 degrees angle at a high rate of speed." Everyone on board the sleek Cessna was surprised and thrilled. Neither Reagan nor Paynter could offer a satisfactory human-based explanation for the UFO, and Ronald Reagan never discussed the incident in public.

"Ronnie" was also rumored to have seen a UFO on a second occasion in California as well, but confirmation is lacking. These notable sightings were of course kept hushed for decades, for the reserved Reagans didn't want to be seen as "kooky," especially while in office (1981-1989). Once he was re-elected president in late 1984, however, Mr. Reagan began mentioning the idea of ETs visiting planet Earth, noting to the United Nations, "I occasionally think how quickly our differences worldwide would vanish if we were facing an alien threat from outside this world. And yet I ask: is not an alien force *already* among us?" It was a stunning statement, one that the Republican leader soon figured he needed to back out of; he quickly claimed that the threat of war itself was this "alien threat," which of course is nonsense.

As president, Ronald Reagan vacationed in the Palm Springs area a whopping total of 41 days, records show. The First Couple had several wealthy friends (some from show business) living in the area, now growing more popular and crowded. In early January of 1984, for example, the Reagans stayed at the same Walter Annenberg mansion that the Nixon's guested in ten years before. During the key February 19, 1984, date, however, President Reagan simply attended to routine business at the White House, taking no mysterious 30th anniversary trips to Palm Springs *or* Edwards AFB. {As it turns out, however, handsome Ron Reagan appeared in some Palm Springs homes – and all across America – the Friday night of the Eisenhower encounter, as a performer on the February 19th, 1954, television drama "*Schlitz Playhouse of Stars*."}

Author Linda Moulton Howe has done considerable research into a special March 1981 Camp David meeting that President Reagan convened with the heads of the CIA, DIA, and NSA. According to rumors, the director of the Central Intelligence Agency briefed Reagan on alien visitation, laying out the details of how at least five or more extraterrestrial races were sending representatives to earth to observe humanity. Some of the information the new chief executive received was allegedly not at all comforting, in that at least *one* of the visiting races were said to have been hostile, prompting a discussion of American defenses in case of an alien attack. Whether the friendly human-like beings that once landed and communicated with Eisenhower were mentioned to or with Mr. Reagan is unknown, but seems in hindsight quite possible.

According to Ms. Howe, at that Camp David site, President Reagan was also briefed by a knowledgeable CIA operative known as "The Caretaker," the so-called "custodian of UFO secrets for thirty-one years." He supposedly informed the fascinated new chief executive that the spaceship crash debris and dead bodies recovered from the July 1947 New Mexico event were hauled initially to Roswell Army Airfield, then to other Air Force installations. One small alien was still alive, however. The ET was treated for some minor injuries and then taken to Los Alamos National Laboratories to reside — just like "Setimus" a year later. The overall matter of alien visitation was/is to be squelched at all costs in order to avoid igniting a media firestorm and a public panic, Reagan was informed, and again that reasoning sounds quite familiar, from the Truman/Eisenhower days.

Oscar-winning movie-maker Steven Allan Spielberg (1946-) is rumored to have been briefed by "a friend with military connections" on the 1954 Eisenhower-ET encounter when readying his script for eventual 1977 classic movie "*Close Encounters of the Third Kind*," where peaceful aliens land in advanced craft on an airbase runway in the western desert of the United States, met by Air Force officials at night. The film plot can't just be coincidental, but the Spielberg connection to our tale herein doesn't stop there...

A whopping 35 years after the fact, Mr. Spielberg at last discussed his special visit on June 27, 1982, to the Reagan White House, to exhibit for the First Couple his newest motion picture, *"E.T., The Extra-Terrestrial."* The film turned out to be one of the biggest smash hits of all time, an instant classic. When the screening ended, the Reagans were visibly moved, so much so that the president stood up, looked around as he composed himself, and then blurted out before many guests (including some astronauts): "We really enjoyed your movie. There are several people in this room who know that everything on that screen is absolutely true." To this Spielberg added in a 2017 interview: "And he said it without smiling." So it was no joke, not to the president who had access to classified UFO files and updated briefings from the military and government officials. Spaceships were on everyone's minds that mid-'82 day; hours earlier the Columbia space shuttle took off from Cape Canaveral in Florida, viewed on White House TVs. Many years after the executive mansion film screening, a presidential staffer recalled that President Reagan asked the assembled movie-viewing group: "How can we be one hundred percent sure that there are no other forms of life out there?" Some in the screening room looked quite stunned in response. {Source: *"Movie Nights with the Reagans"* by Mark Weinberg.}

So let's quickly review what the movie *"E.T."* is all about: a small humanoid-type alien being – who is peaceful, intelligent, and (eventually) speaks English – finds himself cut off on planet Earth from his extraterrestrial family, who take off in a spaceship. The friendly alien is given shelter by a few welcoming Americans and manages to build a communications device to send out high-frequency radio signals to his otherworldly brethren, to come back to

Earth and pick him up. This was the dramatic conclusion of the film story; an advanced alien spacecraft lands and takes the creature to safety in the end.

Does that plot sound just like the "Setimus" situation, or what?

On top of all this, according to the fine research of UFO author Grant Cameron, just a few days after viewing Spielberg's cinematic masterpiece, President Reagan flew on Air Force One to Edwards AFB to watch the landing of Columbia out on the dusty dry Muroc lake-bed. Mr. Cameron also noted that in October of '82, just as the Eisenhower-ET story was making headlines via some newspaper accounts, President Reagan flew to Roswell, New Mexico, and spoke at their old Army Airfield, site of the 1947 UFO crash recovery process. His campaign speech there was to promote a former USAF pilot and Apollo astronaut who had become a U.S. senator. Reagan even stood not far from where the dead bodies of gray alien beings were once said to have been handled, 35 years earlier! And in his delivery, he even mentioned Spielberg's "*E.T.*" movie. Eerie.

As the 1980s continued, Reagan's fascination with the cosmic subject seemed to increase. For instance, in a televised interview, the former Soviet Union's ex-premier, Mikhail Sergeyevich Gorbachev (1931-), said of a November 1985 meeting with then-President Reagan: "From the fireside house, President Reagan suddenly said to me, 'What would you do if the United States were suddenly attacked by someone from outer space? Would you help us?' "I said, 'No doubt about it.'" "He said, 'We too.' So that's interesting." Mr. Reagan, on speaking to Gorbachev, recollected: "I couldn't help but say to him, just think how easy his task and mine might be in these meetings that we held if suddenly there was a threat to this world from some other species from another planet outside in the universe." {Remarks to the students and faculty at a high school in

Fallston, Maryland, on December 4, 1985.} He described the same general extraterrestrial scenario in a speech at the United Nations in New York City on September 21, 1987, and again at a public forum in Chicago on May 4, 1988. No wonder *his daughter*, Patti Ann Reagan (1952-), once remarked that her famous father was "obsessed with UFOs and life on other planets."

But what about his loyal vice president of eight years?

President George Herbert Walker Bush (1924-2018) - and later his son, President George Walker Bush (1946-) - seldom seemed to mention the subject of ETs. Elder Bush was once head of Central Intelligence and knew how to keep classified state secrets. His tight-lipped policy was shown in the fall of 1988 when asked about UFOs by an avid researcher while on the campaign trail in Arkansas; GHWB simply retorted: "I'm very careful in public life about dealing with classified information." On UFO's he replied, "I know some, I know a fair amount," about the subject, before swiftly ending the give-and-take. His one-term administration produced no particular UFO revelations (from 1989 to 1993). Long afterward when out on the campaign trail in 2016, stumping for presidential primary support for his son Jeb, a man in the crowd raised his hand to ask a question, regarding the U.S. government's role in relating the truth about extraterrestrials on earth. "Americans can't handle the truth!" the 91-year-old Mr. Bush suddenly snapped, just before embarrassed event organizers hurriedly put a stop to any follow-up questions.

It should be mentioned that elder Bush – then a young man - consulted with President Eisenhower back in the day, photos show, and that his father – U.S. Senator Prescott Sheldon Bush (1895-1972), Republican from Connecticut – was a fairly close confidante to Eisenhower (and Nixon) during his presidency, becoming golfing buddies in Washington. G. H. W. Bush so enjoyed golf he possibly went along at times... and then he went along with being named President Ford's Director of the Central Intelligence Agency (1976-1977), learning plenty but saying nothing. A former high-ranking CIA employee, Victor Leo Marchetti, Jr. (1929-2018), spoke out in 1979, asserting: "We have indeed been contacted - perhaps even visited - by extraterrestrial beings, and the U.S. government, in collusion with other national powers of the Earth, is determined to keep this information from the general public." {Oddly, Bush and Marchetti died a month apart in the fall of 2018.}

The two-term administration of "the son," fellow conservative George Walker Bush, from 2001-2009, was marred by the terrible 9-11 terrorist attacks in Washington and New York City. Thus the "Second Bush" White House rammed through government secrecy laws and strict regulations on releasing classified materials, meaning any talk of leaking data on UFOs and past presidential encounters was out of the question. Blackout conditions and covert intelligence action behind the scenes "for reasons of national security" became the name of the game in America, and nothing was learned from the Oval Office on the touchy topic of alien visitation. After his presidency, "Dubya" mentioned on a TV talk show that his daughters asked about the subject and he replied that he couldn't tell them anything. *Couldn't...* or *wouldn't?*

Both Bush men were avid golfers; both visited Palm Springs in their day; and both also stopped by Edwards Air Force Base. What they did or learned there is a complete conundrum, unfortunately. Elder Bush visited with retired President Ford when in Palm Springs and golfed aplenty there, which the two ex-chief executives once did on national television with aging comedian Bob Hope, alongside our next elected president of the United States...

William Jefferson "Bill" Clinton (1946-) actually seemed to display a healthy curiosity about aliens in general when in office (1993-2001). Mr. Clinton naturally flew to Palm Springs and golfed there, once even in a trio as mentioned with Ford and elder Bush, at a televised pro-am tournament held on February 15, 1995. Clinton even mentioned in a speech his desire to learn the truth about the 1947 Roswell incident. Several years later, in 2014, ex-President Clinton spoke on an ABC late-night talk show and admitted he had asked for government ET files while in the Oval Office. He added, "If we were visited someday, I wouldn't be surprised." He didn't say if we as a nation had *already* been contacted, but grudgingly summed up on camera: "It's increasingly less likely we're alone."

President Barack Hussein Obama (1961-) and his wife loved visiting Palm Springs, known as "The Playground of Presidents." In fact, it was the Obama's first stop after leaving the White House and a later rally in January of 2017. When searching for a good site to confer with the leader of China back in June of 2013, President Obama arranged a conference in Palm Springs, where he stayed/golfed at Sunnylands. The Obamas visited the Coachella Valley region at least five more times during his tenure (2009-2017), according to media reports. One such visit took place (again at Sunnylands) in mid-February of 2014 to summit with the visiting King of Jordan. *It was just days away from the sixtieth anniversary of the Eisenhower encounter. Very* reminiscent of summiting LBJ and Mateos in '64. Was there another ET treaty expiring and needed secret review or renewal? And why make the King of Jordan travel across *our* country to meet when an East Coast (or White House) confab would have been far less taxing on him and his entourage, arriving in the USA from the Middle East?

The next American president, the controversial Donald John Trump (1946-), was for decades an obsessed golfer and very active businessman who visited Palm Springs several times and hit the links at the upscale, exclusive country clubs there. He was seen - and photographed by the press - in the village as far back as 1991, and two years later participated in the widely televised Bob Hope Desert Classic held there. It is unknown if he visited Edwards Airbase during his tumultuous term (2017-2021). Perhaps it is just a coincidence, but Mr. Trump did initiate his special "Space Force" program through a White House directive dated *February 19*, 2019! And he has also expressed in interviews his great admiration for President Eisenhower. Trump even recalled waving at him when Dwight was passing by in his presidential limousine in New York City when Donald was a boy. His father was reportedly a big Eisenhower booster as well. When asked once by Fox News in 2019 about UFOs, President Trump replied that he "might consider" opening Roswell files but that he was not a believer, yet "anything's possible." His son interviewed him on the same news outlet in June of 2020 and managed to illicit the following response on the possibility of opening UFO files: "So many people ask me that question. There are millions and millions of people that want to go there, that want to see it. I won't talk to you about what I know about it but it's very interesting. But Roswell is a very interesting place with a lot of people that would like to know what's going on." When Trump Jr. pressed his father on whether he would declassify details about the Roswell ET crash of 1947, the president merely said, "I'll have to think about that one."

While sitting and future presidents think about it, we at least have a strong clue what's going on without their assistance, thanks to the now-accumulated data about President Eisenhower's actions, so long ago. Incredibly, Dwight was uniquely positioned to have personally known – and/or perhaps influenced – every U.S. chief executive from the late 1920s' President Herbert Clark Hoover (1874-1964) to the early 1990s (George H. W. Bush). {To be fair, Eisenhower didn't know

Hoover until the 1950s and didn't influence President Roosevelt on anything but military matters in Europe.} But still, Dwight Eisenhower's shadow looms (lightly) even today with Mr. Trump's continuing affection for him.

The bottom line:

When you boil down this presidential UFO topic overall, it is clear that fearless Dwight David Eisenhower knew the alien score much better than all of the other leaders combined, but may have shared only *some* of what he knew in private with them - while the American people were kept *completely* in the dark, essentially lied to "for their own good."

Probably most of our United States chief executives have known the staggering truth but have quite willingly followed the Truman/Eisenhower approach: silence, sidestepping, and shading the facts, to avoid all kinds of possible complications, even after these men get out of office. They feel it's their patriotic duty, and fear what might happen to their legacy and their loved ones should they reveal too much. Life went on, without disruption or upheaval.

Hopefully, an open-minded, knowledgeable United States president will *someday* show the political courage and personal curiosity to read his DIA briefing and report candidly to the entire human race on UFOs/ETs. Until that day all we can do is follow the juicy rumors, clues, and fun facts listed herein and then speculate with reason and logic. What else can thinking human beings do? Invite extraterrestrials to set down and summit with us *on our own,* and then have *them* reveal what went on with American presidents in the past? There may be *dozens* of races coming here, entities that would have stories to tell.

And that leads us to our conclusion...

Paul Blake Smith

EPILOGUE

Final Thoughts

"Complete diplomatic status and recognition to these individuals from beyond our world."

— a 1989 DIA briefing document

Yes, it's a cold, hard, unavoidable fact: no United States president has ever come forward with the complete, candid facts on alien visitation to planet Earth. Likely for fear of mocking ridicule, or triggering a panic, or losing an election, they just won't touch it. From the old Truman/Eisenhower era, to right up to the present day, it's always the same old tiresome evasiveness and misdirection in public when they are pressed on the subject. A skeptical mainstream media is no help, either, barely touching upon the topic without disbelieving snickers and derisive comments.

However, contained within the final assessment summary at the end of the 1989 Defense Intelligence Agency report — a section entitled *"Statement of Position"* - one discovers that since the curious 1940s and '50s human-like visitors to earth — like good ol' "Setimus" - had been deemed tranquil and even helpful with "great and many cultural and technical advances {that} have been derived by such exchanges," privately American leadership has made some very important friends in high places, so to speak. Many of our presidents have been informed of this, it would seem, and all have quietly upheld Dwight Eisenhower's formal treaty with this specific race. *But it's just one species. It's probable there are many more "out there."* And not all of them are very friendly, one can reasonably postulate. And therein lies the problem of disclosure.

Theory: A continuing peace was established by "Ike" in 1954-'55 with an entire race of high-tech humanoid visitors, officially reinforced by Eisenhower-signed agreements, and covertly extended or renewed by other U.S. presidents for decades after. American commanders-in-chief and their top staffers from DIA, CIA, and NSC know much more than what they let on but even in a supposed "open democracy," we the public are kept in the dark for reasons of "national security" and "avoiding panic and social disorder." They have felt it for the overall good. This might be an indication that there are also rotten, soulless ETs in our orbit, entities that would do us harm if they felt so compelled. The Dark Side. It's probably real and we as a planet are in a kind of quarantine from *all* of them. If one kindly race is barely allowed in, to trade with us behind-the-scenes, then that's it, it's all mankind can handle. The other races have been contacted by our "favorites" (by Setimus himself?) and have agreed to barely show up now and then, and remain quite aloof overall. The agreement has held.

That's pure speculation, yes, but not foolishly so.

To try to explain further...

Laid out in the 1989 document, our national behind-the-scenes stance towards visiting *benevolent* extraterrestrials from Eisenhower's day was as follows:

"We hereby grant full, complete diplomatic status and recognition to these individuals from beyond our world. Furthermore, let it be known that we seek to provide shelter, comfort, and aid in all of their peaceful endeavors, so far as these are respective of the laws of our land and the right to self-determination and free will expressed in our national constitution. And until the objectives or methods of either parties in this agreement shall deem otherwise, this bond between our people shall remain in effect."

These might be the very dictated words of President Dwight David Eisenhower in 1954, set into print at some point and signed on behalf of the entire United States government and its military powers (yet apparently not ratified by either house of congress). It was all done in great secrecy and still operates that way. Perhaps the '48-'49 "Diplomat Setimus" cooperation was a template for this '54-'55 agreement and ongoing top-secret exchanges, and the same goes into our future.

So it was mutually beneficial that every U.S. president since Eisenhower remain silent and skeptical in public, and stay that way, today and into the future. If we want the advanced extraterrestrials' goodies, we'll hold to this stated treaty, to put it rather bluntly. It's predicated, of course, on *if* the sympathetic human-like aliens can keep their buzzing about in our skies and their visits on the ground to a brief, bare minimum. To *not* brazenly set down and approach Americans in small or large groups, such as in bustling major cities, scaring the populace into massive, fearful chaos. Then we're good.

But what about all of the other races coming here? Scaly lizard-types; little gray insect types; and huge, blonde Nordic-types, as mere common pop culture examples? They have been seen briefly from time to time, on terra firma and within their spaceships. Again, it is very speculative, but it would seem plausible for the congenial human-type ETs to have taken whatever treaty that was drawn up and signed by Eisenhower (and his top advisers) back to their multi-cultural "floating space lab/apartment complex," (author's description). That is, the three huge, cloaked, undetectable alien mother-ships that are supposedly "parked" outside our solar system, as the 1989 intelligence brief mentions. The site of other intergalactic races of curious visitors, where they live in presumed peace and work (on science projects, evidently), coming and going to earth in much smaller scout ships. They are fascinated by us, and some want to *help* us, while others probably couldn't care less if humanity lives or dies, they simply have their studies to diligently perform.

Did these other races sign the Eisenhower compact too? And possibly hand over advanced technology and advice? If so, it makes Dwight's actions all the more critical and far-reaching, truly worth pursuing and planning over a year in advance. And if so, it would explain why Mr. Eisenhower met in July '54 with ETs, and then again in February of '55, getting all the necessary alien signatures for his deal would have taken time, as corny as it sounds, along with receiving any data and material in return from the races of visitors within the agreement.

Remember, the controversial January '89 DIA document explains that not just humanoids, but *various* alien entities have existed *"in huge interstellar craft,"* or three very large *"mother-ships"* that avoid the strong gravitational pull of physical worlds and are thus *"placed into a "parking orbit" far outside the planetary family (solar system) of any star they approach.*" This trio sounds almost like our man-made, orbiting space stations, or mobile alien office/apartment complexes! Thus different species utilize different types of smaller shuttle crafts that can survive the electromagnetic gravity fields of Earth to come here and dart about, and at times land, like those at the 2/19/54 event. Then they flit on back to their home station in so-called "outer space," undetected by humanity (again, thanks to cloaking techniques). Presumably once there – within their trio of floating, high-tech residence/laboratories - the different races of advanced species – humanoids, grays, "Nords," etc. - examine, log, and compare experiences and scientific data recorded on earth. They monitor our land, our waters, and our skies, worried about our pollution levels. They monitor our human condition and civilizations, our space program, and our arms build-up... but also our tendency towards violence, selfishness, and greed. They monitor our plants, animals, and microscopic lifeforms as well. Even our melting polar ice caps and changing CO_2 levels... perhaps this dangerous and alarming situation *most of all*.

It is conjecture, sure, but perhaps *dozens* of visiting alien species were able to agree to the treaty's provisions, as ever since '54-'55 we've seen only fleeting glimpses of ETs zipping through our skies, sometimes caught on camera, all without any direct, landed involvement - or an invasion. *Eisenhower's dedicated efforts kept us safe*. It's such a mind-blowing concept – all these different visitors with different agendas! - that U.S. presidents simply can't refer to it. It's just too complicated to explain, for the average citizens to handle psychologically, all at once. After all, we still have people in America and around the globe who moronically believe the Earth is flat, and/or don't understand that it revolves in orbit around the sun along with other planets within our arm of the Milky Way galaxy, one of many millions in the incredibly vast cosmos.

Hence the evasive responses, dismissive sarcasm, or mere silence from our American commanders-in-chief. It's much simpler and quicker that way and preserves mankind's sanity and daily order.

Yes, it would Eisenhower was an even greater American/world hero than we imagined. Any trip today to the Dwight Eisenhower Presidential Library and Museum in Abilene, Kansas, will not help the inquisitive among us, seeking proof. Its director remarked in a 2019 interview that his office receives "ten to twelve requests" per month on the Eisenhower-ET incident. He said he tells such researchers that their 29,000 library documents have extremely few references to UFOs - "occasional" papers do for cabinet officials, "such as the National Security Council" - but then admits that many sensitive documents could well have been removed from the presidential files *before* they were even allowed in the building, in the early 1960s. {This author was visited the library/museum some decades ago, and also toured the nearby Eisenhower childhood home.} The Eisenhower library *does* "have proof of the dental work, that part of the story is true," the library/museum director made sure to point out on camera, and he is correct on that point, especially since past UFO researchers have operated *under the wrong date* for the so-called "first contact" theory, Saturday night, February 20, 1954.

Perhaps the most tragic part of this saga is that the human-like ETs who set down at Muroc/Edwards on 2/19/54 in hopes of helping us correct our planet's ecological downward course were rejected by President Eisenhower. That is, their well-intentioned anti-atomic bomb testing advice; their revolutionizing advanced energy technology offer; and perhaps also their fatherly guidance for the rapidly-expanding human race on earth (which *may* have ended up chiseled onto the Georgia Guidestones). Strict policies about the entire highly classified subject of direct contact were considered "Above Top Secret" and that was that. We missed out on plenty.

However...

By late 2020, such restrictive official policy *might* be slowly melting. Citizens worldwide have cellphones and digital cameras. They're recording unusual imagery and placing their UFO home videos online. Many are going viral, impressing the world. TV shows are picking them up and treating them with respect, instead of ridicule. Even military footage and airport radar returns on unexplained craft are hitting the airwaves. "Ancient Aliens" on the History Channel has been helping to shape opinions and open minds, every week for years now. Authentic government documents hinting at, or fully describing, alien visitation have been leaked here and there, in small dribs and drabs. Rock star Tom DeLonge's "To the Stars Academy" has done admirable work in attempting to gain insider access to government sources. Grudging minor admissions and accidental "hot-mic" slips by governmental figures have been slowly mounting. Nowadays it's getting tougher and tougher to deny humanity is being graced by observers from other planets or dimensions. Over 65 years after the '54 Edwards ET affair, citizens of Earth are generally far more accepting and understanding on the topic of celestial entities coming here, conditioned for decades by absorbing UFO/ET-related news stories; paranormal podcasts; documentaries; fictional movies; monthly magazines; and wacky TV sitcoms. The general public at last could well be ready, emotionally... braced up mentally... slowly but surely... for disclosure. Or at least *partial disclosure*. What the CIA used to call "Limited Hangout." Some even feel it is genuinely coming soon, or even quietly underway *now*.

So perhaps in the years to come, a seated United States president, surrounded by a new generation of tech-loving advisers, will make the call to throw open old files and vaults in order to *finally* reveal this unavoidable conclusion: *we're a fascinating race that attracts other races, all of them more advanced, some more friendly than others, keen on studying us and our troubled planet. And that Dwight Eisenhower was a pioneer in this field, leading the way with direct contact and communication.*

Until that hoped-for day of disclosure, the defense rests, and the case is now in the hands of you, the jury, the people of planet Earth. Are you ready to render a verdict?

APPENDIX

SUBJECT: OPERATION MAJESTIC-12 PRELIMINARY BRIEFING
PREPARED: 08 JANUARY 1989
BRIEFING
OFFICER: MJ-1

NOTE: This document has been prepared as a preliminary briefing only.
It should be regarded as introductory to a full operations briefing
intended to follow.

OBJECTIVES

OPERATION MAJESTIC-12 (MAJIC-12 or MJ-12) is a ABOVE TOP SECRET
Research and Development/Intelligence operation responsible directly
and only to the President of the United States. Operations of the
project are carried out under control of the MAJIC-12 Group which
was established by special classified executive order # 092447
of President Truman on 24 September 1947, upon recommendation by
Dr. Vannevar Bush and Secretary of Defense James Forrestal.

Objectives of the Group include the evaluating of risk, control
and containment of the violation of United States air space and of
national security by unknown and possibly hostile aliens of one or
more advanced races of beings presumed to have originated elsewhere
than on the planet Earth. The development of effective countermeasures
and the application of any scientific or technical discoveries made
during the operations is also of the highest concern. The following
are some established aspects of the situation:

* Advanced beings of non-human nature are continuously
  being detected along with their flying-disc craft in
  the controlled space of the U.S. since 07 July 1947.

* The remains of seven (7) flying craft and the bodies
  of twenty-seven (27) deceased non-human beings have
  been recovered as of this briefing date, and are at
  present being studied by MAJIC-12 scientists.

* Three of the recovered craft are nearly intact and
  one such machine has maintained some of its power
  since retrieval in 1948.

* Since 1957, no additional alien craft have been
  available for study. The assessment is that these
  beings have adapted or perfected the machines to the
  conditions of our world, so as to avoid any further
  such revealing crashes.

:TOP SECRET:

HISTORY

As for the history of the MAJIC-12 Group and its membership and investigations, the complete records are available with proper clearance through the office of counterintelligence of the DEFENSE INTELLIGENCE AGENCY and are on microfilm at this time. The written minutes and transcripts of all directorate meetings as well as a full record of all investigations in their original form are located at the MJ-12HQ, codenamed "bigger Command" and situated at the decommissioned nuclear Air Station at Flat Rock, Nevada. This site is now under the covering authority of the Nuclear Regulatory Commission, the story having been circulated widely that this base is involved in the long-term monitoring of residual radiation levels that resulted from the A-bomb testing nearby in the 1950's. With the exception of a monitoring task unit at Wright-Patterson Air Force base, for the sending up of all sightings relayed through the Dept. of the Air Force, all gathering operations are now located at the Nevada site. Over a period of years, all recovered evidence from the crashed alien craft has been transported to underground storage at Flat Rock, making full use of the large complex of fallout shelters built there starting in 1954.

Scientific and technical research and analysis for MAJIC-12 is being conducted at several places around the country. Small monitoring task units remain in place within the command structure of certain other branches of the armed forces. These include NORAD in Colorado and SAC in Nebraska - for reporting of radar sightings, and SEACON in Virginia and FACCON in California for reporting of Naval encounters. The aeronautical research is being carried out by the Redstone Arsenal in Alabama, and linguistic studies are conducted at NASA's Ames research center in California. A team from Johns-Hopkins University and the National Institute of Health is reducing the biological and medical intelligence gathered by the project.

Just as the title implies, MAJIC-12 is headed by a directorate of twelve persons chosen for life (or until retirement), six are military and/or administrative positions, and six are private sector scientists and engineers with long histories of governmental affiliations. All vacancies on the directorate are filled by a unanimous vote of seated directors. The President may recommend an appointment, but while all other decision making lies with this office, membership on the MAJIC-12 directorate is finally decided solely by that group. Such limitation of executive authority is a long-standing historical decision based on the assertion that these twelve persons belong to a small family of deeply skilled experts. Only from within such a family is it possible to have a sense of the "special mindset" required for this very specialized kind of work. It has been said by a former director of the group that the understanding of alien minds requires an alien mind.

DO NOT DUPLICATE

405389

:TOP SECRET:

ORGANIZATION

The organizational structure of OPERATION MAJESTIC-12 is arranged into three (3) tiers or levels, by order of a need-to-know information flow process. These are:

- **DIRECTORATE** - Composed of twelve members sharing equal authority and complete access to all information. The President is accepted to be the thirteenth member of this body, as well as its final authority*.

- **TASK UNITS** - Composed of a variable number of scientific and information gathering groups and/or persons. The complete listing of current consultants in the sciences is available on request. Identities of Military monitoring units and individuals must be requested through the directorate.

- **ENFORCEMENT** - Composed primarily of selected recruits from the Army Special Forces Command. These units are organized into Companies known as "Blue Berets", and are trained and supported by Air Cavalry units based out of DIGGER COMMAND in Flat Rock, Nevada. Purpose includes containment of tactical situations, control of public awareness, panic, evacuation, etc. Originally created for the security of recovery sights during investigations and the transporting of sensitive evidence. Also includes a number of plainclothed operatives whose purpose is the spread of cover stories to avoid public fears about the inability of the Government to control the situation. These members also operate diversions for civilian investigators to discourage such efforts so as to aid in control of public information and interest.

*NOTE: The identities of the directorate, MJ-12 are held in the strictest secrecy. They are known only to eachother and to the seated President of the United States. These names are never to be written down.

The purpose and need for the highly covert and ABOVE TOP SECRET designation of this operation will become apparent with the study of the following reports which led to the forming of OPERATION MAJESTIC-12. Since the time of these events, over forty years ago, the state of our science has advanced to the degree that we may see a measure of short-sightedness in the then-expedient actions of the administration. As a result of actions taken at that time, several sensitive developments have resulted which are of ever-increasing concern to the National Security of the United States of America.

DO NOT DUPLICATE

ROSWELL, NEW MEXICO
(07 JULY, 1947)

On 07 JULY, 1947, a secret operation was begun to assure recovery of the wreckage of an unidentified flying object which had crashed at a remote site in New Mexico. The object was downed approximately seventy-five miles northwest of Roswell Army Air Station (later Walker Field), and was reported to authorities there by a local rancher. During the course of this operation, aerial reconnaissance discovered that four (4) small human-like beings had apparently ejected from the craft at some point before it had exploded. These had fallen to earth about two miles east of the crash site where the wreckage was located. All of the four alien crew members were dead and badly decomposed due to action of predators and exposure to the elements during the approximately one week which had elapsed prior to their recovery. A special scientific team took charge of the removal of the bodies and the recovery of the wreckage of the craft. Civilian and military witnesses in the area were debriefed and news reporters were given the effective cover story that a misguided weather balloon was responsible for the sighting.

A covert analytical effort organized by General Nathan F. Twining and Dr. Vannevar Bush acting on the direct orders of President Harry S. Truman, resulted in a preliminary consensus (19 September, 1947) that the disc-shaped craft was most likely a short range reconnaissance ship. This conclusion was based for the most part on the craft's size and the apparent lack of provisioning. A similar analysis of the four deceased occupants was arranged by Dr. Detlev Bronk. It was the tentative conclusion of this group (30 November, 1947) that although these aliens are generally human-like in appearance, the biological and evolutionary processes responsible for their development has apparently been quite different from those observed or postulated in homo-sapiens (earth humans). Dr. Bronk's team generated the term, since then widely applied, of "Extra-terrestrial Biological Entities", or EBE's, for these creatures, until such that a more definitive designation can be agreed upon. It was the unanimous decision of the scientists involved in this investigation that this craft and its entities most certainly did not originate with the government of any nation on the earth.

The crash near Roswell occured sometime in the evening of 2/3 July
1947. At about 20:47 hours at least two dozen persons in the area
observed a bright yellow or "sun colored" disc-shaped object over the
area. On 3 July 1947, in the early afternoon, the widely scattered
wreckage was discovered by local ranch manager William Brazel and his
son and daughter. The authorities at the Roswell Field Army Air Forces
Base were alerted by Mr. Brazel at 09:18 of 07 July, 1947 and two officers
of the base were guided to the crash site by the ranch manager. These
were Major Jesse Marcel, staff intelligence officer of the 509th. Bomb
Group Intelligence Office, and Captain Lee Cerns of the Counter-intelligence
Corps.

When the two officers returned to Roswell Field with samples of the
crash site material, they immediately reported to Colonel William Blanchard
of Air Tactical Command. It was at this point that the first of many
decisions were made that have gone into the historical posture of this
government's position on the public's need-to-know about the situation.
Colonel Blanchard released an official press statement confirming that
wreckage of a flying disc had been recovered. This was phoned in to an
Albuquerque, New Mexico radio station without approval from higher level
command in the Army Air Corps. Indeed, no one in the Pentagon or anywhere
else was notified or consulted prior to the release of this information.

In defense of Colonel Blanchard's actions, it should be noted that
no established procedure on the issue existed at the time. There were
no Office of Special Investigations, Central Intelligence Agency, National
Security Agency, or Defense Intelligence Agency or any other similar
such organizations at that time. It should be noted that within less
than two years following this incident, and as its direct result, all
of the above agencies were established with the exception of the Defense
Intelligence Agency which was chartered in 1961.

At nearly the same time on the evening of 07 July, two events were
taking the incident in widely different directions at widely separated
locations. In Roswell, Major Marcel was ordered by Colonel Blanchard
to load the debris onboard a B-29 aircraft and fly it to Wright Field
(now Wright-Patterson AFB) at Dayton, Ohio, for examination. As this
was being done, a reporter from the Albuquerque radio station called to
Wright Field to confirm the crash with the commanding general there.
This was Lt. General Nathan Twining, Air Materiel Command, where any such
reported incident should have been filed. In fact, the wreckage and all
persons involved were already on their way to Wright Field. But this
was the first that General Twining had heard of the matter. Twining was
forced to state that he knew nothing of a crashed disc craft.

405389

Upon finally receiving verbal confirmation by open telephone line
- Colonel Blanchard at Roswell Field, General Twining did three things
rapid order in an effort to contain the situation. First, he sent
cial orders by secured teletype to Blanchard at Roswell, instructing
to do nothing and talk to no one until further orders from him.
l, Twining used the same system to contact General Roger Ramey, who
in command at Carswell Army Air Forces Base (HQ-8th. Air Force),
t Worth, Texas, ordering him to direct Major Marcel to vector a
ding for an intermediate stop at Carswell, which was on his flight
h. General Ramey was instructed to: A., remove the recovered debris
- Marcel's aircraft and place it onboard another in sealed crates to
forwarded to Wright Field. B., order Marcel and his crew not to talk
reporters. C., notify the press of a photo conference to be held at
swell where an explanation would be given. D., state at the conference
t the wreckage was only the remains of a weather balloon and its attached
foil radar target and prominently display created evidence of same.
, return Major Marcel at once to Roswell Field. Then General Twining
t an open teletype to the newsrooms at the two Albuquerque radio stations
ning them to cease transmission of the original story and to contact
swell Office of Public Information for the correct release. Finally,
general boarded a plane and flew directly to Roswell Field in New
ico.

At his arrival in Roswell, General Twining relieved Colonel Blanchard
command and ordered troops to set up a secured perimeter around the
sert crash site. He then personally supervised the total policing of
area and removal of all remaining evidence, as well as the four day
briefing of Major Marcel and the six day debriefing of rancher Brazel
m he held incommunicado until the clean-up was complete.

The wreckage recovered at Roswell consisted of three hundred and
enty-seven (327) fragmented pieces of various structural debris. Most
ominent among these were beams of many lengths and ranging in diameter
thickness from just over half an inch, to just under two inches.
ese were found to be composed of a very light and porous metal alloy
posed of extremely pure aluminum and silicon mixed with zirconium
an unknown crystalline structure. The beams were flexible and were
olutely unaffected by both oxyacetylene and oxyhydrogen blowpipe
tting torches. Several of these contained hieroglyphic and alphabetic
tings of unknown type coated onto their surfaces. Also found were many
ces of a thin metallic foil-like material presumed to have been the
ter casting of the crafts hull, or skin.

Following the discoveries near Roswell, New Mexico it became obvious
to the intelligence officers working under the newly appointed Secretary
of Defense, James V. Forrestal, that a special operations group was going
to be needed to coordinate the accumulation & dissemination of data on
this subject. This became known as the Majestic-12 Group when President
Harry Truman chartered them in September, 1947.

The original directorate of the Group were as follows:

- Dr. Lloyd Berkner - Scientist and Executive Secretary of the Joint
  Research and Development Board in 1946 (under Dr. Vannevar Bush).
  Also headed the special committee to establish the Weapons Systems
  Evaluation Group. Was Scientific Consultant to the Central Intelligence
  Agency on UFO's during his years with MJ-12.

- Dr. Detlev Bronk - Internationally known physiologist and biophysicist
  who was chairman of the National Research Council and the Medical
  Advisory Board of the Atomic Energy Commission(later, Nuclear
  Regulatory Commission). Also, Chairman of the Scientific Advisory
  Committee of the Brookhaven National Laboratory.

- Dr. Vannevar Bush - Recognized as one of the United States leading
  scientists. Organized the National Defense Research Council in
  1941 and the Office of Scientific Research and Development in 1943,
  which led to the wartime establishment of the Manhattan Project to
  develop the first atomic bomb. After the war, he became head of
  the Joint Research and Development Board. Was responsible for the
  recommendation, along with Secretary Forrestal, to President Truman
  that the Majestic-12 operation was required. Dr. Bush was a principle
  organizer of the efforts to bring many German scientists, including
  Albert Einstein, to the U.S. before and after the war.

- James V. Forrestal - Served as Secretary of the Navy before he
  became Secretary of Defense under President Truman in July, 1947.
  Among his first acts as the Defense Secretary was the responsibility
  for organizing the crash recovery of the flying disc from Roswell,
  New Mexico, which occurred in the same month he took office. He
  was the first to approach President Truman about the need for an
  operation like MJ-12, and was in charge, along with Dr. Bush, of
  setting up an international intelligence gathering organization
  to monitor world-wide UFO activity. The results of these efforts
  would grow to include the Central Intelligence Agency and National
  Security Agency, both of which were founded shortly after the Roswell
  and Aztec crashes.

As a direct result of circumstances surrounding the Aztec, New
Mexico recovery, Secretary Forrestal suffered a mental breakdown
in March, 1949, & was admitted to Bethesda Naval Hospital under the
cover story of needing a "routine physical check-up". While he was
at that facility, he is supposed to have committed suicide by jumping
from an upper story window in May, 1949. A special committee of
counter-intelligence of the Central Intelligence Agency later
concluded that the highest probability scenario involves his having
been either drugged, tricked, or pushed into his fatal fall. The
presumed reason for this involves details of the Aztec crash which
will follow in that section.

* Gordon Gray - Assistant Secretary of the Army at the time of MJ-12
  Initialization and Secretary of the Army in 1949. In 1950, was
  appointed as Special Assistant on National Security Affairs to
  President Truman. In 1951, headed the Psychological Strategy Board
  for Unidentified Flying Object Impact (PSBUFOI), under Central
  Intelligence Agency Director Walter Bedell Smith.

* Vice Admiral Roscoe Hillenkoetter - Third Director of Central
  Intelligence (DCI) from 1947 to 1950. Founding Director of the
  Central Intelligence Agency, established in September, 1947 to
  direct International information gathering on UFOs. Was covertly
  placed on the board of directors of the civilian UFO organization,
  National Investigations Committee on Aerial Phenomena (NICAP) to
  monitor their activities and control the release of their information
  to the public. Was forced to take an early retirement after he
  broke security making the public statement that "UFOs are real and
  through a process of official secrecy and ridicule, many citizens
  are led to believe the unknown flying objects are nonsense." In
  defense of his position, it must be noted that by this time, the
  events of the Aztec, New Mexico recovery and the death of Secretary
  Forrestal had depressed and demoralized most of the original members
  of the investigating group. By 1951-52, MJ-12 had to be entirely
  reconstructed due to the feelings of many of the directorate that
  the public had a right to know the facts.

* Dr. Jerome Hunsaker - Aircraft designer and head of the Departments
  of Mechanical and Aeronautical Engineering at the Massachusetts
  Institute of Technology. Chairman of the National Advisory Committee
  for Aeronautics. Was in charge of studies of the machined portions
  of the debris recovered from the crash sites. Expert in X-ray and
  microscopic metals analysis.

- Dr. Donald Menzel - Director of Harvard College Observatory and a consultant to the National Security Agency on astronomy. Held a Top Secret Ultra clearance.

- General Robert Montague - Base Commander at the Atomic Energy Commission installation at Sandia Base, Albuquerque, New Mexico from July, 1947 to February, 1951. Was reassigned and transfered following a heated disagreement over National Policy of MJ-12 regarding sightings around nuclear research facilities. Felt the risk to the public health was of greater issue than security and control of the situation.

- Rear Admiral Sidney Souers - First Director of Central Intelligence (DCI) from January-June, 1946. Upon initialization of MJ-12, became Executive Secretary of the National Security Council, in order to control domestic security of UFO information. Following the Aztec, New Mexico recovery and related actions, Souers resigned (1950) his positions in national security and his commission in the Navy. He was retained as a consultant on security to the Executive Branch.

- General Nathan Twining - The principle "ramrod" for high security in the matter of Unidentified Flying Objects and an opponent of scientific release of data or the involvement of civilian scientists. Twining was an outstanding commander of bombing operations in both the Pacific and European theaters in World War II. In 1945 he was appointed Commanding General of Air Material Command, based at Wright Field (Wright-Patterson AFB). Organized Project Sign and Project Grudge (later became Project Bluebook) to control and discredit civilian sightings and civilian investigations. Chief proponent of covert investigation and clandestine contact attempts regarding UFOs and the EBEs (Extra-terrestrial Biological Entities).

- General Hoyt Vandenberg - After an outstanding career in the Army Air Forces, was appointed the second Director of Central Intelligence in 1946 until May, 1947. Following the Aztec, New Mexico incident, he joined General Twining in supporting the sensitive nature of releasing any UFO information to the public. When the Air Technical Intelligence Center published its Top Secret "Estimate of the Situation" indicating the belief that UFOs were interplanetary in origin, in August, 1948, General Vandenberg ordered the document burned before it could be distributed to government scientists with the required clearance. This was directly related to the outcome of the Aztec investigation which began in March of that same year.

It is possible to disclose the identities of the original MJ-12 directorate because they are all deceased. It is necessary in order to understand the climate of confusion and anxiety resulting from the second recovery incident at Aztec, New Mexico in 1948.

DO NOT DUPLICATE

HISTORICAL PRECEDENTS

AT

AZTEC, NEW MEXICO
(25 MARCH 1948)

SECTION C

(10 pages)

AGENCY REPORT NUMBER

405389

AZTEC, NEW MEXICO
(25 MARCH 1948)

On 25 March, 1948 at approximately 16:19 (4:19PM) hours, Mountain Standard Time (local time, or LT), a disc-shaped flying machine came down about twelve (12) miles northeast of the small community of Aztec, New Mexico. The controlled landing occurred in a small desert canyon on the private grazing land of a local farmer and rancher.

The approach of the disc was tracked with the aid of three (3) high powered missile tracking radar stations belonging to the recovery network of the White Sands Test Range and located in classified areas of southwest New Mexico. The disc-craft was first observed in violation of the restricted air space of this facility. The disc was flying on a level glide path and on a heading from the southwest-to-northeast at about 3,200 feet altitude when first detected. This track detection resulted in an Air Defense Command Alert that included the scrambling of squadrons of jet interceptors from the nearby Sandia and White Sands bases. Also, per a recent memorandum issued through Operation Majestic, the Commander-in-Chief of Air Defense Command (CICADC) immediately notified Secretary of State General George C. Marshall.

At 17:53 hours LT (5:53PM,MST) the disc-craft appeared to lose both speed and altitude at nearly the exact moment that it was triangulated by returns from all three (3) radar dish antennae in an effort to vector the interceptor squadrons towards their target. At the time, it seemed to be an evasive tactic on the part of the disc-craft. The current assessment is that the microwaves from these long range radars almost certainly evidenced a damage to the power or flight control systems of the disc-craft.

At 18:02 hours LT, the craft dropped below radar some four (4) minutes before the White Sands jet squadron would have reached intercept point (IP) and engaged-to-disc-craft. Estimates later indicated the disc-craft impacted or landed at approximately 18:19 hours LT. The exact position of the landing zone (LZ) was determined within minutes by calculation of the last radar triangulated tracks and confirmed and by a visual fly-over of interceptors from the White Sands base. The LZ-IP was at the bottom of Hart Canyon, a dry wash area about 12.2 miles northeast of Aztec, New Mexico and 2.3 miles northwest of the Cave Creek bend in the Animas River. This was on private land about 1.7 miles north of the state highway and nearly ½ mile west of unpaved county road 3-141 south.

At 18:26 hours LT (6:26PM, MST), on 25 March 1948, the crash site was visually confirmed by the commander of the 152 tactical fighter wing and relayed to the Air Defense Command officer at Sandia Base, Albuquerque, New Mexico. This information was conveyed at once to the CICADC who contacted Secretary of State Marshall. By 18:35 hours LT, General Marshall had made contact with the Army Air Force's Interplanetary Phenomenon Unit (IPU), a section of the Army Counterintelligence Directorate. The IPU was maintained and supported out of nearby Camp Hale, Colorado and was the closest group able to secure, recover, transport and store a disabled disc-craft. This action was entirely correct in the interval before a MAJESTIC operation could be activated and the preparations of the IPU group while awaiting a MAJICOPS crew saved valuable time.

The IPU was formed after the Roswell, New Mexico crash recovery and was later absorbed into the enforcement division of OPERATION MAJESTIC at the time that the Department of the Air Force was established as an entity seperate from the U.S. Army.

The disc-craft was recovered and the LZ declared secured by 22:45 hours LT through the actions of an IPU scout team sent to the Hart Canyon area. Meanwhile, General Marshall had contacted Dr. Vannevar Bush - scientific head of MAJICOPS - and a joint IPU/MAJICOPS team was assembled under MJ-12 command for the purpose of investigating and clearing the LZ, or crash site. The local rancher who owned the land and ████████████████████ * were held incommunicado while the field analysis and subsequent clean-up was conducted at Hart Canyon. Visiting with the rancher at that time and planning to hunt for game animals on his land, were the owner of a local radio repair shop plus a unemployed oil hunter and inventor. These last two parties were later to get together and tell their story to a columnist from Variety Magazine named Frank Scully. This author later published a book in 1950 detailing parts of the Aztec recovery story. This breach of security was occasioned by the use of a cover story for the IPU/MAJICOPS workers that proved to be ineffective. It was decided to disguise the Aztec efforts as an exploration for oil by a fictional drilling company, a fact that was not in agreement with the knowledge of the unemployed oil hunter who knew that there was no oil in the area. Later both this independent oil hunter and the columnist Scully were discredited by facts leaked to a writer at True Magazine by covert operatives of the MAJESTIC Enforcement Division. This action was unfortunate but very vital in light of the sensational nature of the Aztec discoveries. Fortunately, Scully labeled this fortune hunting oilman as a "scientist" in his book and during the period of the book's sales, this adventurer was convicted of fraud for trying to peddle a device he claimed would find oil. Mostly by luck, the security breach healed itself and the book was quickly forgotten with only minor help from MJ-12.

That evening of 25 March, General Marshall ordered ADC off of alert status and requested that they send teletypes to the radar stations advising them that there had been a false alarm. Time was an important factor here since the disc-craft had landed intact and had the appearance of having been landed under the control of it's operators. No means of entry was immediately evident and members of the IPU scout team considered it possible that some of the crew of the disc-craft might still be alive inside it.

At 01:20 hours LT, 26 March, the team of MJ-12 scientists assembled by Dr. Bush arrived at Durango Air Field, Colorado about thirty-five (35) miles northwest of Aztec. All members of the teams of IPU and MAJICOPS investigators were then sworn to an Ultra-Top Secret security oath. All personal property and identification was left in lockers at Durango and the teams boarded trucks headed for the Hart Canyon site. It must be remembered that the helicopter was still in experimental development at this stage and trucks were the best means of entering the rugged terrain as well as the fact that they would cause far less attention than the noisy and unfamiliar helicopter, which was, however, used to bring in the initial IPU scout team.

* Name withheld to protect a living individual's privacy.

In order to fully follow the course of the Aztec, N.M. recovery and
investigation it is important at this point to detail the names and the
backgrounds of the members of the IPU/MAJICOPS team before returning to a
chronology of the events at Hart Canyon. Only four of these persons were
on the MAJICOPS directorate. These were; Dr. Lloyd Berkner, Dr. Detlev
Bronk, Dr. Vannevar Bush, and Dr. Jerome Hunsaker. Their biographies
may be found in the preceding file of the Roswell, N.M. incident.

The following were selected by the MJ-12 directorate to accompany the
IPU/MAJICOPS recovery team to the Hart Canyon landing site:

- Dr. Carl A. Heiland, Director and senior scientist of the
  Geophysics and Magnetic Sciences Laboratory of the Colorado
  School of Mines. Was instrumental in discovering that sections
  of the Aztec disc-craft were held together by molecular
  magnetic bonding along finely polished seams and determined
  a means for it's disassembly.

- Dr. John von Neumann, former consultant on the Manhattan
  Project (atomic bomb) in 1943 and a close personal friend
  of Dr.'s Bush and Oppenheimer from same. Expert in both
  mathematics and computing machines. His work on the Aztec
  disc eventually led to the binary computer language used
  today in all modern electronic computers.

- Dr. Robert J. Oppenheimer, was Director of the Institute
  for Advanced Studies at Princeton University from 1947
  after a distinguished period of service during the war
  as head of the Los Alamos atomic bomb project. Also, was
  Chairman of the General Advisory Committee of the Atomic
  Energy Commission (later Nuclear Regulatory Commission).
  Acting for his friend, Dr. Bush, who had not yet arrived
  at Aztec, he selected most of the recovery team members
  and arranged with the U.S. Navy for storage in their
  facilities at Los Alamos until permanent sites could
  be prepared.

- Dr. Johann von Roesler, an expert nitrogen chemist whose
  work led to development of Nitrogen Mustard Gas, Nitro-
  glycerin derivatives leading to Trinitrotoluene (TNT) and
  worked with Dr.'s Bush and Oppenheimer on triggering
  devices for the atomic bomb. Originally included as a
  consultant on the possible need to gain forced entry to
  the disc-craft by use of high explosives, he eventually
  worked with Dr. Detlev Bronk on investigating the liquid
  nitrogen cooled cryogenic suspension system used aboard
  the disc-craft by it's crew members.

* Dr. Merle A. Tuve, worked with Bush and Oppenheimer for the Office of Scientific Research and Development. (Manhattan Project) during World War Two. Top pioneer in radio-wave propagation in the upper atmosphere. Later was part of the Bell Laboratories team which developed the principles of laser light physics derived from study of systems found aboard the Aztec disc-craft.

* Dr. Horace van Valkenberg, was Director of the School of Metallurgy at the University of Colorado. Expert in analytical chemistry. Was useful in determining proper materials handling of components of the Aztec disc-craft during investigation and disassembly. Later pioneered science of X-ray crystalography, crystal holography and electron microscopic metals analysis as well as the holder of over thirty (30) patents through Arizona State University in metal alloy processes. Most of the above were the result of research he began after his analysis of the structural materials of the disc-craft.

Although not present during the recovery phase of the Aztec operation at Hart Canyon, it is important we acknowledge the contributions made later by Lambros Callihamos and William Friedman who are experts in language and cryptology and whose analysis of the writings and symbols found aboard the disc-craft led to a degree of understanding of the cryogenic suspension system used to freeze the ship's occupants. Also, Dr. Paul A. Scherer, whose supply of refrigeration and nitrogen cooling and pumping equipment aided greatly in the revival of the suspended occupants aboard the disc-craft at the field laboratory set up at Los Alamos. Both Callihamos and Friedman went on to work for OPERATION MAJESTIC for many years in our Covert Operation Section of the Enforcement Division as deep planted agents within the National Security Agency. Dr. Scherer led an illustrious career as Research and Development Director for Air Research Corp.

The IPU/MAJICOPS convoy took routes to the Hart Canyon site that avoided main roads, and on arrival they set up road blocks and secured a two (2) mile perimeter around the canyon rim and landing site. In exchange for his silence, private land was leased from the farmer who owned the field in Hart Canyon for the construction of a controlled access road to and from the area. Equipment carrying trucks were camouflaged to look like oil and gas drilling rigs and personnel involved wore coveralls with the name of a fictional oil exploration firm created by MAJICOPS for this purpose. Later a fence was constructed around the perimeter of the canyon and bore the name of the oil company and warning of blasting on signs attached to it.

When the time came for removal and restoration of the site, trucks were used that were labeled "High Explosives" and were escorted by Blue Berets disguised as National Guardsmen. The cover story which was very effective in keeping the curious away was spread that these trucks were removing large amounts of nitro-glycerin used in blasting during oil explorations. This was the reason given for the "National Guard" escort; that the governor of the state requested the escort to avoid the theft of the explosives.

:TOP SECRET:

Shortly after sunrise on 26 March 1948 the IPU/MAJICOPS team began
operations at the Hart Canyon location. Measurements of the radiation levels
around the craft and the landing site were taken and proved negative (i.e.,
nothing out of the ordinary). Some high concentrations of potassium chlorate
powder were detected in soil samples surrounding the disc-craft. A fine,
yellowish dust composed of particles less than five (5) microns in diameter
was detected coating the nearby underbrush. Chemical analysis showed that
this was composed of sulfurous substances in an unfamiliar combination having
a bivalent, rhombic crystalline structure and was mixed with an unknown and
extremely highly electro-positive element in the iodide group. It is now
known that this was a form of disinfectant automatically discharged by the
craft upon any touch down to a planet's bioactive soil. Linear calibration
surveys were taken by theodolite (surveyor's transit) and photographs were
taken from every possible angle with a Graflex 4"x5" plate camera equipped
with special calibration overlay masks to register dimensions on the film.
The ship was determined to be 99.983 feet in diameter and 42.638 feet in
height, or thickness, including the 9.451 foot extension of the landing
pods supporting it off of the ground. These three round, hemispheric pods
beneath the craft had obviously been extended from within the hull during
a controlled landing effort. These were measured to form the points of an
equilateral triangle 22.3 feet on a side, center-to-center and were 16.45
feet each from the apicenter of the craft's bottom hull. Both upper and
lower hull surfaces were smooth with no means of entry or even of propulsion
immediately in evidence. The hull was the color of dull, unpolished aluminum
and was apparently metallic in nature with a normal surface temperature.
No seams, hatches, rivets or portholes were obvious. Photographs taken at
closer than fifteen (15) feet were found to be blurred. Later, both infrared
and magnetic radiation fields were found to surround the craft and were
no doubt responsible for fogging of the films in close photographs. Watches
and other ferric (iron-based) tools and instruments left within this zone
around the craft were found to become magnetized.

Eventually the team crawled across the upper hull surface with access
by a scaffold erected around one side of the craft. Upon conducting a close
examination, they discovered a small, hairline crack at the base of a slight
bulge in the domed top of the upper hull. Careful study determined this
crack to be irregular enough as to be a result of accidental impact with
a solid object (much later a civilian witness was debriefed in Albuquerque
who testified that he observed the craft strike the side of a cliff along
the south bank of the Animas River at about the same time the saucer ship
dropped below radar). After banging on the hull and yelling through a
loudspeaker failed to receive any response from the presumed occupants of
the disc-craft, it was decided to attempt to widen this crack in an attempt
to gain entry. At first the discussion was held as to the possibilities
of the craft's internal atmosphere being explosive or that our air could
be poison for the occupants to breath. Finally, Dr. Bush waved all such
debate on the grounds that if some action was not taken immediately, any
chance for survival of members of the ship's crew would run out with the
passage of time.

DO NOT DUPLICATE

First heat from blowpipes was applied in excess of ten thousand (10,000) degrees and finally diamond-tipped drill bits were used until the crack was at last extended longitudinally and finally widened into a gap great enough to shine a small electric light inside and look around. Another plate of material of similar construction seemed to be solidly blocking the view. However, at a seam along the bottom edge of the panel, another breach was located. It was then assumed that the craft was constructed of both an inner and an outer hull separated by only a few inches. After many minutes more of effort, the drill broke through into another empty space. Upon extending this opening and looking in, the research team were surprised to discover the interior to be well illuminated with sunlight. It was discovered that the original opening was forced at the lower corner of a sort of large rectangular window or porthole which had been cracked. These portholes were not visible from the outside, but were extended all the way around the compartment in huge curved rectangles and separated by only a thin structural brace between them. The exception was the cracked one by which the team gained entry; it had turned a milky translucent color like frosted glass. Later testing showed that the entire outer hull was covered in this transparent material that was then blocked off by an opaque inner hull where desired by the ship's designers. This was a thin and inflexible skin barely thicker than four sheets of typing paper and yet direct blows from sledgehammers would not dent or rupture this foil-like substance.

After experimentation with a long, thin rod used to probe at what looked like levers or buttons inside, a panel in the lower hull extended down along what seemed like invisible seams and became a ramp leading up into the craft. When calling out provided no reply, the team obtained flashlights and other equipment and entered the disc-craft. The greatest discoveries were made on the lower level, dubbed the "cargo hold", but the team of investigators did not immediately find the closed door or hatch to this compartment. Instead they found themselves in a small circular chamber about the size of an elevator cab. A spiral ramp of very steep incline led up around a center post to the upper chamber dubbed the "flight deck". Since the team had already observed some details of this upper chamber and had observed the bodies of two (2) small creatures slumped in chairs, it was decided to investigate these first in case they might be alive.

Inside the upper cabin room the team found the bodies of two (2) small humanoids about four feet in height and strapped into seats like those in a jet cockpit (acceleration couches) which faced a row of instrument panels built into a curved countertop circling the cabin just below the portholes they had previously seen from outside. The extraterrestrials were dead. Later study determined that the normal atmosphere inside the cabin was much thinner and colder than our air. When the crack in the windowframe happened the two (2) "pilots" died from sudden increase in pressure and temperature which caused thin hemorrhages like bruises and gave a brownish hue to their skin that first seemed like burns. The seats holding the bodies were found to adjust in size to fit almost any human form and to glide around a track in the floor that followed the instrument panels.

The group soon recognized that the instrument panels were active and some symbols were backlit by a blue-green glow. Some of these were changing as they watched. At this point Dr. Oppenheimer consulted with Dr. von Neumann and suggested that the team proceed with extreme caution since the craft was obviously still under some form of power and it might be activated into operation either by their interference or by electrical automation from within or without by radio control. Dr. Tuve suggested that the team should explore the construction of the controls rather than attempt to operate them on the chance of being able to trace the power to it's source and deactivate same until some understanding of the purpose of each instrument could be determined. This was agreed upon and the work began. Among the first discoveries was that each panel of instruments in the flight deck countertop slide out like a drawer along nearly invisible lines less than 0.2 millimeters wide and in a track or rail composed of a single strip of plastic wrapped in a continuous "S" curve around two metal rollers at the front and rear. There were no ball bearings, springs or motors. And yet each drawer slid both open and shut at the slightest touch of a fingertip as if self-powered. Later it was found that the rear roller bar traveled back-and-forth on a track of it's own as the drawer was operated. This second track was curved so as to balance the force imparted by the bend in the plastic strip and thus created an almost frictionless mechanism. The type of plastic was then unknown to Earthly science, but has since been developed and has what is known as a "molecular memory" of it's ideal unstressed state, to which it will naturally return. Later it was determined that each section of controls or instruments aboard this craft was self-contained as to it's power needs, by some means integrated into it's nuclear structure that gathered electromagnetic and other energy from the space around it; in this case the fields of the Earth. There was no central power system anywhere on the ship and the control, flight and environmental systems drew their power from unknown sources. Instrumentation was eventually found to interconnect and communicate with each other on the molecular level by means of waves or vibrations set up in the atomic structures of each device. No wires or other recognizable electrical components were found.

The sections of the saucer hull which contained both upper and lower deck cabins were joined along microscopic lines by means of electromagnetic locking action engineered into their molecular structure. When Dr. Bush and a team of military engineers found several interlocking key-like devices in a cabinet built into the wall, Dr. Helland determined that these could be used to dismantle the craft into sections. At the joints, the operator of the keys, which linked together for different sized tasks, simply passed the tool over the seam. The device, which looked like a tuning fork and had each tine magnetized with opposite polarity, unlocked the joint when passed over it in one direction and rejoined the sections when it was drawn in the other direction. Even after disassembly and prolonged storage, the seperate sections of this craft still maintain their power and operating capabilities to this day. All attempts to alter the magnetic fields that connect sections of the craft, performed with the use of powerful electromagnets under exacting laboratory conditions, have failed to change the degree of the interlocking effect. Also, kinetic force (repeated blows) has failed to alter molecular magnetic alignment according to crystal holographic imaging tests recently conducted.

:TOP SECRET:-

HISTORICAL PRECEDENTS

AT

AZTEC, NEW MEXICO
(25 MARCH 1948)

SECTION C

(10 pages)

In the process of transfering the frozen EBE bodies from their capsules, in the cargo hold of the disc-craft, to containers of dry ice for shipment, Dr.s Bronk, von Roessler, Scherer and two Army pathologists from the IPU were amazed to discover that one of the small humanoid adults, similar to the "pilots" found deceased on the flight deck, had thawed out with a pulse, limited respiration and had lived in an unconscious state for several minutes before expiring. The shocked scientists then realized that the capsules were actually cryogenic suspension chambers and that the EBE's were still technically alive inside them. Although this concept was almost unheard of in western medicine at that point in time, Dr. Bronk dimly recalled reading about secret experiments conducted in Nazi concentration camps during the war. Such experiments had centered inhumanely on the suspending of the vital life signs and their reanimation by freezing and thawing of the bodies of inmates who were used against their will like laboratory animals.

By this time, the scientists had determined that each section of the ship was able to maintain some operating power even after disassembly. A test showed this to be true for the cryogenic capsules as well. Due to the lack of proper facilities at the landing site, and the lack of a secured holding area for any living EBE's, (or convalescent provisions) it was decided to remove the entire cryogenic section of the craft, and to relocate to better research and medical laboratories on a military compound of some sort before attempting to restore any of the EBE's to consciousness. The story was quickly circulated that, yes, bodies had been found - all deceased, and that these would be removed for later analysis. The bodies of the two small "pilots" were shown to some other members of the recovery team who had heard about them, and then sealed in dry ice chambers, as was the corpse of the EBE who had expired in the cargo hold after thawing. A big display of this was carried out in full view of the other team members, and other dry ice transportation capsules were secretly loaded with dirt and stones before the entire group was loaded into a refrigerator truck labeled "high explosives" for transport. The rest of the craft, in pieces, was loaded onto flatbed trucks, covered with tarpaulins and labeled "explosives". Dr. Oppenheimer arranged for full use and needed remodeling of the restricted Navy Auxiliary Airfield complex at Los Alamos Base. The convoy proceeded at night and by the most unobserved route possible, to these facilities, while units of the IPU/MAJICOPS team assisted by Army Airborne "Rangers" stayed at the Hart Canyon site to effect final clean-up operations. The disc-craft arrived and was put into secured storage for analysis on 5 April 1948.

Two seperate laboratories were set up at the Los Alamos site. One was for the detailed photographing and cataloging of each component of the disc-craft and the effort to decipher the forms of writing found onboard. The second facility was organized around the efforts of teams of doctors led by Dr. Detlev Bronk, to attempt the revival of the craft's occupants. Neither group knew what was the purpose or progress of the other's research. Only Dr. Oppenheimer was in a position, acting as go-between, to see all phases of the work in progress and to disseminate the findings of each to the appropriate investigators within each group. This was done in order to limit the risk of information reaching the public and causing a panic situation based upon a fear of undetectable aliens among them. The thought of riots and murders was on everyone's mind.

:TOP SECRET:

Eventually, the medical team was able to resuscitate one adult Earth-like humanoid male and three (3) Earth-like humanoid infants, all about six (6) months of age; two male and one female. The rest of the infants and one more short, grey-skinned, large-handed humanoid EBE, perished in the attempt to revive them. This was largely the result of Dr_s Bronk and Bush having decided to experiment first on the infants, who were of little intelligence value, in the hope of reviving the short EBE and the adult humanoid for a detailed debriefing.

The adult, Earth-like humanoid male turned out to be, himself, an EBE. But he spoke perfect English with a slight and untraceable accent and exhibited many telepathic and psychic skills as well. This EBE was, in his general appearance, completely human; internally, there were only slight differences in the formation of the heart valves, pancreas, lungs and he possessed two livers and an unfamiliar organ where the gall bladder would be in an earthman. Also, his digestive and gastro-intestinal systems were simpler and less able to process the wide range of foods that earthmen are used to. He was surprised to discover the scientists had unfrozen him alive, but was otherwise undisturbed to find himself in the company of earthmen. He stated within minutes of regaining consciousness that his only surprise would have been if the investigators had not chosen to "hold me captive out of your honest curiosity". After a hasty tele-conference with President Truman, it was explained to the visitor that if his intentions proved to be non-hostile and he cooperated in an information exchange, he would be granted diplomatic status and soon be repatriated to his own kind when the arrangement could be made. To this he readily agreed, provided he was not asked to give away any scientific secrets that could alter the course of our natural cultural development.

All together, the Aztec EBE lived under our protective custody on the Los Alamos complex for nearly a full year, from late April 1948 - until March of 1949. After that, he was sequestered at a private safehouse set-up by Army Intelligence in rural Vermont, during which time he met with the President and other top government and military administrators, prior to his being returned to his people in August of 1949. He gave the scientists and military debriefers a great deal of mostly non-technical information about his civilization and it's motives for being on our Earth; a total of six hundred and eighty-three (683) pages of transcripts were made of recorded conversations. A condensed version of some noteworthy points from these many debriefing sessions follows at the end of this section.

The EBE saw little harm in allowing us to keep the remains of his space craft for study, since he felt our understanding of it would only gradually develop. He did suggest that his people would "probably have to drop one in similar condition in the laps of the Soviet Union - just for the balance of things to be maintained.", and, "You are welcome to take this up with any higher authority you can find willing to listen to you, if you do not approve of this course". The team of scientists were told that the human-like infants were destined for our world anyway, and we were welcome to keep them. On 21 August 1949, the Aztec EBE was returned to his own kind at a meeting site southwest of Kirtland Air Force Base, Texas, and arrangements were made for a future meeting at the same location, to open diplomatic relations.

DO NOT DUPLICATE

Bibliography

A list of the books utilized in researching this publication:

Above Top Secret, 1988, by Timothy Good, William Morrow and Company

The Age of Eisenhower: America and the World of the 1950s, 2018, William Hitchcock, Simon & Schuster

Alien Agenda, 1997, by Jim Marrs, Harper-Collins Publishers

Alien Contact, 1991, by Timothy Good, William Morrow & Company

Aliens Among Us, 1985, by Ruth Montgomery, G.P. Putnam's Sons

An Alien Harvest, 1989/2014, by Linda Moulton Howe, LMH Productions

America's Top-Secret Treaty with Alien Life Forms, 2016, by "Commander X," Timothy Beckley, and Sean Casteel, Global Communications/Conspiracy Journal

The Arrogance of Power: The Secret World of Richard Nixon, by Anthony Summers, 2000, Viking Press

Being Nixon: A Man Divided, by Evan Thomas, 2015, Random House

Beyond Explanation?, 1985, by Jenny Randles, Bantam Books / Salem House

The Case for UFO Crashes: From Urban Legend to Reality, by Timothy Green Beckley, 2013, Global Communications

Close Encounters of the Fatal Kind, 2014, by Nick Redfern, Career Press, Inc.

The Council of Seven Lights, 1958, by George W. Van Tassel, Trade Service Publications

The Day After Roswell, 1997, by Phillip Corso and Bill Birnes, Pocket Books

Eisenhower: The White House Years, 2011, by Jim Newton, Doubleday

The Hidden White House, 2013, by Robert Klara, St. Martin's Press

Ike and McCarthy, 2017, by David A. Nichols, Simon & Schuster

Kennedy's Last Stand: Eisenhower, UFOs, MJ-12, and JFK's Assassination, 2013, by Dr. Michael E. Salla, Exopolitics Institute

Majic Eyes Only, 2005, by Ryan S. Wood, Wood Enterprises

Mandate for Change: The White House Years 1953-1956, 1963, by Dwight D. Eisenhower, Doubleday

Movie Nights with the Reagans, 2018, by Mark Weinberg, Simon & Schuster

Need to Know: UFOs, the Military, and Intelligence, 2007, by Timothy Good, Pegasus Books

Palm Springs Babylon, 1993, by Ray Mungo, St. Martin's Press

Real Aliens, Space Beings, and Creatures from Other Worlds, 2011, by Brad Steiger and Sherry Hansen Steiger, Visible Ink Press

The Presidents and UFOs: A Secret History from Roosevelt to Obama, 2015, by Larry Holcombe, St. Martin's Press

The Roswell Incident, 1980, by Charles Berlitz & William Moore, G.P. Putnam's Sons

Sage-ing While Age-ing, 2007, by Shirley MacLaine, Atria Books

Secret History: Conspiracies from Ancient Aliens to the New World Order, 2015, by Nick Redfern, Visible Ink Press

The Source: Journeys Through the Unexplained, 1999, by Art Bell & Brad Steiger, Paper Chase Press

They Knew Too Much About Flying Saucers, 1956, by Gray Barker, published by University Books USA.

The Untold History of the United States, 2012, by Oliver Stone & Peter Kuznick, Gallery Books

Watergate: The Hidden History, 2012, by Lamar Waldron, Counterpoint Press

Winston S. Churchill, Volume 8: Never Despair, 1945-1965, 1988, by Sir Martin Gilbert, Rosetta Books plus a thesis: *Research Study #8*, 2004, by Dr. Michael Salla

{I'd have listed some websites on this subject besides majesticdocuments.com and earthfiles.com, but the those online pages are often so distorted and inaccurate on the topic I found them not worth my trust or time, and probably not yours. But you be the judge.}

ABOUT THE AUTHOR

Paul Blake Smith is the sole author of "**President Eisenhower's Close Encounters**." He previously authored the popular books "**MO41, The Bombshell Before Roswell:** *The Case for a Missouri 1941 UFO Crash*" and "**3 Presidents, 2 Accidents:** *More MO41 UFO Crash Data and Surprises*," released at opposite ends of 2016. {He'd like to inform readers as of mid-2020 that he no longer believes his original "April 12th, 1941" dating for the Cape Girardeau, Missouri, UFO crash; it was simply "one night in late April '41."}

This is Paul's fourth nonfiction UFO book and his sixth book overall. In 2017 Paul also authored the fictional comedy novel "**Sexy Alien Races**" which utilized factual UFO cases in the Nevada area. In 2018 Paul released his nonfiction book, "**JFK and the Willard Hotel Plot***: The Explosive New Theory of Oswald in D.C.*," shedding startling new light on previously unnoticed aspects of the assassination of President John F. Kennedy.

Paul was a four-year Mass Communications Major with an English Minor at Southeast Missouri University in his hometown of Cape Girardeau, Missouri. A fan of history, sports, and the paranormal, Paul spends his days writing mostly nonfiction books and movie screenplays, and can be found on the internet through his website www.mo41.info, and on Facebook with "*Cape Girardeau's 1941 UFO Crash, America's First*" and "*JFK and the Willard Hotel Plot.*" Plus the Facebook page: "*President Eisenhower's Close Encounters,*" via @EisenhowerEncounters. Additionally, he and/or data on this book can be found on Linked-In, Twitter, and Pinterest.

More Books from Foundations Books Publishing

The Mor
By Steve Soderquist

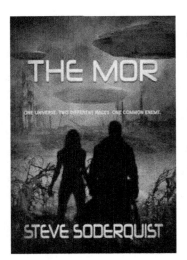

"An ACTION-PACKED read that will pull you along from the first page to the chilling end."

One universe. Two different races. One common enemy. When the benevolent race known as the Illuminous visited Earth back in the 1950's, they weren't aware of the aliens who had attached themselves to the hull of their ship. The Mor, also known as Seeds, found Earth to be a poor choice for a new home, but a home, nonetheless. Years later, three brilliant college students inadvertently stumble on a formula that enhances the Mors' ability to communicate and grow at an incredible rate... and now the race is on to reverse what was done before all life is destroyed.

The Mor is a "fast-paced" and "tightly written" standalone Sci-fi Thriller.

Royalty
By Laura Ranger

Rayne Martin is a typical teen excited to go off to college.

However, the school she chooses at random is anything but typical and she begins to doubt she will ever fit in at Brighton College. Rayne grew up in the Bible belt and attended church whenever her parents wanted her to. She considered herself to be a good Christian. When she truly commits to being a believer, she embraces the fact that she is a daughter of the King and therefore, Royalty.

Now God is calling on her to wage war against the demons and Satanists threatening to overrun Brighton. Rayne is sure He is mistaken. How can someone who has never even been in a fight lead in battle?

Where will she find others willing to risk their lives to stand with her against such evil?

Captivate Me
By S.J. Pierce

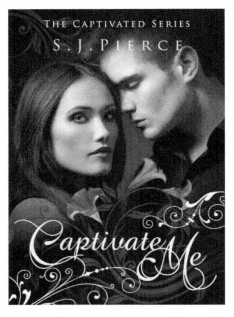

Welcome to Midland Pines High, school for the paranormally gifted. Shifters, illusionists, and elementals are welcome. No humans allowed.

I once thought humans were the monsters, but my kind has something even more terrible to fear.

Growing up half angel with telekinetic powers should have made life a breeze...until the humans at my old school found out and labeled me a witch. Fearing for my safety, my parents shipped me off to Midland Pines High, where I met new friends and fell for an illusionist named Levi, though he's not the only one hell bent on captivating my heart.

But now...none that matters, because someone wants us dead. Shadows have been watching us from the woods surrounding the school, and one by one, kids go missing. Judging by the faceless visitor in my dreams and the strange gifts I'm left at night, I might be next.

Too bad for them, they've messed with the wrong school.

Jasper
By T.K. Lawyer

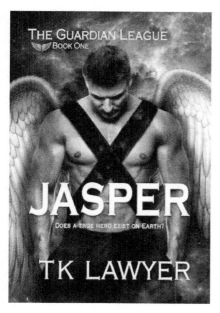

Jasper wasn't seeking a mate. His only intention was to rescue Tatiana from a near-fatal car accident and move on to his next assignment, but we all know intent and reality don't always coincide.

Saving this fiery vixen altered his world, and now he can't tear himself away... though he know he should. She's not supposed to know he even exists.

Printed in Great Britain
by Amazon